The Icelandic Legend of Saint Dorothy

Edited by
KIRSTEN WOLF

The volume presents an edition of the Icelandic translation of the legend of Saint Dorothy, extant in a single manuscript, Copenhagen, Arnamagnaean Institute AM 429 12mo, written in the Benedictine convent at Kirkjubær in Síða around 1500.

The introduction examines the origin and development of the legend of Saint Dorothy as well as vernacular translations and adaptations of the legend and its reception by modern authors and artists. Particular attention is given to Scandinavian and Icelandic adaptations of the legend and evidence of the cult of Saint Dorothy in the North.

The analysis of the German, English, and Scandinavian renderings of the legend as well as the Icelandic translation reveals that Jacobus de Voragine's *Legenda aurea* version, which has been posited as the source for virtually all of these, including the Icelandic translation, is not the direct source, for certain deviations from the *Legenda aurea* version in the Icelandic translation are found also in some of the German and English texts. Some of these deviations appear in a Latin version of the legend represented by a manuscript in the University Library in Bologna, Codex 2800, from the mid-fifteenth century, the text of which is edited in an appendix to the study.

Illumination of Saint Dorothy
Copenhagen, Arnamagnaean Institute AM 429 12mo, folio 48v

STUDIES AND TEXTS 130

The Icelandic Legend
of Saint Dorothy

Edited by

KIRSTEN WOLF

PONTIFICAL INSTITUTE OF MEDIAEVAL STUDIES

ACKNOWLEDGEMENTS

This book has been published with a grant from the Humanities and Social Sciences Federation of Canada, using funds provided by the Social Sciences and Humanities Research Council of Canada.

Cataloguing in Publication Data

The Icelandic legend of Saint Dorothy

(Studies and texts, ISSN 0082-5328 ; 130)
Includes bibliographical references and index.
ISBN 0-88844-130-4

1. Dorothea, Saint, d. 311 – Legends. 2. Christian saints – Biography – Early works to 1800. I. Wolf, Kirsten, 1959– . II. Arnamagnaeanske institut (Denmark). Manuscript AM 429 12mo. III. Pontifical Institute of Mediaeval Studies. IV. Series: Studies and texts (Pontifical Institute of Mediaeval Studies) ; 130.

PT7299.D6I34 1997   270.1′092   C97–932025–9

© 1997
Pontifical Institute of Mediaeval Studies
59 Queen's Park Crescent East
Toronto, Ontario, Canada M5S 2C4

PRINTED IN CANADA

CONTENTS

Acknowledgements   vii

INTRODUCTION
1   *The Legend of Saint Dorothy*   1
   1.0 The Origin and Development of the Legend □ 1
   1.1 The Legend in the Vernacular □ 19
   1.2 Artistic Representations of the Legend □ 45

2   *Saint Dorothy in the North*   47
   2.0 Her Cult and Legend in Scandinavia □ 47
   2.1 Her Cult and Legend in Iceland □ 58

3   *Dorotheu saga*   64
   3.0 Transmission □ 64
   3.1 AM 429 12mo □ 64
   3.2 The Sources □ 74
   3.3 The Translation □ 76

THE TEXT   87
   A Note on the Present Edition □ 87
   De sancta Dorothea □ 88
   Dorotheu saga □ 89

APPENDIX
   Bologna, Biblioteca Universitaria Cod. 2800   104

BIBLIOGRAPHY   108
INDEX OF MANUSCRIPTS   121
INDEX OF NAMES   123

Acknowledgements

The main portions of this study and edition of the Icelandic legend of Saint Dorothy were completed with the help of a research fellowship from the University of Manitoba's Institute for the Humanities in 1994–95, which released me from teaching duties in the spring of 1995. A grant from the Social Sciences and Humanities Research Council of Canada enabled me to spend several months in the Stofnun Árna Magnússonar in Reykjavík.

Several scholars have been generous with their assistance and time. I wish to thank especially Jakob Benediktsson, who answered a number of questions concerning the 2325d text in *Bibliotheca Hagiographica Latina*. Stefanie Würth kindly made available to me photocopies from rare German books, Britta Olrik Frederiksen provided me with information about the manuscript transmission of some Old Danish and Swedish texts, and Jón Hallur Stefánsson let me consult and use his unpublished edition of the Icelandic rendering of *Den hellige Dorothea*. Finally, I wish to thank Phillip Pulsiano, who read the entire introduction; I am grateful to him for incisive criticism and staunch support of this and other research projects through the years.

INTRODUCTION

1 THE LEGEND OF SAINT DOROTHY

1.0 *The Origin and Development of the Legend*

The origin and provenance of the legend of Saint Dorothy, one of the "quattuor virgines capitales,"[1] are obscure. A patroness of brides, newly-weds, midwives, florists, and also miners and brewers, Saint Dorothy is believed to have suffered martyrdom during the Diocletian persecutions on 6 February 287 or 304 at Caesarea in Cappadocia.[2] Her body is believed to repose in the church which bears her name in Trastevere in Rome, although also other churches, notably those of Bologna and Cologne, claimed to possess her relics.[3] Only her name and martyrdom have been historically verified, however. There are no historical details of her life; her surviving acts are legendary.

Unknown in Greek tradition, Saint Dorothy has in the West been venerated since the seventh century, and her feastday (*dies natalis*, that is, [heavenly] birthday) on 6 February has been celebrated since the eleventh century (Wimmer 1966: 186). According to the oldest breviaries, her feastday was celebrated with three *lectiones*.[4] Early signs of the suppression of her feast are, however, evident from a decretal issued on 18 May 1854 by Pope Pius IX (1792–1878), in which 6 February is associated with Saint Titus. In the new Roman Calendar published in 1969 after the Second Vatican Council (1962–1965), her feast was expunged.

The first mention of the Cappadocian virgin, along with Theophilus, is found in the *Martyrologium Hieronymianum* (ed. Rossi and Duchesne

---

1. The other three "great virgins" are Saints Barbara, Catherine of Alexandria, and Margaret of Antioch.

2. The year of her martyrdom is uncertain; also 311 has been suggested.

3. See *Acta Sanctorum*, February, vol. 1 [1966], 773.

4. I am indebted to Robert Godding, SJ, of the Bollandists (personal correspondence, 1995) for this information. He notes, however, that one exception is known to him: "Je ne connais qu'une exception, sans doute assez récente: notre bibliothèque possède deux éditions différentes d'un feuillet imprimé vraisemblablement au siècle dernier (mais non daté) et intitulé *In festo S. Dorotheae v. m. patronae principalis civitatis Piscien* [= Pescia, prov. Pistoia, Toscane]: la fête de Ste Dorothée y est un *duplex 1. class. cum Oct.*, avec neuf lectures."

1894), falsely attributed to Saint Jerome (ca. 341–420), which was drawn up in northern Italy in the second half of the fifth century. The oldest manuscripts of this work date from the eighth century and depend upon a single Gallican recension that was made in Auxerre between 592 and 600 or at Luxeuil between 627 and 628. The original text was compiled from three principal sources: the work of the *Chronographer of 354* (an almanac containing, along with other listings, a *Depositio episcoporum* and a *Depositio martyrum*) continued to 420, the *Syriac Breviary* or *Calendar of Antioch* compiled between 362 and 381, and an African calendar, as well as other as yet unresolved sources (Brun 1967: 317). Like the calendars, the *Martyrologium Hieronymianum* ordinarily mentions only the martyrs' or saints' names, the dates of commemoration, and the places of martyrdom or cult. In the entry for 6 February, the martyrology about Saint Dorothy reads: "IN achaia. Saṭnini Revocatę. Scae Dorotheae. Ethiofili. Scolastici" (*Codex Bernensis*; Rossi and Duchesne 1894: 17). The *Codex Wissenburgensis* assigns the place of suffering to Caesarea in Cappadocia ("In cesaria cappadocię paṡ sc̄ę dorothae. Et in opoli scolastici"; Rossi and Duchesne 1894: 17), whereas the *Codex Epternacensis* does not give a specific place, stating simply "alibi" ("alibi revocatae dorotae teofili scolastici"; Rossi and Duchesne 1894: 17). Disagreement is also found in regard to the day of her martyrdom: both 6 and 12 February are given as the day on which Saints Dorothy and Theophilus received the crown of martyrdom. In the entry for 12 February, however, only the names are mentioned.

The legend of Saint Dorothy seems not to have come into existence until the Middle Ages. The oldest known version of the legend is found in Saint Aldhelm's (639–709) didactic tract *De laudibus virginitatis*, addressed to Abbess Hildelitha of Barking Abbey, Essex. The work, which borrows heavily from Saints Cyprian's (ca. 200–258) *De habitu virginum*, Ambrose's (339–397) *De virginibus ad marcellinam*, *De virginitate*, *De institutione virginis*, and *Exhortatio virginitatis*, Augustine's (354–430) *De sancta virginitate*, and the works of Jerome, serves as an elaboration of almost every patristic idea subsequently advanced by medieval writers of England on virginity and reinforces the patristic exhortations for the life of virginal perfection. After a lengthy and elaborate encomium of virginity, which he illustrates by the simile (taken from Saint Ambrose) of the chaste bee which gathers honey but does not undergo intercourse, Saint Aldhelm presents as encouragement to contemporary nuns a series of compact lives of male and female virgin saints.[5] Especially prominent are those women who "cum virginitatis palma et martyrii corona paradisi præmia possessuræ ... ad Christum pariter perrexerunt" (1850: 150) and therefore served as models for the nuns of Barking Abbey. Included among these illustrious *exempla* is Saint Dorothy:

> Porro Scholastica ac Christina simulque Dorothea apud Cæsariam oriunda in provincia Cappadociæ, licet dispari sæculorum serie sequestrarentur, pari tamen integritatis tiara a Christo coronabantur. ... Tertiam vero cum Sapricius orthodoxorum cruentus carnifex non solum ad nuptias, sed ad nefandas quoque idolorum culturas et ineptas gentilium cæremonias cogere nequiret, confestim furibundus catastarum crudelitatem exercuit, lividas palmarum vibices exhibuit, torrentes lampadarum flammas applicavit. Duabus quoque feminis, quæ nuper a fide naufragaverant, et a Christi consortio apostataverant, eamdem tradidit depravandam, sed versa vice earumdem probrosas apostatarum cicatrices pœnitudinis medicamento ita salubriter curavit, ut statim ordine præpostero doctricem propriam ad martyrii palmam præcederent. Verum cum egrederetur crudele prætorium, Theophilo cum cachinnanti cavillatione flagitanti, ut de paradiso sponsi cœlestis, ad quem se properare fatebatur, grata fructuum munuscula mitteret, quod cum calumniæ gannitura prolatum, in veritate completum est. Nam pridie quam pateretur, et cruentis mucronibus truncanda subderetur, tria mala cum purpureis totidem rosis ad eumdem Theophilum destinasse describitur, qui, hujus rei gratia propriæ occasionem salutis adeptus, rubicundis martyrii sertis coronabatur (1850: 146–147).

These model lives of the saints were to demonstrate to the nuns that virginity entailed struggle, aggressive defence, but ultimately great apocalyptic and eschatological rewards.

Mention of Saint Dorothy's martyrdom is also found in the Venerable Bede's (673–735) martyrology from around 720. Bede's work differs from the martyrologies then in vogue in that it is a "historical" martyrology, because to the information furnished by the *Martyrologium Hieronymianum*, Bede often added a brief account of the saints' lives and a large number of names taken from Eusebius of Caesarea's (ca. 260–239) *Eccle-*

---

5. Cf. Lapidge: "One wonders why Aldhelm should have included both male and female virgins: possibly the answer lies in the fact that Barking, the immediate destination of Aldhelm's treatise, was a double monastery" (Lapidge and Herren 1979: 56–57).

siastical History, the Scriptures, legends, and the writings of the Church
Fathers. His work was continued at Lyons, first by an anonymous cleric,
who around 800 compiled a new martyrology by adding numerous notices
to those of Bede (BN Lat. 3879; see Quentin 1908: 131-221, esp. 156-157
for his study of Saint Dorothy's *passio*),[6] and later by the deacon Florus
of Lyons (d. 860), who around 850 completed the former's work.[7]
However, the information provided about Saint Dorothy is scanty: "D.
Cæsarea Cappadociæ S. Dorotheæ virginis et Theophili scholastici" (1843-
1844: 4, 34).

Bede's work, as well as martyrologies and passionals, the *Liber pontificalis*, the *Dialogues* of Gregory the Great (ca. 540-604), and the works of
Gregory of Tours (539-594), served also as the basis for the martyrology
of Rabanus Maurus (776/784-856), Archbishop of Mainz, written between
843 and 854. Rabanus Maurus adds a number of details to Bede's brief
account; of note is especially that the two apostate women mentioned in
Saint Aldhelm's legend of Saint Dorothy are here her sisters, Christa and
Calista, who are put to death in a boiling cauldron:

> In Caessaria Cappodochiae passio sanctae Dorotheae uirginis et
> Theophili sub Sapricio praefecto, quae cum duabus sororibus, id est
> Christae et Calistae, quae a fide nuper apostatabant uitae doloribus,
> commendata est, ut eam auerterent a Christo; eas iterum conuertit ad
> Christum, ita ut in cuppam missae per praefectum incensae ad martyrii
> palmam peruenerunt. Postea uero Dorothea ducta ad locum poenarum,
> ubi et passa est. Cum a Theophilo quodam scolastico inrideretur, quod
> ad paradisum uadens a sponso suo Christo rosas et poma et rosas
> florentes sibi mitteret, hoc citius impetrauit. Quod cum uidisset
> Theophilus mox Christum confessus est uerum Deum, et martirizauit
> sub eodem profecto capite plexus (1979: 20).

But one or two decades later, between 853 and 860, Ado (ca. 800-875),
Archbishop of Vienna, compiled a new martyrology "ut supplerentur dies
qui absque nominibus martyrum, in martyrologio quod venerabilis Flori
studio in labore domni Bedae accreverat, tantum notati erant" (quotation

---

6. This martyrology in turn served as the basis for the *Martyrologium Fuldense*
from the end of the ninth century (Quentin 1908: 683; Dubois 1978: 40).

7. Ed. Dubois and Renaud (1976). Florus's martyrology in turn served as the basis
for Wandalbert of Prüm's verse martyrology (ed. Dümmler 1884: 578-602) written
around 848 (Quentin 1908: 15, 683; Dubois 1978: 59). For a discussion of Florus's
martyrology, see Quentin (1908: 222-408, 683).

from Quentin 1908: 17). Nine-tenths of this martyrology was taken from Florus of Lyons; the remaining text Ado claimed to have derived from an ancient collection copied by him in Italy at Ravenna, but this portion of the text has been condemned as sheer forgery on Ado's part.[8] Nonetheless, Ado's work exercised much influence and was used by Notker Balbulus (ca. 840–912), monk of St. Gall Abbey in Switzerland, who conflated the texts of Rabanus Maurus and Ado,[9] and Usuard (d. 877), monk at Saint-Germain-des-Prés in Paris, who conflated the texts of Florus of

8. Ado writes for 6 February: "Apud Caesaream Cappadociae, natale sanctae Dorotheae virginis, quae sub Apricio, provinciae ipsius praeside, primum equulei extensione vexata, dein palmis diutissime caesa, ad ultimum capitali sententia punita est. Cumque egrediens de praetorio duceretur ad mortem, Theophilus quidam scholasticus ait ad eam: Eia tu sponsa Christi, mitte mihi mala de paradiso sponsi tui. Quae statim promisit se esse missuram. Ubi ergo ventum est ad locum in quo iugulanda erat, paulisper oratione facta, protulit orarium suum; et vocato ad se quodam puerulo annorum sex, misit Theophilo dicens: Dic ei, Dorothea ancilla Dei mittit tibi mala de paradiso sponsi sui Christi. Accipiens ille et gratias agens quod petitionem eius implesset, coepit sibi faciem tergere, tantaque repente suavitate perfusus est, ita ut tota mente mutatus cum grandi exultatione et clara voce saepius replicaret: Benedictum nomen Domini mei Iesu Christi; ob quam confessionem mox et ipse tentus, ac suspensus in equuleo tanta crudelitate tortus est, ut omnes circumstantes horrescerent; novissime caeso capite martyrium consummavit" (Dubois and Renaud 1984: 81).

9. Notker's martyrology, written in 896, is fragmentary; November and December are missing. It is considered a careful compilation, but it never became widely known outside the Benedictine order. The entry for 6 February reads: "Apud Cæsaream Cappadociæ nativitas S. Dorotheæ virginis; quæ cum duobus sororibus Christe et Calliste, quæ a fide nuper apostatabant, victæ doloribus, commendata esset, ut eam averterent a Christo, ipsas iterum convertit ad Christum: ita ut a præfecto in cupam ferventem missæ, ad martyrii palmam pervenerint. Postea vero ipsa sub Sapricio provinciæ ipsius præside, primum, equulei extensione vexata, dein palmis diutissime cæsa, ad ultimum capitali sententia punita est. Cumque egrediens de prætorio duceretur ad mortem, Theophilus quidam scholasticus ait ad eam. 'Eia tu, sponsa Christi, mitte mihi mala de paradiso Christi tui.' Quæ statim promisit se esse missuram. Ubi ergo ventum est ad locum in quo jugulanda, erat, pauper parumper oratione facta, protulit orarium suum, et vocato ad se quodam puerulo annorum sex, misit Theophilo, dicens; 'Dic ei: Dorothea ancilla Dei mittit tibi mala de paradiso Christi sui.' Accipiens ille et gratias agens quod petitionem ejus implesset, cœpit sibi faciem tergere. Tantaque repente suavitate perfusus est, ut tota mente mutatus cum grandi exsultatione, et clara voce sæpius replicaret: 'Benedictum nomen Domini Jesu Christi.' Ob quam confessionem mox et ipse tentus ac suspensus in equuleo, tanta credulitate tortus est, ut omnes, circumstantes exhorrescerent. Novissime vero cæso capite martyrium consummavit" (1884: 1043–1044). The poet, chronicler, and monk of Reichenau, Herimannus Contractus (1013–1054), in turn conflated the texts of Ado, Rabanus Maurus, and Notker for his martyrology (Quentin 1908: 683).

Lyons and Ado. Usuard in fact depends to such an extent on Florus and Ado that his version may be considered an abridged edition of their works, although he appears to have borrowed also from Pseudo-Jerome, Bede, and the anonymous martyrologist at Lyons. In his entry for 6 February Usuard writes as follows about Saint Dorothy:

> Apud Caesaream Cappadociae, natalis sanctae Dorotheae virginis, quae, # primum equuleo vexata, dein palmis diu caesa, ad ultimum capite punita est. In cuius confessione, quidam Theophilus scolasticus conversus, # et mox equuleo idem acerrime tortus, novissime gladio caesus est (Dubois 1965: 175).

Usuard's work became the model for every later Roman martyrology and the direct ancestor of the one published as official for the universal Church by Pope Gregory XIII (1572-1585) in 1584 with the bull *Emendatio*.[10] The *Martyrologium Romanum* gives the following information about Saint Dorothy:[11]

> Caesareae in Cappadocia natalis sanctae Dorotheae virginis et martyris, quae sub Sapricio illius provinciae praeside primum equulei extensione vexata, dehinc palmis diutissime caesa, ad ultimum capitali sententia punita est; in cuius confessione Theophilus quidam scholasticus ad Christi fidem conversus, et mox equuleo acerrime tortus, novissime gladio caesus est (1940: 51).

---

10. The *Martyrologium Romanum* was republished under Pope Sixtus V (1585-1590) with the notes and treatise on the martyrology by the cardinal and church historian Baronius (1538-1607). It was frequently revised, especially in 1630 under Pope Urban VIII (1623-1644), who reorganized its structure and introduced recently canonized saints, but also under Pope Clement X (1670-1676) in 1681 and Pope Benedict XIV (1740-1758) in 1748. The revision in 1924 is characterized by attempts at a complete reform. The more recent editions have merely added new feasts and newly canonized saints.

11. Schade (1854: 12-13) notes that in the *Martyrologium Romanum* (Venice, 1597) in the entry for 6 February there is a reference by Baronius to a Latin hymn about Saint Dorothy: "Dorotheae res gestas et sociarum sacer hymnus celebrat qui extat in breviario Toletano" (73; quoted from Schade 1854: 12-13). He is, however, doubtful that this hymn is the same as the one found in Josse Clichtove's *Elucidatorium ecclesiasticum, ad officium ecclesiæ pertinentia planius exponens* (Paris, 1548; cf. also Chevalier [1892-1920]: 1, 444, no. 7409]), which he prints in its entirety (13-14).

One must assume that the legend of Saint Dorothy belongs to those legends termed "les passions épiques" (as opposed to "les passions historiques") by Delehaye (1966: 223–226), which in the fourth and fifth centuries were invented for the names of the saints listed in the various calendars so as to provide a legend for the respective saints' feastdays. Whether the legends of Saint Dorothy and Theophilus had been conflated before the appearance of their names in the calendars or whether the fact that they were listed together led to the association of one with the other cannot be ascertained.[12]

As far as the central point of the legend, the heavenly fruits and flowers, is concerned, one is likewise forced to rely on suppositions. As Günter (1949: 103) notes, gifts of this kind are common in the legends. However, only the legend of Saint Justina of Tergeste is comparable with that of Saint Dorothy in this respect.[13] At Saint Justina's execution, a spectator by the name of Zeno mocked her, saying: "Bride of Christ, send me apples from the garden of your spouse." Before receiving her death-blow, Saint Justina instructed a child to give Zeno her sudarium and say: "Justina, the bride of Christ, sends you the apples you requested from the garden of her spouse." As Zeno in jest holds it to his face, he is overcome with love for Christ, confesses himself a Christian, and receives the crown of martyrdom under Diocletian in 289. Although Günter classifies these similarties as "Gleichartigkeit ohne Entlehnung," it is difficult not to suspect the influence of the legend of Saint Justina on that of Saint Dorothy, or vice versa. Indeed, Stadler and Hein (1858–1861) comment that "[d]ie Bollandisten glauben zwar, es seien hier sonst unbekannte Martyrer mit der Legende der hl. Dorothea ausgeschmückt" (554). Busse (1930: 6) considers it probable that the meaning of the name Dorothy – dōron (gift) and theos (god), that is, Saint Dorothy received a gift from God – contributed to the creation of this particular aspect of the legend.[14] Whether or not the roses and apples have symbolic meaning

12. Cf. Delehaye (1927: 37–38).
13. Stadler and Hein (1858–1861: 3, 553).
14. The same may be seen in the legend of Saint Agnes, whose name resembles the word agnus (lamb). In her legend, it is related that her parents and relatives, watching beside her grave on the eighth day of her execution, saw a chorus of angels clothed in shining gold garments, and in their midst Saint Agnes, similarly clad and with a lamb whiter than snow standing at her right hand. Accordingly, Saint Agnes's principal iconographic emblem is a lamb. See also Carlé (1981: 45).

cannot be ascertained; Busse (1930: 7) notes that the roses may signify Saint
Dorothy's martyrdom and the apples her eternal life.

Despite its brevity, the legend, as related by Saint Aldhelm, very
clearly conforms to the pattern of the ficticious legends that came into
existence in the fourth and fifth centuries. For it contains the four essential
structural elements outlined by Delehaye (1966: 173–218): characters (the
protagonists Saints Dorothy and Theophilus and their persecutor Sapricius
as well as a couple of minor characters); dialogue (Sapricius's offer of
marriage, his instructions to worship heathen idols, and Saint Dorothy's
refusal); tortures (the beating, burning, and execution of Saint Dorothy);
and miracles (the apples and the roses). As Gad (1961: 20) notes, the
arrangement of these four parts is quite deliberate: it seeks to impart to the
passion a dramatic structure.[15]

The legend of Saint Dorothy was not included in the *Legenda aurea*
compiled between 1252 and 1260 by Jacobus de Voragine (ca. 1230–1298),
a scholarly friar and eventual archbishop of Genoa, and is, in Graesse's
edition (1890) relegated to a sort of appendix ("legendae superadditae"; *BHL*
2324),[16] because her legend probably cannot be ascribed to Jacobus, but
was added to the *Legenda aurea* by a later author or authors. (That the
legend existed independently of the *Legenda aurea* is clear from *BHL*.) In
fact, the *Legenda aurea* seems to have continually expanded to include additional lives. Cult interest is, of course, a major reason for these additions,
but the specific needs of monastic communities must also have been a primary factor. Legends were the most commonly used literature in daily com-
munal readings, and the "original" corpus of the *Legenda aurea* could provide only about 170 at the most for this purpose. Williams-Krapp (1986a:

15. Gad admits, however, that there are many differences between the legends of
the martyrs and dramatic works: "legenderne er ikke bestemt til opførelse, de savner
spænding om udfaldet; der er ingen konflikt i heltens sind, han er ubetinget god og
modstanderen ubetinget ond osv. – men jeg vil tro, at når disse fortællinger gennem
over tusind år er blevet læst og fortalt og kopieret og udvidet og resumeret igen og
igen, så var den faste komposition medvirkende hertil. Legenderne giver religiøs
belæring og beretninger om utrolige mirakler og grusomme lidelser, men de bringer
ikke disse elementer i tilfældig blanding, men indordnet i en dramatisk handling, kam-
pen mellem helten og hans modstander" (21).

16. Graesse's source, identified in his preface only by a reference to Ebert's *Allge-
meines bibliographisches Lexikon* ("Lexic. Bibliogr. T.I, p. 872, sq. nr. 10672[b]"), is among
the earliest editions of the *Legenda aurea*; Seybolt (1946a: 328) lists it as number six.
Although the printer seems not to have been identified, Gaiffier (1958: 470) identifies
the place of publication as Basel.

231) notes that an anonymous Latin *Legenda aurea* printing of around 1470 contained no fewer than 448 saints' lives.

Reames (1985: 160) draws attention to the fact that the promise in the legend of Saint Dorothy, as represented by *BHL* 2324, that those who honor her memory will receive both remission of their sins at death and deliverance from all earthly tribulations, including false accusations and poverty,[17] seems inconsistent and incompatible with Jacobus's rather consistent purification of the old legends of such concessions to the flesh. In fact, Jacobus was not the only cleric to take exception to such excesses, which could impair the religious and social usefulness of a legend. When Nicholas of Cusa (1401–1464) set out to reform the diocese of Brixen in the Tyrol around 1450, he forbade his clergy to teach the people such "superstitiosa" as were found in the *Legenda aurea* accounts of Saints Barbara (*BHL* 916), Blaise (*BHL* 7 Epitomae), Catherine of Alexandria (*BHL* 1667), Dorothy, and Margaret of Antioch (*BHL* 5309).[18] As Reames (1985) observes: "There is not much question about his meaning, for the chapters singled out as examples have one thing in common: they promise in unequivocal terms that acts of devotion to the saints in question will magically guarantee one's deliverance from certain evils, among them illnesses, poverty, and damnation itself" (50).

The version in *BHL* 2324, based on an eleventh-century manuscript (Wimmer and Binding 1985: 1318), represents, in plot and essential details, the legend in its full-fledged form. It may be summarized as follows.

During the reign of the Roman emperors Diocletian and Maximian, when the Christians were persecuted, one Christian family, Dorus and

---

17. "Cum autem venit ad locum decollationis, rogavit dominum pro omnibus, qui ad honorem sui nominis suae memoriam passionis peragerent, ut in omnibus salvarentur tribulationibus et praecipue a verecundia, paupertate et a falso crimine liberarentur et in fine vitae contritionem et remissionem omnium peccatorum obtinerent, mulieres vero parientes nomen ejus invocantes celerem sentiant in doloribus profectum" (*Legenda aurea*, 911). As in the cases of, for example, the legends of Saints Barbara, Blaise, Catherine of Alexandria, and Margaret of Antioch, the guarantee is requested just before the saint's martyrdom and ratified at once by a voice from heaven.

18. "Item ne populo praedicentur superstitiosa, quae in legenda lombardica habentur de S. Blasio, Barbara, Catharina, Dorothea, Margarita, etc." (*Synodi Brixinenses, saeculi XV*, ed. G. Bickell [Innsbruck, 1880], 41; quotation from Reames 1985: 233). See also Schreiner (1966: 41). Similar sentiments were expressed by the compilers of the *Acta Sanctorum*. In the legend of Saint Dorothy, they said, "hyperbolice exaggerata quaedam, ut propterea haud multum absimilia apocryphis videri possint" (*Acta Sanctorum*, February vol. I [1966], 772).

Thea and their two daughters, Christen and Calisten, fled to the city of Caesarea in Cappadocia, where a third daughter, Dorothy, was born and secretly baptized by a bishop. The exceptional beauty of Dorothy inflamed with love the prefect of the place, Fabricius. Having declared his love and offered marriage, he was refused by Dorothy, who said that she was the bride of Christ. In his anger, Fabricius caused her to be cast into a vessel of burning oil, but she emerged from it miraculously unharmed. He then starved her in prison for nine days, but she was sustained by the heavenly consolation of angels and emerged more beautiful than ever. Brought before Fabricius as judge, she was threatened with hanging if she did not sacrifice to idols. He set up a pillar and placed his god on top of it, but angels cast down the idol and utterly destroyed it, while the voices of devils complaining about the harm Dorothy was doing were heard. Fabricius next commanded that she be hung upside down on a gibbet, lacerated with hooks, and scourged, and that her breasts be burned.

Half dead, she was returned to prison, but the next day she appeared unscathed. Fabricius pitied her, but ascribed her preservation to the mercy of his own gods. He sent her two sisters, now apostates from Christianity, to plead with her, but instead she converted them, and they professed their faith before the prefect, who had them bound back to back and burned. When Dorothy professed her love for Christ, "in cujus horto deliciae, et rosas cum pomis colligam et laetabor cum ipso in aeternum," Fabricius had her face beaten to a pulp, but again on the next day she appeared unharmed. Fabricius then ordered her to be decapitated. On the way to the place of execution, a scribe or protonotary, Theophilus, mocked her, requesting her to send some roses and apples from the garden of her spouse. She promised to do so, although it was winter. At the place of execution, she kneeled and prayed for all those who would be her clients, "ut in omnibus salvarentur tribulationibus et praecipue a verecundia, paupertate et a falso crimine liberarentur et in fine vitae contritionem et remissionem omnium peccatorum obtinerent, mulieres vero parientes nomen ejus invocantes celerem sentiant in doloribus profectum." A voice from heaven was heard welcoming her as spouse. A child, barefooted, with fair curly hair, clothed in a purple garment ornamented with gold stars, appeared and offered her a gold basket containing roses and apples. She asked him to take them to Theophilus, and then bowed her head to the executioner. Theophilus received the gifts, and he and most of the city were converted. Fabricius ordered him to be tortured and his body torn into small pieces and thrown out to be devoured.

As is evident from the summary above, the legend of Saint Dorothy in *BHL* 2324 has been fleshed out through the addition of many details. Thus, a few lines about the persecution of Christians, Saint Dorothy's parents' flight from Rome, and Saint Dorothy's birth and youth have been added.[19] Moreover, the legend has been molded to conform to what appears to be the general narrative and structural pattern common to legends of female martyrs. As Gad (1961: 31) observes:

> Legenderne om de *kvindelige martyrer* indtager en særstilling blandt martyrlegenderne, fordi amplifikationerne af passionsmønsteret her er særlig talrige. Med meget eftertryk skildres det, hvorledes troen får de svage unge piger til at blive helte og bære pinsler og trodse forfølgerne med mandsmod. 'Viriliter age' lyder det også til de kvindelige martyrer, og virkningen af martyrens mod er så meget større, når det viser sig, at den svage kvindelige natur kan udholde det samme som de mandlige krigere for troen.

As in the legend of Saint Dorothy, some of these legends of female martyrs add to the passion a new motif: the woman defends not only her religious belief, but also her chastity, and, by extension, her independence, so that she dies not only a Christian, but also a virgin, who has preserved her chastity for the sake of her heavenly spouse.[20] As such, there is a

---

19. Busse (1930: 6–7) draws attention to the fact that the child's appearance is described in detail: barefooted, with fair curly hair, and clothed in a purple garment with gold stars. She suggests that pictorial representations of possibly the Child Jesus may have influenced the legend and refers to late-medieval artistic works in which the child with the basket is indeed Jesus Christ (see p. 45).

20. The notion of the corporeality of female nature can be traced to Aristotle, who defined women through their bodies alone as beings lacking in reason. Saint Augustine tried to reconcile Plato's gender-neutral view of the soul with Aristotle's and concluded that while men's and women's souls were equal, their bodies were not; women had a conflict of body and soul that men did not, and as the flesh was inferior to the soul, so were women subordinate to men. Saint Jerome was one of the many proponents of the view that women could transcend their female nature only by denying it, that is, by preserving their virginity. Accordingly, the virginal religious life was by patristic theology viewed as the most acceptable state of life open to the woman; the second was continent widowhood, and the third marriage (which was regarded as a remedy for the sin of lust in addition to being the natural institution for the procreation of "souls" to love and honor God). Only as a virgin could a woman rise to spirituality, personhood, and equality with the male, but, as Ruether (1974: 164) emphasizes, in order to do so she had to transcend not just her body (as men who chose celibacy did), but her entire female nature.

kind of ambivalence in the legends: the discourse glorifies virginity as a prerequisite for female salvation, but through narratives whose story line places the saint's virginal status, her *integras*, in continuous jeopardy (Cazelles 1991: 44). The saint's sanctity is not achieved by virtue of her virginity, but at the risk of it; it is only a beleaguered virginity that is able to gain the crown. In most legends, the matter of the saint's *virginitas intacta* does not dominate the entire legend, however, but serves primarily as a starting point.[21] Thus, in the legend of Saint Agatha (*BHL* 4 Epitomae), for example, Quintianus, the consular official of Sicily, pursues the highborn virgin, but she rejects his advances. Accordingly, he turns her over to a procuress and her daughters, but since they are unable to overcome Saint Agatha's resistance, Quintianus summons her before the court, where he himself is the judge; the rest of the legend is a conventional *passio* with dialogues, tortures, and miracles (Gad 1961: 31–32).

The legend of Saint Agnes (*BHL* 9 Epitomae), possibly one of the oldest legends of virgin martyrs (Gad 1961: 19, 31), and the legend of Saint Dorothy (as represented by *BHL* 2324; see p. 19) differ in this respect, in that the two motifs, chastity and *passio*, are closely connected throughout. In the legend of Saint Agnes, it is related that the prefect's son made her an offer of marriage, which she refused because of her commitment as *sponsa Christi*. The young man fell ill with lovesickness, and Agnes was brought before the prefect, who told her of his son's condition, but she assured him that she could not violate her covenant with her betrothed. The prefect then gave her two choices: to make a sacrifice to the goddess Vesta or be thrown in with harlots. Upon her refusal to perform the sacrifice, the prefect had her stripped naked and taken to a bordello, but God made her hair grow so long that it covered her. When she entered the brothel, an angel was waiting for her; his radiance filled the place with light and formed a shining mantle about her. The prefect's son came in

---

21. See Carlé (1980: 81), who also argues that some of these legends of female virgin saints "should not be read as examples of a female attitude of disdain and suppression of the sex, but as examples of chastity as a female potential." In her view, "[t]hese legends present us with a picture of women who used Christianity as a reinforcement of their strife for a society where female sexuality was not a mattter of disgrace, but a source on which to draw" (86). Carlé's view seems to be based on a misunderstanding of the idea of female virginity, because, as McLaughlin (1974: 234) points out, a woman's virginity is not an affirmation of her being as a woman; her salvation involves a complete negation of her nature, both physically and mentally, and an assumption of the nature of the male, which is identified with the truly human: rationality, strength, courage, steadfastness, and loyalty.

with other young men and invited them to take their pleasure with her, but they were terrified by the light. He scorned them as cowards and rushed in to force himself upon Agnes, but the same light engulfed him. When the prefect heard about his son's death, he insisted that Agnes should prove her innocence by bringing him back to life with her prayers. Agnes prayed, and the youth came back to life and began to preach Christ publicly. The priests of the temples stirred up a tumult among the people, and the prefect, wishing to set her free, but fearing that he would be outlawed, put a deputy in charge. The deputy had Agnes thrown into a roaring fire; but when the flames left her unscathed, he had a soldier thrust a dagger into her throat, killing her.

The similarity between the two legends (such as the prefect's or the prefect's son's infatuation with the saint and the prefect's insistence that the saint sacrifice to heathen idols) suggests that the legend of Saint Dorothy was influenced by that of Saint Agnes, although these motifs appear with varying degrees of similarity also in other legends, including those of Saints Agatha, Anastasia (*BHL* 2 Epitomae), Margaret of Antioch, and, not least, Justina.[22] As Delehaye (1927) observes: "Bien des épisodes saillants ... ne sont que des réminiscences, traits flottants qui s'attachent tantôt à un saint, tantôt à un autre" (26–27). The fact that both Saint Dorothy and Saint Agnes are highborn does not necessarily suggest a connection, for the Latin legends attribute an aristocratic background to their subjects almost as a matter of course (Heinzelmann 1977), and the saints' noble status often functions as a narrative device that provokes the first encounter between them and their tormentors. Similarly, beauty is another typical characteristic of female martyrs; it is precisely because the saint is beautiful, because she remains *virgo intacta*, that she is attractive and will be forced to suffer and die.[23] Finally, the rejection of a suitor's

22. The similarities between the legend of Saint Dorothy and the legend of Saint Justina are quite striking (see p. 7). Concerning Saint Justina it is related that she was born to Christian parents and that when she reached the age of fourteen, she was courted by many men. Because she repeatedly rejected the offers of marriage due to her commitment as *sponsa Christi*, she was brought before the prefect Fabianus, who demanded that she sacrifice to the heathen gods. She refused, claiming that the gods were demons, and was then given the choice between worshipping the gods or being subjected to tortures.

23. Cf. Cazelles (1991): "The physical and social distinctions that characterize all the heroines commemorated in hagiographic romance serve to stress their vulnerability, since these very qualities attract the attention of the surrounding community, thereby contradicting their desire to avoid unchaste gazes. These saintly maidens seek, in

offer of wealth may be said to be a commonplace; since the saint's life is
to be an *imitatio Christi*, the renunciation or rejection of material
possessions is a general prerequisite for and a first step toward sanctity
(Heffernan 1988: 268).

Other episodes in the legend of Saint Dorothy suggest a kinship with
the legends of Saint Agatha and Saint Christina (*BHL* 4 Epitomae): the
procuress and her nine daughters, to whom Saint Agatha is turned over in
an attempt to make her change her mind, bear some ressemblance to Saint
Dorothy's two sisters; and the heathen idol that collapses into a heap of
dust in the legend of Saint Christina recalls the idols destroyed by angels
in the legend of Saint Dorothy.[24] As Delehaye (1927: 95) notes, borrowings from other legends are common: "Les Vies de saints remplies d'extraits
d'autres. Vies de saints sont très nombreuses, et il en est qui ne sont guère
autre chose qu'un centon hagiographique." Often a compiler of a saint's
life had only scanty information about the saint in question, and, in order
to satisfy the devout curiosity of pilgrims and others and to create edifying
narratives from such paucity of fact, he would take the only course open
to him and make liberal use of the method of amplification used in the
schools, or else fall back on borrowings from other writers.[25]

Delehaye (1927: 89) comments that it is the martyr's physical sufferings
that lend themselves most readily to amplification: "Ils [les hagiographes]
multiplient les supplices, sans beaucoup se préoccuper de la limite d'endurance de la nature humaine; car on fait intervenir la puissance divine, pour
empêcher le saint de succomber à l'excès des souffrances et permettre à
l'hagiographe d'épuiser sur lui tous les tourments que son imagination ou
le souvenir de ses lectures lui suggèrent" (cf. also Gad 1961 quoted p. 11).
And indeed, the nameless editor of the legend of Saint Dorothy, as it
appears in *BHL* 2324, was not sparing in the details of Saint Dorothy's

---

principle, to remain invisible; yet the logic of the narrative goes counter to this aspira-
tion, and their ordeal can be best described as a process of forced visibility" (50).

24. Günter (1949: 143–144) observes that the destruction of idols as a hagiographical *topos* of the victory over demonic powers is found in many legends.

25. "Avec plus ou moins d'imagination et de faconde, d'innombrables hagiographes
se sont résignés à suppléer au silence des sources, en racontant, sur la matière, ce qui
leur paraissait vraisemblable ... Il s'agit, par exemple, d'un martyr. Le cadre de la narra-
tion est nettement dessiné. D'abord, une description plus ou moins détaillée de la persé-
cution. Les chrétiens sont partout recherchés; un grand nombre tombent aux mains des
soldats, et parmi eux le héros du récit; il est arrêté et jeté en prison. Mené devant le
juge, il confesse sa foi et endure d'affreux supplices. Il meurt, et son tombeau devient
le théâtre d'une foule de prodiges." (86–87)

sufferings, many of which recall spectacular accounts of tortures by pagan tormentors, full of gore and eloquence, in the lives of other female saints.[26] Saint Barbara, for example, was first beaten with ropes, lacerated with sharp combs, and imprisoned; she was then burnt; her breasts were cut off; and finally, she was led naked through the city. Saint Anastasia was thrown into a dreadful prison to be starved to death and then bound to a stake to be burned alive. Saint Juliana (*BHL* 3 Epitomae) was first stripped and beaten; secondly, she was hung up by the hair and had molten lead poured on her head; later she was bound in chains and shut up in prison; next, she was stretched on a wheel until all her bones were broken and the marrow spurted out; and finally, she was put in a tub filled with molten lead. Saint Justina's face was beaten to a pulp with a cane after which her breasts were mauled. Saint Agatha was first stretched on a rack and tortured; later, the executioners twisted her one breast and severed it; she was then sent to prison to be starved; and finally, she was rolled naked over potsherds and live coals strewn on the ground. Saint Margaret of Antioch was hung upon a rack, beaten with rods, and lacerated with iron rakes, then stripped of her clothes and burned, and finally bound and put in a tub full of water. Saint Christina was first torn with hooks; next, she was thrown into an iron cradle fired with oil, pitch, and resin; thirdly, her head was shaved and she was led naked through the city; fourthly, she was

26. Most scholars who have studied the legends of female virgin martyrs are struck by the extraordinary emphasis on the saint's physcial sufferings and the writers' lingering over these episodes. Robertson (1991) suggests that the legends incorporate the contemporary view that a woman's relation with God could be realized only through the body, and further, that physical suffering identified the female saint with Christ's sufferings: "Because a woman can never escape her body, her achievement of sanctity has to be through the body. Her temptation by the devil will be through the body and most probably will be sexual. She can overcome that sexual temptation only through her body, primarily by countering her physicality with her endurance of extreme physical torture. A woman further achieves redemption through her identification with Christ's physical suffering, through her dependence on Christ, and most important, not through her transcendence of earthly desire, but through her transference of physical desire to Christ" (269). Robertson, who bases her theory on a study of the thirteenth-century Middle English life of Saint Margaret of Antioch, draws attention to the fact that the legend of Saint Margaret (as that of Saint Dorothy) ends with the saint's prayer for women in childbirth, which she sees as underlying the significance of physical suffering as the central theme of the text. Robertson comments: "It may seem odd that a chaste saint should be the patron saint of childbirth, but given this life's exploration of the particularly physical aspect of female spirituality, such a link is quite appropriate" (285).

thrown into a furnace with asps, wipers, and cobras; and finally, her breasts were severed and her tongue was cut out. Fides (*BHL* 5 Epitomae), one of Saint Sophia's three daughters, was punished by being beaten, by having her breasts torn off, by being thrown on a red-hot gridiron, and by being put in a frying pan full of oil and wax. Spes (*BHL* 5 Epitomae), the second daughter, was put into a cauldron full of pitch, wax, and resin. Caritas (*BHL* 5 Epitomae), the third daughter, was first stretched on the rack until her limbs broke, then beaten with clubs and scourged with lashes, and finally thrown into a fiery furnace.[27] It appears that certain

27. A number of scholars have commented upon the apparently sexual orientation of the tortures. Atkinson (1983) draws attention to the fact that while men and women were beaten and burnt, women saints were also sexually humiliated and assaulted, stripped naked, taken to brothels, and subjected to tortures such as the mauling of their breasts. Since male saints were spared corresponding tortures, she claims that it is "difficult to avoid the conclusion that such passages were experienced as erotic" (189). Gad (1971) comments on "den utilslørede sadisme, der ikke skjuler hvilke instinkter genren også vender sig til, og som hos Agatha er af mere klart sexuel karakter end i andre" (58; cf. also 42). Carlé (1980) goes so far as to assert that these legends may have served as a kind of pornography: "The pornographical details are especially numerous, though extremely unvaried in details, in the last part of each legend, when the woman is tortured and humiliated in various ways in order to break her down and make her sacrifice to the Roman gods. Keeping in mind that the story began with a conflict concerning the sexual integrity of the woman, the writers of the legends could gain some pornographic value from these situations as well. The most common examples will be about women who are raped in prison, or undressed in court; the amputation of the woman's breasts is also rather common. On the whole, the legends could be described as 'yellow' literature, sadistic scenes, staged on the great theatre of society" (82). A similar assertion is made by Atkinson (1983): "On the highest level they [the legends of female saints] inspired faith and courage, perhaps especially in women, for whom these were the only models of active and heroic femininity ... . But on the lowest level, their indulgence – perhaps even delight – in the details of sexual abuse can only be described as pornographic" (190). The possibility that the legends are a by-product of some libidinal repression that generates vivid sensual fantasizing under the guise of anti-sensual polemics cannot be denied. Nor can the possibility be denied that the underlying idea behind these punitive measures was to destroy the woman's physical attractiveness so that she was no longer desirable to any man (including Christ).

Nonetheless, if we take into account (1) the medieval theology of womanhood which taught that women were created inferior to men and only through virginity could achieve the highest spiritual development possible; and (2) the characteristics of the legends as a literary genre, these comments appear to reflect a superficial reading of the legends and ignore the underlying idea behind the sufferings. As Delehaye (1927: 38) notes, in the legends, the abstract is made concrete, and ideas are replaced by pic-

borrowings from the lives of some of these saints have taken place. However, as Delehaye (1927) points out: "Au moyen âge, on se souciait assez
peu de passer pour plagiaire" (83). Indeed, Heffernan (1988) argues that the
authors or editors of saints' lives made deliberate use of borrowings to
stimulate the reader's associative faculty or recognition: "This substitution
of motifs from other sacred biographies, this *amplificatio*, was viewed as an
act of filial *pietas* and not one of literary theft. There is little evidence to
suggest that the sacred biographer was consciously deceiving his readers
into believing that an embedded selection was in fact from the writer's
own hand" (114).

Whatever the reasons for Jacobus's omission of the legend in his *Legenda aurea* and despite Nicholas of Cusa's scepticism concerning the "superstitiosa," it appears that it was exactly the promise in the legend of Saint
Dorothy's intercession at the hour of death which brought about an in-
crease in her popularity (Künstle 1926–1928: 2, 188). Indeed, in some areas
it caused her to be included among the fourteen or fifteen holy helpers.
These holy helpers or auxiliary saints (in missals called "auxiliatores,"
"adiutores," and "legitimi adiutores") constitute a group of saints who
enjoyed a collective cult in the Rhineland in the fourteenth and especially
the fifteenth centuries. From the Rhineland area the cult spread to the rest
of Germany, Hungary, and Scandinavia (the devotion seems to have had
little following in France and Italy). The names of the saints varied from
place to place, and in some areas their number was increased, but the principle of their selection seems to have been the efficacy of their intercession
against various diseases, and especially at the hour of death in view of

---

tures. It is in the light of these features that the *topoi* in the lives of female virgin saints
(such as nakedness, stripping, and the mauling, cutting, piercing, burning, and severing
of a woman's breasts), must be seen: the woman is defeminized in a visual and concrete
manner; Christ will love her as a redeemable "soul," but in a way that excludes her
bodily functions as a woman. As Ruether (1974) points out: "The angelic life demands
the male to rise above his body, but it demands that woman rise above her 'nature,'
crushing out from herself all that pertains to her 'femaleness'" (176). This also explains
why not a single male saint is described as being castrated in the legends of the saints
(Origen, who castrated himself to ensure chastity, is an isolated example, and, interestingly, he was condemned by the Church for this "unnatural act"). It seems unneces-
sary to view the mutilation of the female saint's breast as a *topos* of transformation, as
Heffernan (1988) does: "the virgin becomes the bride of the God, and finally the
mother of the God, while retaining her virginity. Her breasts as the symbol of her
maternity are mutilated and finally severed, to underscore the miraculous metamor-
phosis of the virgin into a nurturing mother, virtually a deity in her own right" (283).

supposed revelations that their clients would thus obtain salvation. The list generally comprises Saints Acacius, Barbara, Blaise, Catherine of Alexandria, Christopher, Cyricus, Denys, Erasmus, Eustace, George, Giles, Margaret of Antioch, Pantaleon, and Vitus. For one or other of these were sometimes substituted Antony, Leonard, Nicolas, Sebastian, Roch, or, in areas of Germany and Scandinavia, Dorothy (Franz 1902: 171–172). Liebgott (1982), however, comments that Saint Dorothy was not really a "true" holy helper: "Nogen 'rigtig' nødhjælper var Dorothea ikke. Hun havde ikke i samme grad som de andre et 'speciale,' men havde dog i sin dødsstund hos Gud sikret sig bønhørelse for alle, der ville påkalde hende under vanskelige forhold" (79–80).

The later inclusion of the legend of Saint Dorothy in the *Legenda aurea* was no doubt the most significant contribution to the spread of the legend (see Fleith 1991: 462). Williams-Krapp (1986b: 403) lists no fewer than eleven legendaries from Germany and the Netherlands alone that include the legend of Saint Dorothy; he also notes thirteen texts independent of these legendaries.[28] Most of the later adaptations of the legend, whether in prose or in poetry, in Latin or the vernacular, seem to be derived from the more concise version in *BHL* 2324 or versions closely related to it, although, as Schachner (1903: 157) remarks, longer and divergent versions are found.

28.   The legendaries are: *Bebenhauser Legendar, Das Buch von den heiligen Mägden und Frauen, Darmstädter Legendar, Die elsässische Legenda aurea, Der Heiligenleben Hermanns von Fritzlar, Der Heiligen Leben, Harburger Legenda aurea I, Der Heiligen Leben (Redaktion), Mittelfränkische Heiligenpredikt, Die niederdeutsche Legenda aurea,* and *Die Thalbacher Legenda aurea.* Only two of the texts independent of these legendaries have been edited, see Williams-Krapp (1968b: 403). Of particular interest here is *Die elsässische Legenda aurea,* which, as noted by Kunze (1973: 27), was read especially in convents, for "[d]ieselbe Schreiberin, welche um 1450 die elsässische Legenda aurea in Handschrift Licht. 70 schrieb, legte (u. a.) auch Handschrift Licht. 69 zu Karlsruhe an, welche 57 Legenden weiblicher Heiliger enthält und daher den Titel *büch von den heilgen megden vnd frowen* trägt (f. 10ʳ)" (30). Included among the legends of female saints is Saint Dorothy. Concerning the source of these legends, Kunze notes, however, that "[d]ie Vorlagen müssen für jede einzelne der 57 Legenden gesondert bestimmt werden. Ich kann hier nur einige allgemeine Hinweise geben. Obwohl die Verfasserin die elsässische Legenda aurea eigenhändig abgeschrieben hat, benutzte sie sie für ihr 'Buch von den hl. Mägden und Frauen' nur selten. Häufiger gibt sie eigene Übersetzungen von großen Partien aus der lateinischen Legenda aurea. Doch oft genügen ihr die kurzen Fassungen des Jacobus de Voragine nicht, und sie vergleicht und übersetzt zusätzlich Teile aus den unverkürzten ursprünglichen Legenden" (35–36).

One may distinguish between two main versions of the legend: (1) a longer and earlier version of the legend represented by the *Acta Sanctorum* (*BHL* 2323) and (2) a later and, by comparison, abridged version represented by *BHL* 2324. The longer version does not include the names of Saint Dorothy's parents, and does not mention the flight from Rome, Saint Dorothy's baptism, and the date of her martyrdom. Instead, Saint Dorothy's many virtues and her saintly life are emphasized. The saint's virginity does not dominate the narrative, and her refusal to make sacrifices to the heathen gods is correspondingly more prominent in this version; in fact, it leads to an elaborate debate between the prefect and Saint Dorothy, who on several occasions quotes from Scripture. Indeed, the longer version is characterized by lengthy dialogues, not only between the saint and the prefect, but also between Dorothy and her sisters and, especially, between Theophilus and the prefect; the episode concerning Theophilus's conversion and martyrdom takes up almost one third of the legend, whereas it occupies only a few lines in *BHL* 2324.

In general, *BHL* 2323 is considerably less fanciful than *BHL* 2324. The appearance of the child-angel is not described in as much detail as in *BHL* 2324, although in contrast with *BHL* 2324, he is specified as being four years old. Finally, the order in which the incidents occur differs from *BHL* 2324. In the longer version, Saint Dorothy is, after some parleying with the prefect, placed on the rack, then led to her two sisters, and, after the sisters' execution, again placed on the rack, then burnt with torches and beaten with fists in the face, and finally beheaded. In *BHL* 2324, Saint Dorothy is, as noted above, put into a cauldron of burning oil, starved in prison, lacerated, scourged, and burnt, and imprisoned again; her sisters are then sent to her and are executed, whereupon she is beaten with staves and cudgels, imprisoned, and finally beheaded.

1.1 *The Legend in the Vernacular*

The oldest extant vernacular renderings of the legend of Saint Dorothy appear to be from Germany, where, especially in the fourteenth, fifteenth, and sixteenth centuries, Saint Dorothy was exceedingly popular. In addition to the numerous prose versions of her legend (see n. 28), which all seem to be based on *BHL* 2324, there are a number of recensions in verse. One of these is the *Dorotheen passie* of East Middle German origin from around 1400 (ed. Busse 1930: 15–24). The poem has been transmitted in a number of manuscripts and printed editions, the texts of which differ considerably;

UUB C 497 from the fifteenth century preserves the most original text.[29]
According to Schade (1854: 7) and Busse (1930: 8), the ultimate source of
the *Dorotheen passie* is *BHL* 2324. (That the poem is based on a written
source is evident from the reference "Als ich in dem buche las" [34].)[30]
However, as Eis (1935: 93) observes, Saint Dorothy's parents are here
named Dorotheus and Theodora (and not Dorus and Thea as in *BHL*

---

29. The other manuscripts and printed editions are: (1) Braunschweig, Stadtbibliothek Fr. 87 from the fifteenth century (fragmentary; ed. Gärtner 1977: 63); (2) Dessau,
Zweigstelle der Universitäts- und Landesbibliothek Sachsen-Anhalt Cod. Georg. 24 8to
from the fifteenth century; (3) Hannover, Niedersächsische Landesbibliothek Cod. 84a
from 1474 (ed. Stammler 1921: 75–79); (4) Munich, Bayerische Staatsbibliothek Cod.
Germ. 478 from the fifteenth century; (5) Praha, Narodní Knihovna České Republiky,
Cod. IV D (fragmentary); (6) a Magdeburg imprint by Simon Mentzer from 1550 (cf.
Falk 1890: 89; ed. Wegener 1878: 8–14), (7) a Marienburg imprint by Karweyß from
around 1500 (cf. Falk 1879: 89), (8) a Cologne imprint by Ulrich Zell from about 1502
or 1503; (9) a Nürnberg imprint from around 1505; (10) a Cologne imprint by Heinrich
von Nuyß from 1513 (cf. Falk 1879: 89); and (11) a Cologne imprint from about 1513
(ed. Schade 1854: 11–12). Finally, Williams-Krapp (1980: 212) draws attention to a
Cologne imprint by Koelhoff from 1499, which is probably now lost. The Praha fragment and the Nürnberg imprint were not used by Busse (1930) in her edition of the
poem, and the Braunschweig fragment and the Cologne imprint edited by Schade (1854)
were unknown to her. Schade (1854) was unaware of the other manuscripts and editions and thus argued that the poem had its origin in Cologne. He draws attention to
the fact that in Cologne the legend of Saint Dorothy was of particular interest, because,
as noted by Gelenius in connection with the feast on 6 February, relics of the saint
were kept in the church in Cologne: "S. Dorotheae virginis et martyris cujus multae
reliquiae apud Ubios et imprimis mandibula in ecclesia Beatae Mariae virginis de monte
Carmelo honoratur (*De admiranda sacra et civili magnitudine Coloniae Claudiae Agrip-
pinensis Augustae Ubiorum urbis libri IV. Colon. Agripp.* [1645]: 668; quoted in Schade
1854: 11–12). In *Dat liden der hilger Machabeen* (ed. Schade 1854: 366–393), in which the
Cologne relics are listed, reference is also made to Saint Dorothy: "... sent Barbaren vin-
ger zant geiselong und sent Agneten, / Cecilia Dorothea Cristina Clara van sent Mar-
gareten" (vv. 849–850). The monastery where these relics were kept was founded in
1304. Schade (1854: 12) considers it likely that its relics were acquired at the time of or
soon after its establishment and that the poem was composed in Cologne at this time.
It may also be noted that one of the Carmelites' confraternities in Cologne carried
Saint Dorothy's name; the confraternity was ratified in 1464 (Lindberg 1923: 212).

30. In three of the above-mentioned manuscripts, the legend of Saint Dorothy
appears together with the other *virgines capitales*: (1) UUB C 497, (2) Dessau, Zweigstelle der Universitäts- und Landesbibliothek Sachsen-Anhalt Cod. Georg. 24 8vo, and (3)
Munich, Bayerische Staatsbibliothek Cod. Germ. 478. For a discussion of the *Passienbüchlein von den vier Hauptjungfrauen*, see Jefferis and Kunze (1989) and Williams-
Krapp (1986b: 29–30).

2324),[31] which points to *BHL* 2325d as the source of the legend.[32] Moreover, as in *BHL* 2325d, the details about the date of Saint Dorothy's death is placed after the angel's visit to Theophilus, not before: "Noch gotes gebort czweihundert iar / Unde siben unde achezig, das ist war, / In dem manden alzus, / Der do heiset Februarius, / Lit den tot di reine mait / Dorothea, von der ich han gesait" (371–376).[33] Unlike both *BHL* 2324 and 2325d, the poet presupposes the apostasy of Saint Dorothy's two sisters: "Der tuvel hatte ouch dar oberhant / Gewunnen mit sinem spotte, / Das si an beten di abgote. / Nicht lange wart do gespart: / Sine tochter wurden beide vorkart, / Wenne si vorchten den tot / Unde der grosen marter not, / Di den luten wurden getan, / Di di abgote nicht beten an" (70–78); the lacuna in the Latin, in which the two sisters are neglected until Saint Dorothy converts them from their apostasy, is thereby filled. One other detail, which has no equivalent in the Latin, is added: Theophilus's chopped-up body was thrown to beasts and birds ("Tyren und vogelen werfen vor" [362]).

Another version in verse is the Middle Low German *Sunte Dorotheen passie* (ed. Priebsch 1904: 376–384), which is believed to have been composed in Ostfalen around 1400, but which is extant only in MS Brussels, Koninklijke Bibliotheek F II, from 1476. The poem is, according to Busse (1930: 24) and Williams-Krapp (1980: 213), a free rendering of *BHL* 2324 with many additions or a version of the legend closely related to it. For example, the brief mention in the Latin of the persecution of Christians is elaborated at length (5–18) after the poet's introduction (1–4). Generally, however, amplification of material is limited to important episodes in the legend, including the conversation between Theophilus and Saint Dorothy (362–391), the conversation between Saint Dorothy and the child (465–483), and, not least, Saint Dorothy's prayer before her execution:

31. Cf. Willenberg (1880: 25): "Ich neige zu der annahme, dass die namen *Dorus* und *Thea* jüngeren ursprungs und nur zu dem zwecke von *Dorotheus* und *Theodora* abgeleitet sind, den namen der h. Dorothea als eine zusammensetzung aus den namen ihrer eltern darzustellen."

32. *BHL* 2325d is represented by Bologna, Biblioteca Universitaria Cod. 2800, fols. 65r–66v. See the appendix, pp. 104–107.

33. Line references to versions of the legend in verse, here and elsewhere in the introduction, are provided in parentheses. The Cologne edition edited by Schade (1854) gives the date of Saint Dorothy's execution as "nae godes gebort zwei hundert jair / ind seven und seszich dat is wair / in deme maende der uns alsus / genant is Februarius" (372–375). Eis (1930: 93) comments: "Der deutsche Dichter muß einen Text vor sich gehabt haben, der zwei X weniger hatte als die Leg. aur. [*BHL* 2324]."

Dar vel se up dat ertrike
Und bad gode so innichliken
Vor alle de dar dachten an or pyn
Dat god on dede hulpe schin
Und se [lose?] van aller drovicheyt,
Syn ewige trost sy on bereyt.
De scrifft uns ok dat leret:
We se des daghes (ok) gherne eret
Und begheret oren trost
Van hovet sunden wart he lost,
Van valschem richte und armode
Wart he lost myt orme gode,
Und ok umme willen der edelen juncfrauwen
So krighet de mynsche ware ruwe
Und deyt lutter sine bycht
Van aller schult de ome ane licht.
Wan ome dat leuent schal ave ghan
De licham Cristi wart ome dan,
Des wart he nicht berovet
Ghensliken we dat louet.
Ok frauwen de dar sin myt eyner bort beswert
Und orer hulpe dar to begheret
De werdet snel ghelost
Und van der bort gelost.
Auer spreket de scrifft also:
In welkem hus (sy) or belde io
Ghemalet effte gescreuen is,
Des so schal me syn ghewis,
Dat schande, dwelinghe noch mord
Wart snelle van dem huse vort.
Ok de snelle, gaye doyt
Mach dar nycht scaden affte yennick noyd.
Wan wy eret de reynen maghet
Und unsen kummer or claghet
Und unsen kummer so mannich:
Des werde wy alle ewich (396–431).

The description of miraculous events, such as the destruction of the idols (170–205) and the healing of Saint Dorothy after she has been thrown into a vessel of burning oil (115–125), are also amplified. Moreover, what is implicit in the Latin is made explicit in the poem. Thus, the Latin nowhere specifies that Fabricius became angry when Saint Dorothy converted her sisters, although it is evident from the context; the poem, by contrast, makes it explicit: "Do Fabricius horde dusse dyngh. / Mit grotem torne he u*m*me ghingk, / Dat se de suster hadde bekart" (270–272). The poet also uses similes, especially in the description of Saint Dorothy: "Alse de rose in dem dauwe / So schone was de edele joncfrauwe" (56–57); "Me nam dar de juncfrauwen syn, / Clare alse der sunnen schyn" (108–109); "De juncfrauwe stunt dar so eyn lam / Dat dar manigk den wulven were bevan" (160–161). As in the older *Dorotheen passie,* the names of Saint Dorothy's parents are Dorotheus and Theodora; however, her sisters' apostasy is not mentioned until Fabricius brings them to her in an attempt to make her abandon her Christian faith. Unlike both the *Dorotheen passie* and *BHL* 2324, but like *BHL* 2325d, the nameless bishop who baptizes Saint Dorothy is called "Apolonius" (48). Finally, the description of Theophilus's martyrdom is abridged, and the factual details about the date of Saint Dorothy's execution and her feastday are omitted.

The fragmentary *Von sent Dorothea* (ed. Busse 1930: 30–41) is believed to have been composed in Bavaria in the first half of the fourteenth century.[34] The poem, which, according to Busse (1930: 27), was composed by "[e]in Kleriker allerdings, der auch weltliche Literatur kannte und selbst für ein feingebildetes Publikum schrieb," is, according to Williams-Krapp (1980: 213), based on *BHL* 2324, although the names of Saint Dorothy's parents are those of *BHL* 2325d. It differs considerably from the two poems mentioned above: details from other sources have been added, and the narrative exploits the dramatic potential of the events; the work is marked by its realistic characterization and by its attempts to probe the motivation of the principals. As such, it attests the beginnings of a trend toward a more belletristic form of sacred legends. Stylistically, too, it shows influence of Konrad von Würzburg (d. 1287) and familiarity with courtly literature, especially Wolfram von Eschenbach's (ca. 1170-ca. 1220) *Parzival.* Saint Dorothy's father is described almost as a chivalric knight (55–59), and the detailed and dramatic account of the flight from Rome to Caesarea contains a brief vignette of wild animals fighting dragons to which the family is witness (155–161). As Busse (1930: 26) observes: "Diese Schilderung dürfte aus dem ritterlichen Abenteuerroman inspiriert sein." The same may apply also to the episode in which Fabricius requests Saint

---

34. The poem has been transmitted in Klagenfurt, Landesarchiv Cod. 6/30 (seven leaves) and Nürnberg, Germanisches Nationalmuseum Cod. 8601 (three leaves).

Dorothy to worship the heathen gods: "'Dorothea, chera wider,' / Sprach er, 'und chnie palde nider, / Ruef an Machmeten minen got / Und Apollo, von des gebot / Die sunne schinet durch den tac; / Machmet schatz dir geben mach, / Und pris und ere Tervigant" (372–377).[35] The poet also draws on biblical imagery and allusion. Saint Dorothy quotes examples from the Old Testament to demonstrate God's power (255–269), and her sisters express the hope that they will be forgiven as were Saints Peter and Mary Magdalen (667–685). It is, however, in psychological characterization that the poem distinguishes itself from other adaptations of the legend. The character of Fabricius in particular is rich in nuance; he is not the traditional brutal tyrant, the archetypal heathen persecutor, but very human in his love for Saint Dorothy and in his frustration and anger at her stubbornness. So, too, the rigid features of her character are softened. She is not abrupt in her rejection of Fabricius's offer of marriage; rather, she tactfully explains to him their incompatibility and advises him to marry a heathen woman instead.

The *De Dorothea*, extant in St. Gall, Stiftsbibliothek Cod. 1006 (ed. Busse 1930: 42–46), combines *passio* and prayer and thus presents a very different rendering of the legend of Saint Dorothy.[36] The poem consists of an enumeration of the saint's ten tortures, described in vivid detail and greatly amplified in comparison with the accounts found in *BHL* 2324 and 2325d.[37] The ending of the poem discloses the date of composition: "DO man mit worten wol gestalt / Von der geburt Kristi zalt / Dusent und fierhundert jar / Und drißig, daz ist war, / da ward gedichtet dis gedicht / Und us latin in düsche gericht" (337–342). According to Busse (1930: 42), the poem has its origin in Alemannia; Williams-Krapp (1980: 214) draws

---

35. Busse (1930): "Diese Gottheiten kehren häufig in den ritterlichen Epen als die heidnischen Götter wieder, und dieser seiner Lektüre hat der Dichter sie wohl auch entnommen" (27).

36. Williams-Krapp (1980: 214–215) mentions Munich, Cod. Lat. Mun. 22309, which preserves a poem based on the same source as the poem in the St. Gall manuscript. This poem has its origin in Bavaria and was, according to Williams-Krapp, composed in the first half of the fifteenth century.

37. Cf. Busse (1930): "Hier zeigt sich die Neigung des Spätmittelalters zum Realismus, wie sie uns vielfach auf Altarbildern mit Legenden- oder Passionsszenen entgegentritt. ... Von Bedeutung für uns sind die Hinweise auf bildliche Darstellungen der Dorothea: Wo ein Bild der Heiligen im Hause ist, kann weder Diebstahl noch Feuersbrunst Schaden anstiften. Hier haben wir eine Erklärung für die Beliebtheit, welcher Dorothea sich mit zunehmendem Spätmittelalter erfreute, und für die Holzschnitte, die gerade in der zweiten Hälfte des XV. Jahrhunderts so zahlreich verbreitet waren" (41–42). See also Saint Dorothy's prayer in *Sunte Dorotheen passie* quoted p. 22, which agrees more with *BHL* 2325d than *BHL* 2324.

attention to the reference to "sant Jergen" (5) and suggests that it was composed in the St. Gall Benedictine convent of St. Georgen.

A verse paraphrase from Bavaria or Austria, *Die Erzählung vom Martyrium der lobesamen Jungfrau St. Dorothea*, is preserved in Klosterneuburg, Stiftsbibliothek Cod. 1079, from the fifteenth century (ed. Ludwig 1928: 1–51). The poem seems to be based on an expanded version of *BHL* 2325d, but differs from it in a number of details. The *passio* is preceded by an invocation of the Trinity and the Virgin Mary and a plea for aid in the composition of the work. And in the account of Saint Dorothy's imprisonment after her tortures, the Savior himself appears and consoles her, saying that she will be joining him soon in heaven. The apostasy of the two sisters is mentioned at the beginning of the legend; and to the account of the three sisters' conversation a newly invented speech by Calisten, who expresses Fabricius's views, is inserted. Saint Dorothy's final prayer is also expanded. She now becomes the patron of captives and travellers, sick and distressed; homes where she is honored will be spared the birth of deformed children, and those who read her passional will be granted their prayers. A number of miracles are added: men and women are cured with the help of the heavenly apples and recover from ailments at her grave; her body causes the pictures of the heathen gods on the walls of Theophilus's hall to fall to the ground. Busse (1930: 47), who argued that the poet based his work on an oral German version of the legend, was challenged by Menhardt (1930), who remarks: "Daß der Verfasser 'nach einer mündlichen Verdeutschung erzählte' ... glaube ich nicht" (448).[38]

Meistersinger Michel Schrade's poem about Saint Dorothy (ed. Busse 1930: 50–58), composed in Schwaben (Augsburg?) in the second half of the fifteenth century, is by contrast indisputably based on a written vernacular source, *Der Heiligen Leben,* of which it is a fairly close rendering (Williams-Krapp 1986b: 344).[39] The text deviates slightly from the source in response to the demands of meter and rhyme; in the only substantial addition in the last stanza, the poet names himself as he calls upon Saint Dorothy.[40]

38. Cf. the comment in the story: "pey den czeytten wazz ein man / cze Ron als ich gelessen han / gesessen Theodorum was seyn nam" (4).

39. Michel Schrade's poem is preserved in Heidelberg, Universitätsbibliothek Cod. Pal. Germ. 392, from the fifteenth century. Cf. n. 28 above.

40. "Dorothe, ich bit durch deiner martter ere, / An meinem end so solt du mir auch wone bey; / Bit got fur mich, und das ich werd der sinde frey, / Das im kain böser gaist auch nit da schedlich sey; / Ich, Michel Schrade, das beger / Von sant Dorothe here" (396–401).

It is also possible that a vernacular text served as the source for Heinrich der Teichner's (ca. 1310-ca. 1375) poem about Saint Dorothy (ed. Niewöhner 1953-1956: 1, 238-241, no. 216).[41] The poem follows the *BHL* 2324 or 2325d versions closely, but omits mention of the names of Saint Dorothy's parents and sisters as well as the names of the prefect and the scribe and does not include the details about the date of her martyrdom. As in Michel Schrade's poem, the only substantial addition occurs at the conclusion of the poem, when the poet names himself.[42]

Finally, Williams-Krapp (1980: 215) draws attention to two fragmentary versifications of the legend of Saint Dorothy independent of the ones mentioned above. One is extant in Dresden, Sächsische Landesbibliothek Cod. M 249, which contains only the account of the execution of Saint Dorothy and the miracle of the roses and apples. The other is extant in Wolfenbüttel, Herzog-August-Bibliothek Cod. 1231 Helmst. The author of this poem was interested only in the execution and the last miracle; previous events in the narrative are restricted to a few sentences.

Dramatizations of the legend of Saint Dorothy are found in a number of places, but appear to have been especially common in Germany. The records of the town hall in Bautzen testify to the popularity of the plays:

> Am 8. februar 1413 gab der rector scholae wie alle jahre am sonntag vor Dorothea mit consens des domstiftes und rats mitten auf dem markte eine Comoedie de Passione S. Dorotheae. Als das spiel fast über die hälfte war und der vorwitzige pöbel in grosser menge bey dem seigerthurme, auf dem thum oder markte, auf der gewandladen ziegeldach gestiegen war, so brach es mit den leuten ein, und stürzte ein stück ziegelmauer herunter, dass über 30 personen erschlagen wurden, die man folgendes tags mit grossen weinen und wehklagen begrub. Viele waren sehr beschädigt, viele blieben an händen und füssen lahm (Schachner 1903: 158).

---

41. Heinrich der Teichner's poem is preserved in Vienna, Österreichische Nationalbibliothek Poem. Germ. 2901, 2819, and 2848.

42. "ez ward an dem selben tag / offt ein sel hintz himel pracht, / daz sand Torothe dervacht, / daz si furt den sturm van. / sich haet nieman martern lan, / hiet si nicht den spitz gehalden / und dez vestichleich gewalden. / si ueber vacht den cheiser schon. / dez trait si *die* hime*l* chron / ewichleich an alle swaer. / also sprach der Teychnaer" (236-246).

The phrase "wie alle jahre am sonntag vor Dorothea" shows that by 1413 these performances were already well established. The Saint Dorothy plays also seem to have been an attraction in many areas of Bohemia. Referring to the list of expenditures of the city of Eger for the year 1455, Gradl (1895: 141-142) notes that on Saint Dorothy's feast day, grammar school children walked about in the city singing Saint Dorothy songs under the direction of their teacher. From around 1500, grammar school children also performed a fullfledged Saint Dorothy play in the town hall and perhaps also in the school; the last such performance was in 1544. It is known that Saint Dorothy plays were also performed in Lambach (1366), Kulm (1436), Mergentheim (1498), Dresden (1498 and 1523), Butzbach (1517), Zwickau (before 1535; see below), and, in the Netherlands, in Nimwegen (1414).[43] As Krogh (1940) points out: "I dette Stof var alt, hvad hin Tids Publikum med Rimelighed kunde forlange: Et Par Omvendelsesscener, forskellige Mirakler og flere rystende Tortur- og Henrettelsesscener" (50).

Only a fragment of one such a play has been preserved: the *Ludus de Sancta Dorothea*, found in Kremsmünster, Stiftsbibliothek CC 81 (ed. Schachner 1903: 186-193; Ukena 1975: 2, 337-349). Composed around 1350, it has been consigned to Upper Saxony or northern Bohemia by Schachner (1903: 171) and Creizenach (1911-1923: 1, 126).[44] Apart from the prologue, the *Ludus* is a close rendering of *BHL* 2324, according to Schachner (1903: 173-174).[45] However, as in the *Dorotheen passie, Sunte Dorotheen passie, Von sent Dorothea*, and the *Erzählung vom Martyrium der lobesamen Jungfrau St. Dorothea*, the names of Saint Dorothy's parents are Dorotheus and Theodora,[46] and, as in the *Dorotheen passie* and the *Erzählung vom Martyrium der lobesamen Jungfrau St. Dorothea*, the translator pre-

43. Wimmer and Binding (1985: 1318); Linke (1978: 741, 760); Ukena (1975: 2, 351). See further Feifalik (1864: 81-166).

44. Cf. Ukena (1975): "Die Sprachuntersuchung in Schachners Ausgabe charakterisiert den Text als ursprünglich einer ostmitteldeutschen Mundart angehörig, in der vorliegenden Form aber von einem österreichischen Schreiber mit dessen Dialekt vermischt. Der Lokalisierung auf ostmitteldeutschem Gebiet kann zugestimmt werden; es handelt sich um ein frühes Zeugnis schlesischer Mundart" (2, 328).

45. Schachner (1903): "Der zusammenhang unseres bruchstückes mit der legende ist so auffallend, dass man annehmen kann, sie sei vom dichter direkt ohne mittelglied benützt worden" (174). See also Ukena (1975: 1, 47).

46. Schachner (1903: 175) draws attention to the fact that the editors of the *Acta Sanctorum* version (*BHL* 2323) note that in François Lahier's *Le grande Menologe des saintes, bienheureuses et venerables Vierges* (Lille, 1645), their names are Theodorum and Theodarum.

supposes the apostasy of Saint Dorothy's sisters; Schachner (1903), who attributes this to the poet, comments: "Es muss aber als geschickter griff des dichters bezeichnet werden, dass er sich durch diese kleine eigenmächtigkeit für eine spätere scene den weg ebnete" (175; see also Ukena 1975: 1, 47). Since this deviation from *BHL* 2324 (and 2325d) occurs in other vernacular renderings, the attribution of this alteration to the author of the *Ludus* is questionable. What may, however, be attributed to the poet is the introduction of the character "Primus miles Grim," who serves as Fabricius's knight; the "cursor" or "nuncius" Ewer, also in the service of Fabricius; the "primus tortor" Notopolt, and the "secundus tortor" Tarant; as well as three pagans, a demon, and an angel. Among the *dramatis personae* are groups of walkers-on: "milites," "pagani," "angeli," and "populus." The fragment does not cover the episode involving Theophilus and the child.

The legend also inspired the German Chiliani Equitis Mellerstatini (Kilian Reuther von Melrichstadt), who, in 1507, produced his drama *Comedia gloriose parthenices et martiris Dorothee agoniam passionemque depingens.* As Creizenach (1911–1923: 2, 50) points out, "daß Reuter sich gerade Dorothea unter den heiligen Jungfrauen auserwählte, ist wohl durch die Beliebtheit der Dorotheenspiele in den sächsischen Landen zu erklären".[47] Kilian's Latin play, a product of German renaissance humanism,

---

47. Indeed, the Lutheran Joachim Greff from Zwickau says about the Saint Dorothy plays (which he, in terms of value and impact, equates with the passion plays) that they teach how in times of persecution and sorrow one must be true to God: "Vnd ist kein spiel so klein noch so geringe / man kan vnd sol was daraus lernen / wie man sich hüten sol / itzt für hurerey vnd vnzüchtiger lieb / itzt für fressen / sauffen / spielen / vnd dergleichen / alles zu vnser besserung. Also auch vnser lieben vorfahren habens gut gemeinet vorzeiten / mit dem spiel der passion / wolten vns zu andacht vnd fromigkeit reitzen. Dergleichen auch andere mit S. Dorotheenspiel / darinn sie haben angezeigt vnd zuuerstehen geben / wie wir vns mit nichte / vnd durch keinerley weise von Gott / odder von seinem Göttlichen worte vnd seiner liebe / wedder durch verfolgung odder einige trübsal solten lassen abwendē / gleichwie die heilige Dorothea gethan / die ir leib vnd leben lieber vmb Christi vnd seines worts willen verlieren hat wollen / deñ das sie die Abgötter solt angebetet haben / vnd von Gott solt sein abgefallen. Solch ein spiel ist auch gewesen von des heiligen Johannis des tauffers enthaubtung / vnd viel andere mehr / wie jederman bas weis / denn ich sagen kan. Alles zu vnser besserung (habe ich gesagt) sey solches geschehen / beide von vnsen vorfharen / vnde von den alten klugen / weisen leuten / poeten vnd allen viel andern Scribenten, die es on zweiuel fast gut gemeint haben ..." (Schachner 1903: 161–162, who quotes from Greff's preface to his translation of Plautus's *Aulularia* [Magdeburg, 1535]).

is in prose, but is prefaced by an *argumentum* (an overview of the contents) and a prologue in verse. It follows the *BHL* 2324 version closely, although it clearly relies on other sources as well. In the preface, Kilian himself claims that the *Comedia* is influenced by the Latin plays by Hrotswitha, the tenth-century Benedictine nun of Gandersheim in Saxony: "Sacrimonialem secutus Rosphitam." Indeed, there are many parallels between Kilian's *Comedia* and Hrotswitha's *Dulcitius* and *Sapientia*, especially in the account of Fabritius's offer of marriage and his threats, in the description of Saint Dorothy's conversion of her two sisters, and in Saint Dorothy's words to Runchardus, her executioner (Spengler 1898: 126–128). There are other borrowings from earlier Latin literature. The opening of the *Comedia*, in which the warrior Metellus comes from Caesarea with a letter to Fabricius and is received at the door of Fabricius's house by his servant Orestes, appears to be drawn from the *Amphitruo* (4.1 and 2) by Plautus (c. 250–184). The language of Metellus's description of Saint Dorothy's beauty, appears to be indebted to the *Metamorphoses* by Apuleius (second century). Certain innovations may, however, be ascribed to Kilian himself. These include the account of the soldiers' breaking into Saint Dorothy's home and her mother Thea's lament, as well as the appearance of Pluto, a representative of Hell, with the fury Alecto. Saint Dorothy's description in hexameters of the joys of Paradise, which carries the title "Mantuanus," may be derived from Frater Baptista Mantuanus Carmelita Theologus's epic *De beata virgine*, which, incidentally, accompanies the *Comedia* in the copy of Kilian's play housed in the library of the Znaimer Gymnasium (Spengler 1898: 129; see also Toldberg 1958: 253). Otherwise, Kilian seems to have learned little from his predecessors: he concludes his play rather clumsily by having the tyrannical Fabricius order a meal to be accompanied by music after the bloodbaths he has just helped bring about (Creizenach 1911–1923: 2, 50).[48]

48. Søholm (1972: 105) interprets the concluding lines differently. He argues that Fabricius's final act is not necessarily just a crude and inelegant conclusion to the play, but demonstrates the self-delusion of the tyrant: "Magtmennesket har lidt nederlag og står tragisk alene. Men udadtil kan og vil han ikke drage konsekvensen af denne erkendelse. Tværtimod demonstrerer han sin afmagt som den, der kun kan slå legemet ihjel, ved at beordre dette gjort eftertrykkeligt. Alle kristne skal efterstræbes og pines. Det er den lovlydige romerske blodhund, der giver sin ordre, men det er på den indre front nederlagets mand, der søger at fortrænge erkendelsen af at være det. Den afsluttende festattitude er en illusion, selvbedragets demonstration – og ikke nødvendigvis *blot* en 'rå og kluntet' slutning, som Creizenach kalder den."

The continuing influence of the legend of Saint Dorothy in Germany
is evident from Nikolaus Hermann's (ca. 1480–1561) *Ein schön new geistlich
Lied von S. Dorothea* (Maltzahn 1875: 99 no. 642; Breslauer 1908: 45 no. 98
and 59 no. 136),[49] the poem *Dorothea und Theophilus* recorded from oral
tradition by Arnim and Brentano in the early nineteenth century;[50] the
play *Sancta Dorothea virgo, Cesareae in Cappadocia martyrio affecta a
Sapritio tyranno: tragicâ scenâ producitur a iuventute Cremiphanensi* (1651;
see Schachner 1903: 193–196); Clemens Brentano's (1778–1842) cyclical
poem *Die Monate* (1852–1855: 2, 575–603), in the "Februar" section of
which he refers to the saint ("Gib Dorothea Rosen, meinem Kind, zur
Lust" [2, 602]); Pailler's play *S. Dorothea: Legende in zwei Aufzügen* (1899:
121–166); and not least from Gottfried Keller's (1819–1890) *Sieben Legenden*
(1872), in which he included the story *Dorotheas Blumenkörbchen*. It is generally believed that it was Ludwig Kosegarten's (1758–1818) *Legenden*
(1804), a collection of stories from the *Vitae patrum*, the German *Passional*,
and the *Legenda aurea*, which inspired Keller's interest in the legends and
prompted him to adapt them to a nineteenth-century readership. Keller
succeeds in secularizing the legends: dispensing with the pious tone of
Kosegarten, he imbues the saints with very human qualities and gives to
heavenly matters the air of wordly concerns (Banasik 1986: 285). Thus he
recasts the figure of Theophilus in a sympathetic new light as Dorothy's
earthly lover and provides a vivid description of his heartfelt grief at her

49. For references to seventeenth-century editions containing poems about Saint
Dorothy, see Maltzahn (1875: 318 no. 794 and 321 no. 816) as well as Breslauer (1908:
63 no. 144).
   50. Arnim and Brentano (1987: 2, 305–307). Erk, who prints the poem and the
accompanying melody ("In Dorotheae festo gaudete"), notes that the poem is a revision
of Nikolaus Hermann's poem: "Es ist die Umarbeitung und Kürzung eines Liedes, das
der Cantor Nik. Hermann für seine tochter Dorothea gedichtet hat und steht in dessen:
'Evangelia auf alle Son- und Test-Tage ... für die lieben Kinder in Joachimsthal
aufgestellt. Wittenberg 1560'" (Erk [1893–1894]: 3, 812–813; see also Crecelius 1884: 63
and Rieser 1908: 391–394). Erk (ibid, 313) also notes that the melody shows that
Nikolaus Hermann appears to have based his poem on a Latin hymn: "Aus der Tonan-
gabe folgt, daß Hermann sein Legenden-Lied nach einem lateinischen Gesange dichtete"
(see also Bode [1909: 560–561]). On the whole, the poem follows the standard (*BHL*
2324 or 2325d) version of the legend closely; only the description of the appearance of
the boy-angel has been altered and amplified: "Der helle Morgen lichtet, / Ein Knäblein
stehet draus, / Geschwingt mit goldnen Flügeln / Reichts Rosenkörbchen dar, / Ver-
schwindet auf den Hügeln, / Von wo es kommen war. / Und auf den Rosenblättern
/ Da steht geschrieben klar: / 'Mein Christus ist mein Retter, / Und er mir gnädig war,
/ Ich leb in Freud und Wonne, / In ewger Herrlichkeit!'" (Arnim and Brentano 1987: 2,
306–307).

tortures. Their conversation before her execution serves as an example of the informal tone of the narrative:

> Leichten Schrittes ging sie einher, gefolgt von dem gedankenlosen und lärmenden Volke. Sie sah den Theophilus am Wege stehen, der kein Auge von ihr wandte. Ihre Blicke begegneten sich, Dorothea stand einen Augenblick still und sagte anmutig zu ihm: "O Theophilus, wenn du wüßtest, wie schön und herrlich die Rosengärten meines Herrn sind, in welchen ich nach wenig Augenblicken wandeln werde, und wie gut seine süßen Äpfel schmecken, die dort wachsen, du würdest mit mir kommen!"
>
> Da erwiderte Theophilus bitter lächelnd: "Weißt du was, Dorothea? Sende mir einige von deinen Rosen und Äpfeln, wenn du dort bist, zur Probe!" (78–79).

Keller is respectful of the religious substance of the legend and does not compromise the narrative value of the miraculous elements, which he clearly regarded as essential and unequivocal components of the stories. Nonetheless, he is insistent on his depiction of the worldly and humorous elements, as evident from his description of Theophilus and the basket:

> Theophilus hielt das Körbchen, das nicht verschwunden war, wirklich in Händen; die drei Äpfel fand er leicht angebissen von zwei zierlichen Zähnen, wie es unter den Liebenden des Altertums gebräuchlich war. Er aß dieselben langsam auf, den entflammten Sternenhimmel über sich (80).

Finally, by way of rounding off the story, Keller invents a happy ending, in which the two lovers are united.

> So war Theophilus noch am gleichen Tage für immer mit Dorotheen vereinigt. Mit dem ruhigen Blicke der Seligen empfing sie ihn; wie zwei Tauben, die, vom Sturme getrennt, sich wiedergefunden und erst in weitem Kreise die Heimat umziehen, so schwebten die Vereinigten Hand in Hand, eilig, eilig und ohne Rasten an den äußersten Ringen des Himmels dahin, befreit von jeder Schwere und doch sie selber. Dann trennten sie sich spielend und verloren sich in weiter Unendlichkeit, während jedes wußte, wo das andere weile und was es denke, und zugleich mit ihm alle Kreatur und alles Dasein mit süßer Liebe umfaßte. Dann suchten sie sich wieder mit wachsendem Verlangen, das keinen Schmerz und keine Ungeduld kannte; sie fanden sich und wallten wieder vereinigt dahin oder ruhten im Anschauen ihrer selbst und schauten die Nähe und Ferne der unendlichen Welt. Aber einst gerie-

ten sie in holdestem Vergessen zu nahe an das kristallene Haus der
heiligen Dreifaltigkeit und gingen hinein; dort verging ihnen das
Bewußtsein, indem sie, gleich Zwillingen unter dem Herzen ihrer
Mutter, entschliefen und wahrscheinlich noch schlafen, wenn sie in-
zwischen nicht wieder haben hinauskommen können (80–81).

In France, Saint Dorothy seems to have been less prominent than some
of the other legendary virgin martyrs. However, her legend is included in
the Franco-Italian writer Christine de Pizan's (ca. 1365-ca. 1430) *Livre de
la cité des dames* (ed. Curnow 1975) written between 1404 and 1407. One
of the most important contributions to the early fifteenth-century "querelle
des femmes," the book is an explicit and systematic defence of women
against the standard charges of the misogynistic tradition by adducing some
two hundred examples of extraordinary achievement by women in virtually every area of human endeavor. Inspired in large measure by Saint Augustine's *De civitate Dei* and Boccaccio's (1313–1375) *De mulieribus claris*
(in French translation), Christine describes the foundation and building of
an allegorical *Cité des dames* to give visible proof of the positive qualities
of women and to serve as a refuge for all virtuous ladies of the past,
present, and future. The form of the work is significant: it is an allegorical
dream vision in which the three personified virtues, Dames Raison,
Droiture, and Justice reply to the criticisms of women and give Christine
the directions and building material for the *Cité des dames*. In the first part,
Dame Raison initiates the process with a number of examples in politics,
law, war, and the arts and sciences. In the second part, Dame Droiture
continues the process with a list of women who display exemplary moral
virtue. In the third part, Dame Justice completes the work by relating
stories of women who are exemplary in the spiritual realm, that is, female
saints and holy women, and it is here (in chapter 9.3) that Dame Justice
narrates the story of Saint Dorothy:

"Item, la benoite vierge Dorothee pareillement souffry plusieurs mar-
tiers en Capadoce. Et pource que elle ne vouloit prendre nul homme
a mary et tant parloit de son espoux Jhesu Crist, le maistre des escolles,
qui estoit nommé Theophillus, luy dist par moquerie quant on la men-
oit decoller que au moins quant elle seroit devers son espoux, qu'elle
luy envoyast des roses et des pommes du vergier de son mary. Et elle
dist que sy feroit elle. Dont il avint que si tost que elle ot parfait son
martire, un tres bel petit enffant, comme de l'aage de .iiij. ans, vint a
Theophillus et apportoit un petit paneret plaine de souverainement
belles roses et pommes a merveilles bien flairans et belles, et dist que

la vierge Dorothee les luy envoyoit. Adonc fu celluy esmerveillez, car
il estoit yver ou moys de fevrier. Si se converty et puis fu martirés
pour le nom de Jhesu Crist" (Curnow 1975: 999–1000).

While Boccaccio is considered to be the primary source for the first two
parts, it is generally believed that Vincent of Beauvais's (ca. 1190–1264)
Speculum historiale (in Jean de Vignay's [ca. 1282-after 1340] French
translation) and possibly also Jean de Vignay's *Légende Dorée*, a French
version of the *Legenda aurea* made at the request of Jeanne de Bourgogne,
queen of Philippe VI de Valois (1293–1350), in 1333–1334, provided the
material for the third part,[51] although Christine relied also on other
sources, including Boccaccio's *Decameron* and *De casibus virorum illus-
trium*.[52]

51. See *BHL* 2325 (3. Epitomae). Cf. Dame Justice's words: "Se de toutes les saintes
vierges qui sont ou ciel par constance de martire te vouloye racompter, longue hystoire
y couvendroit: si comme sainte Cecille, sainte Agnés, sainte Agathe et inffinies autres.
Et se plus en veulx avoir, ne t'estuet que regarder ou *Mirouer historial*: la assez en
trouveras" (Curnow 1975: 1000). Vincent of Beauvais's version of the legend is as
follows: "Eodem tempore passa est apud Cæsaream Cappadociæ Dorothea virgo, sub
Sapricio Præside 8. Idus Februarij. Hæc tradita duabus sororibus Christæ, & Calistæ,
quæ apostatauerant; iterum eas conuertit, quæ postea sunt in dolium missæ, & in con-
spectu eius incensæ. Post illarum autem passionem Beata Dorothea leuatur in catasti,
& ait: Nunquam sicut hodie lætata sum in vita mea. Tandem ducta est ad decollandum.
Cui dixit Theophilus Scholasticus: Eia tu sponsa Christi, mitte mihi rosas aut mala de
Paradiso sponsi tui. Quæ respondit: Plane sic faciam. Cumque orasset, ecce puer ante
eam apparuit, ferens in sportario tria mala optima, & tres rosas. Cui illa: Obsecro te
inquit, vt hæc Theophilo scholastico deferas. Cum ergo Theophilus narraret circunstan-
tibus promissionem Virginis irridens: Ecce puer ante eum stetit, & ait: Ecce tibi petenti,
mittit Dorothea virgo sacratissima, quod promisit; Qui accipiens statim conuersus est
ad fidem Christi: eratque mensis Februarius, quando rosæ illæ missæ sunt, & totam
Cappadociam glaciale frigus tegebat. Videbatur autem puer pulcherrimus, & perbreuissi-
mus non plusquam quatuor annorum. Mox ergo Theophilus in eodem equuleo suspensus, & acerrime tortus dicebat: Ecce modo Christianus factus sum, quia in cruce suspensus sum. Nam equulei factura, crucis similitudinem gerit, tandem gladio consummatus
est" (Liber XII, cap. 47).
52. The *Livre de la cité des dames* was translated into Flemish and English. The
Flemish version, the *Stede der Vrouwen*, was completed in 1475 at the command of Jan
de Baenst (d. 1485), an official in the government of Bruges under Phillip the Good.
The English version, the *Boke of the Cyte of Ladyes*, was translated by a certain Bryan
Anslay and was printed by Henry Pepwell in 1521 on behalf of George Grey, Earl of
Kent. For discussions of the Flemish and English translations, see Lievens (1959) and
Curnow (1974), respectively.

In England, the life of Saint Dorothy is found in the *Gilte Legende* and in William Caxton's *Golden Legend*. The *Gilte Legende*, a collection of 178 legends, is a translation made around 1438 of the *Légende Dorée*. Several manuscripts of the *Gilte Legende* were later expanded by saints' lives not included in the original *Gilte Legende*: there are unique additions to BL Addit. 35298 and to Lambeth Palace 72, but a larger group of texts, as found in BL Addit. 11565 and 35298, Lambeth Palace 72, and Southwell Cathedral VII, was (except for the legend of Saint Dorothy) drawn from a manuscript of the *South English Legendary*[53] closely related to BN Nouv. acq. lat. 3075 (Görlach 1972: 14).[54] As pointed out by Görlach (1972: 35), the legend of Saint Dorothy is the only additional legend drawn from an earlier Middle English prose translation and not from the *South English Legendary*. This original translation, which is now lost, is, according to Horstmann (1880: 319) and Görlach (1972: 35), a rendering of *BHL* 2324. The translation, which was made at the beginning of the fifteenth century, survives in three garbled copies: BL Royal 2. A. xviii, Lambeth Palace 432 (ed. Horstmann 1880: 325–328),[55] and Chetham

---

53. Görlach (1986: 304) argues that in its original form the *South English Legendary* was a collection of the Sarum type and close to the surviving Exeter Ordinale of 1337, which was reworked into a rhymed legendary, including some very short and imperfect stories, in the diocese of Worcester around 1270. Immediately after the completion of this first draft or even in the course of its compilation, the legendary was revised, possibly by Dominicans in Oxford or at Gloucester, with the *Legenda aurea* serving as a model for some of the legends of the *pars hiemalis*. When the *South English Legendary* spread to other areas and to other orders, the collection split into a number of textual traditions (see Görlach 1972: 13). In the earliest extant form, Oxford, Bodleian Library, Laud. Misc. 108, the legendary consists of a random arrangement of 64 legends (ed. Horstmann 1887). The edition by D'Evelyn and Mill (1956–1959), based on Corpus Christi 145 and BL Harley 2277, contains ninety items. None of these manuscripts contains the life of Saint Dorothy.

54. The additional legends in the *Gilte Legende* are the lives of Saints Edmund of Abingdon, Bridget of Sweden, King Edmund of East Anglia, Frideswide, Edward the Martyr, Archbishop Alphege of Canterbury, Archbishop Augustine of Canterbury, Bishop Oswald of Worcester, Dunstan, Aldhelm, Theophilus, Bishop Swithun of Winchester, Kenelm, Bishop Chad of Mercia and Lindsey, Bishop Cuthbert of Lindisfarne, Fides, Dorothy, Bishop Leger of Autun, Brendan, Michael (II), and Archbishop Thomas à Becket of Canterbury (II). Görlach (1972: 29) notes that these legends represent a rather complete selection of what the *South English Legendary* had to offer in the way of supplement to the *Gilte Legende*.

55. According to Horstmann (1880: 320), the original Middle English translation of Saint Dorothy is a prose rewriting ("prosa-umdichtung") of the verse legend in BL Harley 5272 and Arundel 168 (see below). Horstmann's conjecture was, however, re-

8009. None of these manuscripts is a copy of another.[56] The legend of Saint Dorothy in the additional legends to the *Gilte Legende* seems to be derived from a text close to, but independent of, BL Royal 2. A. xviii.

The French *Légende Dorée* was modified twice during the fifteenth century: first around 1402 when forty-two "Festes Nouvelles" were added, and again sometime in the last decades of the century, when the traditional order of the chapters was altered and several additional saints' lives were incorporated. This revised collection William Caxton set out to translate in his *Golden Legend*, the last full-scale hagiographical compendium published in England before the Reformation, which was first issued from Caxton's press at Westminster in 1483. Although the *Légende Dorée* forms the basis of the *Golden Legend*, it is clear that Caxton also made use of the *Gilte Legende*, that is, a version containing the additional legends, and the *Legenda aurea*, especially for texts not contained in the *Légende Dorée*. Among the additional legends drawn from the *Gilte Legende* is the legend of Saint Dorothy, which was not contained in Caxton's Latin and French exemplars nor in any English manuscripts of the *Legenda aurea* (Butler

---

futed by Peterson (1910: 52), who states: "the sources of the two poems were Latin texts of the G-type [*BHL* 2324], diverging from the sources of the English prose versions as well as from the text published by Graesse."

56. Görlach (1972: 35, n.2) notes that the version edited by Horstmann (1880), that is, Lambeth Palace 432, is the poorest of the three extant texts. At the end of the legend of Saint Dorothy in this manuscript, there are two Latin prayers to Saint Dorothy: (1) "Gaude virgo Dorothea, ex stirpe nata nobili: Esto aduocatrix, queso, mea, in hac valle flebili. Gaude quia reliquisti prefectum ffabricium Et in sponsu assum*pcisti Cristum dei ffilium. Gaude quia in feruentis olei missa dole*um, De calore nichill sentis dei per auxilium. Gaude carcerata fameque cruciata Pulcryor 7 magis grata sis quam vnquam antea. Gaude quia, columpna facta et distrecto ydoleo, Demonum gen⟨s⟩est subacta, conuersio multo populo. Gaude quod post exquisita tormentorum genera ffax fferuenter et ignita appo*nitur ad v⟨is⟩cera. Gaude quia conuertisti sorores ad dominum Et ffactas martires misisti ad ipsum patrem hominum. Gaude ffacie vulnerata seuo ictu ffustiu*m, In crastino sic es sanata quod no⟨n⟩ paret vestigeu*m. Gaude quia propter ffructus 7 rosas temporandas *Per te scriba est adductus ad Cristi ffamulias. Gaude quia impetrasti cunctis te uenerantibus Quidquid eis [Horstmann notes that a word is missing here] et precipue pregnantibus. O preciosa margarita, virgo sancta Dorothea, cor mundum in nobis crea." (2) "O Omnipotens sempiterne deus, in cuius nomine gloriosa virgo 7 martir Dorothea multorum tormentorum genera superauit, te supplices exoramus ut eius meritis et precibus cuncta pericula devitamus et ipsam scelerem adiutricem nostris nessessitatibus senciamus, per xpm dominum nostrum amen" (Horstmann 1880: 328).

1899: 83; Görlach 1972: 38). Caxton's *Gilte Legende* exemplar is now lost, but Görlach (1972: 38) demonstrates that it must have been based on the exemplar common to BL Addit. 11565 and 35298 and Lambeth Palace 72, that is, the lost exemplar of the compiler of the additional legends. Görlach draws attention to the fact that the texts of the additional legends (BL Addit. 11565 and 35298 and Lambeth Palace 72) all contain a garbled version of Saint Dorothy's father's name:

> The right gloryous virgyn & martyr Seynt dorothe was borne of the noble blode of the Cenatours of Rome her ffade*r* hight Theodra[57] In that tyme the p*er*secuc*i*on of cristen people was wonder grete in the londe of Romaynes wherefore this blessid theodra dispysyng the ydols forsoke Rome w*ith* alle his possessiouns as ffyldis vinis castels & howsis and saylid with Theodora his wiffe & with his ij doughters Crystyne & Calystyne to þe Realme of Capodoce in to the cyte of Cesarem wherein thaye dwellyd & brought forth his holy doughter seynte dorothe and when this holy virgyn was cristenyd of the holy bysshopp appolynar he namyd hir dorathe (BL Addit. 35298, fol. 80v).

Caxton, possibly by way of attempting to correct the confusion caused by Saint Dorothy's father's name (see n. 57), made Saint Dorothy old enough to counsel her parents to leave Rome, and rather than being born in Caesarea, she is sent to school there:

> The glorious virgin and martyr S. Dorothy was born of the noble lineage of the senators of Rome, her father hight Theodore. In that time the persecution of the christian people was great about Rome, wherefore this holy virgin S. Dorothy, despising the worshipping of idols counselled her father, her mother, and her two sisters, Christine and Celestine, to forsake their possessions, and so they did and fled into the realm of Cappadocia and came into the city of Cæsarea wherein they set S. Dorothy to school, and soon after she was christened of the holy bishop S. Appollinarius, and he named her Dorothy (1900: 7, 42).

In connection with the additional legends and the *Gilte Legende*, mention must also be made of the Middle English prose legend of Saint Dorothy in Trinity College 319 (fols. 2v–4v, 15r–16v). According to Gerould

---

57. BL Addit. 35298 originally read "dorothea"; the scribe crossed out "doro," altered o^2 to *a*, and added "dra," which extends beyond the right margin; thus "dorothea" > "theodra." The text was altered by the main scribe. I am indebted to Phillip Pulsiano for this information.

(1916: 195; cf. 1912: 259), this legend represents a text of the additional legends. Görlach (1972: 27, n. 10 and 36, n. 4), however, argues that the legend of Saint Dorothy in this manuscript is a completely different translation than the one from which the legend of Saint Dorothy in the *Gilte Legende* is derived (see also Hamer 1978: 33). Indeed, the opening of the legend in Trinity College 319 differs greatly from the text of the additional legends (see above):

> Thys gloriouse virgyne and martyr Dorothea whos fadirs name Dorotheus and her moders Theodora whyche was comen of the noble progeny of the most famouse and worthyest senatoures of Rome. In whos dayes grewe full gretly the greuous persecucion of crystyn peple euerywhere but most specyally amonge the Romaynes whyche causyd thys blessyd Dorotheis ffader of thys holy vyrgyne hatyng and despysyng the cursyd and abhominable mawmetry of the Romaynes forsoke the contre and felyshyp of the lothsome Romaynes with all hys possessyons of castelles houses londes rentes and vynes wyth all other rychesses and passyd ouer the see with hys good wyfe Theodora and hys two doughtres whos names were Crystem and Calystem and came to the region of Capadosy And entryng into a feyre cyte of that region called Cesarea and dwelled theryn wherein a gracious doughter was begoten of whos lyfe nowe wyth goddys grace we purpose to speke of (Görlach 1972: 36, n. 4).

The legend is also included in *Legendys of Hooly Wummen* (ed. Serjeant-son 1938), a collection of the lives of thirteen women saints by Osbern Bokenham (ca. 1393–ca. 1463), who, during the period of his literary activity, was at Clare Priory in Suffolk, East Anglia, the oldest Augustinian establishment in England. The legendary, containing the lives of Saints Margaret of Antioch, Anne, Christina, Ursula (and the 10,000 virgins), Fides, Agnes, Dorothy, Mary Magdalen, Catherine of Alexandria, Cecilia, Agatha, Lucy, and Elizabeth of Thüringen, is preserved in a single manuscript, BL Arundel 327, written in Cambridge in 1447 for the friar Thomas Burgh.[58] As Delany (1992) observes: "Bokenham's *Legend* is

---

58. In referring to the prologue to the life of Saint Catherine of Alexandria, in which Bokenham apostrophizes "all those who shall read or hear this treatise" ("alle þo þat redyn or here / Shal þis tretyhs"; Serjeantson 1938: 173), Delany (1992: xxxiv) points out that Bokenham probably anticipated separate circulation of individual lives for recitation at home or convent. She also mentions the fragment of the life of Saint Dorothy (in BL Addit. 36963), which seems to confirm this hypothesis. Delany (1992: xxi) also suggests that Chaucer's *Legend of Good Women* provided a model for Boken-

unique in the history of hagiography, for it is the first all-female hagiography in any language" (xxvii).[59] The legendary, which is composed in
several verse forms, is thought to be based on the *Legenda aurea*. However,
the legend of Saint Dorothy it contains differs in some details from *BHL*
2324. As in the Middle English renderings and a number of the German
adaptations mentioned above, Saint Dorothy's mother is named Theodora
and her father Dorotheus and is said to be descended by senators from the
high and noble blood of Romulus ("In Rome dede dwellen a wurthy man,
/ Wych by senatours descendyd fro / The hye & noble blood Romylyan,
/ Wych hycht, as þe story telle can, / Dorotheus, & egal to hys dygnyte,
/ Theodora clepyd, a wyf had he" [4744–4749]); that Saint Dorothy was
named after her parents is nowhere mentioned. The bishop, who baptized
Saint Dorothy in Caesarea and who is not named in *BHL* 2324, is, as in the
Gilte Legende and Caxton's *Golden Legend*, here called "Apolynar"
(4763).[60] These divergences point to *BHL* 2325d rather than *BHL* 2324
as the source for Bokenham's legend, as do some of the details of Saint

---

ham in the selection and arrangement of the female saints. She points out that the cor-
respondences with Chaucer's mock-legendary are consistent throughout the first ten
lives; that their order follows the order of Chaucer's *Legend;* and that their number is
statistically beyond coincidence. She admits, however, that the central episode in the
legend of Saint Dorothy, the story of the roses and apples, has no parallel in the
Chaucerian tale.

59. Delany (1992) notes, however, that there were partial models and antecedents,
among them Aldhelm's treatise *De laudibus virginitatis*, which is divided into male and
female virgins; the Franciscan friar Nicole Bozon's (late thirteenth-early fourteenth centuries) lives of nine female saints (Saints Lucy, Mary Magdalen, Margaret of Antioch,
Martha, Elizabeth of Hungary, Christina, Juliana, Agnes, and Agatha), although it is
not known if they were intended as a set; and Christine de Pizan's *Cité des dames*, in
which stories of a group of women saints form a small portion. Delany (1992: xxvii)
concludes: "While it might therefore be overstating the case to claim that Osbern
Bokenham invented the female legendary as such, nonetheless it is certainly fair to say
that he reinvented it – not as a system of classification, not to illustrate the value of virginity, not subsumed within another form, but as a free-standing, carefully crafted instance of
the demanding genre of hagiographical verse." To Delany's examples of female legendaries
may be added the German *Passienbüchlein von den vier Hauptjungfrauen* (see n. 30) and *Das
Buch von den heiligen Mägden und Frauen* (see n. 28), as well as the Danish *De hellige Kvinder*
and the Icelandic MS AM 429 12mo in the Arnamagnaean Collection (see below).

60. Cf. the *Sunte Dorotheen passie* (discussed above), in which the bishop is named
"Apolonius"; the *Erzählung vom Martyrium der lobesamen Jungfrau St. Dorothea*, in
which he is named "Appollonaris"; and below for the Danish "bøn aff ionfrw Sancta
dorotea" in *Visdoms Spejl*, in which he is named "apolore."

Dorothy's last prayer, in which she asks God that any religious house owning her passionary would never be endangered by fire or lightning ("noon hous where were hyr passyonarye / Wyth feer ner lyhtnyng shuld neuyr myskarye" [4909–4910]);[61] these details have no equivalent in *BHL* 2324, but are found in *BHL* 2325d, although *BHL* 2325d specifically has "imago." Moreover, Bokenham also adds that Theophilus's body was thrown "to bestys & fowlys" (4966),[62] and whereas in *BHL* 2324 Saint Dorothy is sent to her two sisters ("misit eam ad duas sorores suas"), in Bokenham, as in the *Gilte Legende* and Caxton's *Golden Legend*, her sisters are sent to her ("And þer-wyth anoon hyr sustrys tweyne, / Trystem & kalystem, he to hyr dede sende" [4848–4849]).[63] Finally, we are told that Saint Dorothy died on 16 February 288 ("The yere of grace two hundryd & eyhghty, / If eyghte þer-to men doon applye, / Of februarye þe syxten day suthly" [4933–4935]), not on 13 February 287 as in *BHL* 2324 ("anno domini CCLXXXVII Idus Februarias");[64] as in *BHL* 2324, however, this information is given immediately after the account of Saint Dorothy's execution. Willenberg (1889: 26) argues that the divergences from *BHL* 2324 are sufficient proof that Bokenham's legend of Saint Dorothy is not based on *BHL* 2324: "Ich halte alle diese verschiedenheiten gerade in bezug auf

61. Cf. the *De Dorothea* (Busse's comment quoted in n. 37); the *Gilte Legende*: "also she prayed that, where her lyff were writtyne in ony place or house, that hit myght be kepte frome all maner of parellis, of thunder, lightenyng or any other myschaunce" (Lambeth Palace 432; Horstmann 1880: 327); Caxton's *Golden Legend*: "Also she prayed to God that where her life was written or read in any house, that it should be kept from all peril of lightning and thunder, and from all perils of fire" (1900: 7, 46); and the Danish prayer "Een bedhe aff sancta Dorothea" in AM 418 12mo, in which it is stated that "huilket hws henne belethe er screueth wthi Thet hws maa ey wothe ild skadhe."

62. Cf. the *Gilte Legende*: "to be cast to wilde beestis and byrdis, to be deuourid" (Lambeth Palace 432; Horstmann 1880: 328), and Caxton's *Golden Legend*: "the pieces were cast to birds and beasts to be devoured" (1900: 7, 47).

63. Cf. the *Gilte Legende*: "And thane he sent to hirre two of her susters, Crysteane and Callestyne, the whicche for drede of deth were turnyd away ffrome Crist Jhesu: and thay shuld laboure to her suster Dorothea ffor to withdrawe her frome the ffeythe" (Lambeth Palace 432; Horstmann 1880: 326), and Caxton's *Golden Legend*: "And then the provost sent for her two sisters which were named Christine and Celestine, which for fear of death forsook the faith of Jesu Christ, and went to S. Dorothy and counselled her to obey to the provost's desire and forsake her faith" (1900: 7, 44).

64. In Caxton's *Golden Legend*, Saint Dorothy died on 6 February 288: "And thus she suffered death and passed to our Lord full of virtues, the sixth day of February, the year of our Lord two hundred and eighty-eight" (1900: 7, 47). The *Gilte Legende* has: "CClxxxVIII yere of oure lord god" (Lambeth Palace 432; Horstmann 1880: 327).

namen und daten für wesentlich genug, um die vermuthung zu rechtfer-
tigen, dass Bok[enham] bei dichtung dieser legende nicht auf der von
Graesse mitgetheilten lateinischen version gefusst habe." Willenberg draws
attention to the fact that the early Middle English prose translations now
extant in BL Royal 2. A. xviii, Lambeth Palace 432, and Chetham 8009,
display the same divergences from *BHL* 2324 as Bokenham's legend. Since
Bokenham specifically states that his work is a translation, Willenberg
(1889: 27) suggests that both the early Middle English prose translation and
Bokenham's legend of Saint Dorothy are based on a hitherto unknown
Latin legend.[65]

Finally, there is a mid-fifteenth-century poem of Saint Dorothy (ed.
Horstmann 1878: 191–197), which survives in two manuscripts, BL Harley
5272 and Arundel 168. Gerould (1916: 271), at least tentatively, ascribes the
poem to Bokenham's Cambridge friend John Capgrave (1394–1464), Prior
Provincial of his order, the Augustinian, in Britain (1453–1457) and a proli-
fic producer of religious, and occasionally historical, works. Gerould (1916:
271–272) argues that the poem is an undistinguished translation of *BHL*
2324 without any striking characteristics. Nonetheless, it should be noted
that also in this text the names of Saint Dorothy's parents are Dorotheus
and Theodora, while the bishop is called "Appol(i)nary" (36). Several
details familiar from other versions are repeated here. Saint Dorothy's
sisters are sent to her ("send Cristem and Kalixtem, hire sustress bothe"
[174]); she prays that any house or dwelling place owning the story of her
passio will never be destroyed by fire ("And where the story is of my
passione, / In howse or eny dwellynge place, / Neyther fyre ne leven hit
ouercome!" [265–267]); and Theophilus's body is thrown to beasts and
birds ("He leet hewe his body in pecis smale, / And cast hit in dyuerse
partie, / That wilde bestis to hit schulde falle / And oþer fowlis devowre

---

65. "Es fragt sich, ob wir nun infolge dieser bemerkenswerthen übereinstimmung
zwischen der prosalegende und Bok.'s gedicht annehmen dürfen, dass erstere Bok.'s
quelle gewesen sei, dass er also einfach jene englische prosa in reime gebracht habe:
diese möglichkeit indessen wird durch des dichters eigene versicherung ausgeschlossen,
dass sein gedicht eine *translacyoun* (v. 245) sei. So bleibt uns meiner ansicht nach nur
übrig, in Bok.'s gedicht die buchstäbliche paraphrase einer lateinischen legende zu er-
blicken, die nahezu vollständig mit einer andern lateinischen version derselben legende
übereingestimmt haben muss, welche ihrerseits in der in Anglia III veröffentlichten pro-
saversion eine übersetzung ins Englische erfahren hat. Hiernach dürfte es also fast zwei-
fellos sein, dass sich Bok. auch bei abfassung der legende von der h. Dorothea – seinem
sonstigen verfahren getreu – mit sclavischer genauigkeit an eine lateinische legende, die
uns allerdings bis jetzt unbekannt geblieben ist, angeschlossen haben muss."

hit alle" [vv. 330–333]). As in the other Middle English versions and as in *BHL* 2324, the date of Saint Dorothy's execution, "The VIII day from the Idus of Februarij; / The date from Cristis incarnacione / IIC IIIIXX VIII yeris were gone" (291–293), is given immediately after her execution and not at the end of the legend.[66]

The legend also inspired *The Virgin Martyr*, a tragedy by Thomas Dekker (ca. 1570-ca. 1632) and Philip Massinger (1583–1640).[67] The play is something of an anomaly in the history of early seventeenth-century English drama, for while plays on the lives and martyrdom of the saints continued in France and other Catholic countries long after the Reformation, such plays were suppressed and virtually lost in England. As Craig (1955) points out, the "legend of St. Dorothea, one of the oldest and most popular of all miracles plays, seems to have been an exception" (376–377). The play, written for the Red Bull Theater, was registered in 1621 and published in the following year under the title *The Virgin Martir: A tragedie. As it hath bin divers times publickely acted with great applause, by the seruants of his Maiesties Reuels; Written by Phillip Messenger and Thomas Decker*. Koeppel (1897) argues that the source is a Cologne martyrology of the year 1576 (*BHL* 2323) and Peterson (1910) that it is a combination of *BHL* 2323 and 2324;[68] howsoever, the emphasis in this play is on the

---

66. The following Latin verse lines, which appear to represent a version of the chant listed as no. 8740 in Chevalier (1892–1920: 1, 523), are appended to the poem: "In quacunque domon⟨ome⟩n fuit vel imago / Virginis eximie Dorothee virginis alme, / Nullus abortiuus infans nascetur in illa / Nec domus nec ignis furtique pericula sentit. / Nec quisquam inibi poterit mala morte perire, / Celestique pane moriens qui moriatur." Then follows a "Deuota oracio ad sanctam Dorotheam": "Sancta Dorothea virgo & martir, o castitate fallerata, humilitate coronata, paciencia ornata, virtutum floribus fulcita, temperancia pollita, o preciosa margarita, sancta virgo Dorothea, cor mundum in nobis crea" (Horstmann 1878: 197).

67. Here reference is made to Bowers's edition (1953–1961: 3, 365–480).

68. Koeppel (1897: 82) says: "Um zu der Quelle der englischen Dramatiker zu gelangen, brauchen wir jedoch vermutlich nicht weit zurückzugehen – fast alle von ihnen aufgenommenen stofflichen Elemente der Legende könnten sie einem grossen Martyrologium des 16. Jahrhunderts entlehnt haben: *De Probatis Sanctorum Historiis ... nunc recens recognitis ... per F. Laurentium Surium Carthusianum. Tomus primus, complectens Sanctos Mensium Januarii et Februarii. Coloniae Agrippinae, Anno MDLXXVI*; fol. 896 ff.: *Martyrium S. Dorotheae Virginis*." Koeppel (1897: 83, n. 1) points out that in both Surius's version (*BHL* 2323) and in *The Virgin Martyr*, the prefect of Caesarea is called Sapritius, whereas in the *Legenda aurea* (*BHL* 2324) he is named Fabritius. Koeppel admits, however, that Massinger (and Dekker) may have known other versions of the

clash of Saint Dorothy's and Theophilus' personalities, and there are many
digressions and additions. Thus, Dekker and Massinger invented the hope-
less love of Antoninus, son of the prefect Sapritius, for Saint Dorothy and
that of Artemia, Diocletian's daughter, for Antoninus; they even fabricated
a scene (4.1) in which first Antoninus and then a slave are urged to rape
her on stage, but Antoninus refuses at the crucial moment, and even the
slave reveals himself too noble to commit such a beastly act. They also
added the devil Harpax, who follows Theophilus, here a persecutor, in the
shape of a secretary, and the two morality figures Hircius, a whoremaster,
and Spungius, a drunkard, representing the two sins most abhorrent to the
maiden purity of their mistress. In many respects, Dekker and Massinger's
Saint Dorothy displays a more secular virtue of chastity than she does in
other adaptations of the legend; indeed, her defence of Christianity takes
the form of an attack on the lusts of the pagan gods, which owes more to
Ovid than to Christian martyrology (McLuskie 1981: 175):

Yet *Venus* whom you worship was a whore,
Flora the Foundresse of the publike Stewes,
And has for that her sacrifice: your great god,
Your *Iupiter*, a loose adulterer,
Incestuous with his sister, reade but those
That haue canoniz'd them, youle find them worse
Then in chast language I can speake them to you (3.1.139–145).

---

legend: "Doch fehlt es nicht ganz an Indicien dafür, dass die Dramatiker auch noch
andere Versionen der Legende kannten. Macrinus sagt von Dorothea, dass sie reich und
die Tochter eines römischen Senators sei (*though her birth be noble, / The daughter to
a senator of Rome, / By him left rich...*). Bei Surius [*BHL* 2323] ist von der Abstammung
der Dorothea nicht die Rede, die Märtyrerin ist losgelöst von allen irdischen Bezie-
hungen, der erste Satz der bei Graesse gedruckten Legende hingegen lautet: *Gloriosa
virgo et martir Dorothea ex patre Doro et matre Thea fuit progenita ex nobili sangue senatorum*, und zwar, wie der Context zeigt, aus dem Blute römischer Senatoren. Mög-
licherweise giebt es eine mir nicht bekannte Version der Legende, welche sowohl Dorothea's Abstammung meldet, als auch den Namen Sapritius bietet." Peterson (1910: 108)
argues that "no one alone of the two versions of the legend can have been the source
of the story presented in the drama. The two versions of the legend, although similar
in many points, contain some features of marked difference, and several of these individual peculiarities of both versions are found reflected in the drama. ... We must, therefore, conclude that the author of the 'Virgin Martyr' was familiar with both versions
of the legend. Whether this familiarity was based on a knowledge of the two types
independent of each other, or of a combined version of the legend ... must be left
undecided."

Dekker and Massinger developed other aspects of the tradition as well. From the mere mention of a boy carrying a basket of heavenly fruits and flowers in earlier versions of the legend emerges the exquisite conception of Saint Dorothy's child-servant, who reveals to her his angelic nature only at the hour of her martyrdom. They also clearly recognized certain similarities between the legend of Saint Dorothy and that of Saint Agnes (see p. 13). Indeed, many of the digressions and additions in *The Virgin Martyr*, such as the prefect's son's infatuation with the saint, who declares herself pledged to another lover, his subsequent lovesickness, the attempted rape, and also Saint Dorothy's child-servant Angelo, appear to be drawn from the legend of Saint Agnes (Peterson 1910: 53).

In addition, the legend of Saint Dorothy inspired a number of poets. In fact, the legend became a favorite of the Pre-Raphaelites: Dante Gabriel Rossetti (1828–1882), Christina Georgina Rossetti (1830–1894), Edward Burne-Jones (1833–1898), William Morris (1834–1896), Algernon Charles Swinburne (1837–1909), and Gerard Manley Hopkins (1844–1889) all represented Saint Dorothy in their art. Among Dante Rossetti's early unfulfilled designs for pictures is found a study in pencil illustrating an episode in the martyrdom of Saint Dorothy (Sharp 1882: 270, 434; Surtees 1971: 12, no. 43). Christina Rossetti used the legend as a basis for her poem *A Shadow of Dorothea* (ed. Rossetti 1906: 216–217), although she did not adhere closely to the story; in the poem, the speaker is a human soul, not as yet confirmed in saintliness, appealing to the boy-angel, or, perhaps rather, to Christ (Rossetti 1906: 474). In 1861 Edward Burne-Jones made a design for embroidery of Saints Cecilia and Dorothy (Goodwin 1975: 107 [plate 1]), and in 1867 he completed a watercolor of Saint Dorothy (subsequently exhibited as "St. Theophilus and the Angel" [Goodwin 1975: 108 [plate 2]).[69] William Morris composed a poem, *The Story of Dorothea*, for inclusion in his *The Earthly Paradise* (1868–1870), but later discarded it, and the tale exists only in manuscript form. Goodwin (1975: 93) notes that Morris's source was either Caxton's *Golden Legend* or Bokenham's poem,[70] which, however, he treated rather freely by supplying a number

69. See Goodwin (1975: 100–101, n. 8).

70. According to Goodwin (1975: 92), Morris's interest in the legend of Saint Dorothy may have been aroused in 1857, when Morris visited Manchester and saw the Pre-Raphaelite paintings in the Manchester Art Treasures Exhibition. It is possible that Morris saw there the late fifteenth- or early sixteenth-century oak panel of "SS. Peter and Dorothy" (presented in 1863 to the National Gallery and now NG 707) by the

of details. Morris developed the characters of Saint Dorothy's two sisters, who, in his account, decline into prostitution through avarice and vanity, but who are redeemed when Saint Dorothy later preaches to them in prison; and he invented a faithful and cunning slave, who, on Fabricius's behalf, conducts negotiations with yet another invented character, a gossip or bawd, who works in the sisters' house, in order to secure an interview with Saint Dorothy.

Algernon Charles Swinburne, who wrote his poem *St. Dorothy* (published in his *Poems and Ballads* [1866: 274-291]) in an attempt – as he writes to Lady Pauline Trevelyan (1816-1866) in a letter of 19 January 1861 – to try his "heathen hands at a Christian subject ... and give a pat to the Papist interest" (ed. Lang 1959-1962: 1, 38), followed Morris in stripping away the spurious accretions, retaining as a miracle only the account of the heavenly basket. He set the story in Rome rather than in the city of Caesarea, omitted Saint Dorothy's two sisters entirely, assimilated Saint Dorothy's would-be lover and the man who requested her to send a sign from heaven into one person, Theophilus, and fabricated a new character, the emperor Gabalus, for the role of condemning her to death. In Swinburne's version, the pagan worship that Saint Dorothy rejects is centred on the goddess Venus, and includes an annual parade of twelve naked maidens. The poet also transforms Theophilus's appeal for a sign into a sincere, half-believing request. The sign itself appears on earth only after Saint Dorothy's execution as in *The Virgin Martyr*, not before, and becomes a basket containing not merely roses and apples, but white and red roses, marigolds, the "flower that Venus' hair is woven of," apples, peaches, poppies, and lilies. Finally, Gerard Manley Hopkins, whose aim was "to revitalize the medieval legend of St. Dorothea" (Bump 1982: 66),[71] composed his *For a Picture of St. Dorothea*, which has survived in several forms. Gardner and Mackenzie (1967) print three versions: an early version, *For a Picture of St. Dorothea* (19-20), written in 1864, a version in sprung rhythm, *Lines for a*

---

painter known as the Master of the S. Bartholomew Altarpiece. Goodwin (1975: 93) also notes that Morris was undoubtedly aware of Burne-Jones's work on the legend.

71. Bump (1982: 68) further notes that at "the time he was revising his Dorothea poem he was agonizing about his religious vocation and no doubt was aware that some of the most popular Victorian writers were clergymen – indeed, two of the most successful were Anglican priests who had gone over to Rome. Moving in the same direction himself, Hopkins was in fact experiencing two simultaneous and related conversions; he felt the necessity of restoring not only the medieval religion but also some of the oral traditions with which it was identified."

Picture of St. Dorothea (35–37), which, according to Mariani (1970: 15), can be dated to 1868, and an expanded version in dramatic form, *St. Dorothea* (344–345), which, again according to Mariani, was written mid-way between the other two.[72] The two first-mentioned versions of the poem center on St. Dorothy's apparition before the sceptical Theophilus, carrying a basket of "Sweet flowers" (Hopkins substitutes lilies, larkspurs, and a quince for the roses and apples in the legend); in the last-mentioned, the exhange between Saint Dorothy and/or her angel is expanded.

1.2 *Artistic Representations of the Legend*
Saint Dorothy became a favorite subject especially for German artists of the late fifteenth and early sixteenth century (Braun 1943: 196; Kirschbaum and Bandmann 1968–1976: 6, 89–92). She is usually depicted as a distinguished-looking young woman wearing a wreath of flowers around her head, as exemplified by the wooden statue in Muggensturm in Baden (Künstle 1926–1928: 2, 188, fig. 86); and holding a basket of fruits and flowers (Braun 1943: 197), as exemplified by Tilmann Riemenschneider's (1468–1531) stone statue from around 1506–1508 in the Marienkirche in Würzburg (Tönnies 1900: 266, fig. xxixa).[73] Not uncommonly, a child (whom some artists portray as Jesus Christ) kneeling or standing beside her is sometimes holding the basket (see Reinach 1905–1923: 2, 683; Schreiber 1927: 80–83, nos. 1395, 1396, 1398, 1398b, 1401, 1403, 1404a). Occasionally, Dorothy herself is holding a book and/or a palm, as in the wooden statue in the Erzbischöfliche Museum in Utrecht (Vogelsang 1911: 2, fig. VII: 4).

Sometimes, Saint Dorothy is depicted in the company of other saintly men and women; in a painting by Stephan Lochner in Nürnberg, Saint Dorothy is standing next to the crucifix together with other saints (Reinach 1905–1923: 2, 447); in a large painting in Klosterneuburg from 1516, Saint Dorothy, holding her basket, is sitting next to the enthroned Madonna (Reinach 1905–1923: 2, 332); and in two alterpieces from the Walpurgiskirche in Soest, Konrad von Soest depicts her together with Saint Odilia (Künstle 1926–1928: 2, 188–189). Other artists focused on Saint Dorothy's martyrdom. Her sufferings are described in detail, for example, on the Dorothy altar in the Danzig town museum (Ehrenberg 1920: 86, fig. 73 and 74). Her execution is depicted by Holbein the Older in the S. Maria

---

72. Bump (1982: 74) argues that Hopkins's *The Starlight Night* (66–67) represents his ultimate revision of the Saint Dorothy poem.

73. For further examples, see Künstle (1926–1928: 2, 188), Schreiber (1927: 80–84: nos. 1393–1404m), and Kirschbaum and Bandmann (1968–1976: 6, 90–91).

Maggiore basilican painting in the Augsburg gallery (Künstle 1926–1928: 2, 189, fig. 87). In front of Saint Dorothy the Child Jesus is standing holding a basket with fruits and flowers, and behind her the executioner is raising his sword. On the speech bands between Saint Dorothy and the Child Jesus is written "dorothea, ich bring dir da" and "ich bitt dich, herr, brings theophilo dem schriber."

Although Saint Dorothy is patroness of the diocese of Peschia, she seems to have had less appeal to Italian artists. She is, however, depicted by the artist Ambrogio Lorenzetti on an alterpiece now housed in the Siena Gallery (Venturi 1907: fig. 581) and also on a painting, likewise in the Siena Gallery and by the same artist, of the Madonna, who is surrounded by Saint Catherine of Alexandria, Saint Dorothy, the four Church Fathers, and a number of angels (Venturi 1907: fig. 582). The picture of Saint Dorothy, dressed in fine clothing and with a wreath around her head, in the van Horne collection in Montreal, Canada (Mayer 1922: 323, fig. 240), attests to her cult in Spain.

In England, Saint Dorothy figures commonly in stained glass and in screen-paintings especially of the fifteenth and early-sixteenth centuries. In the area of Somerset alone, Saint Dorothy is to be seen with a basket of flowers and a palm in the east window of Langport and in the tracery lights of the second window from the east in the north aisle at West Pennard (Woodforde 1946: 33, 56, 62). She is also found in the west window of the north aisle of Mark and in the tracery lights on the south side of Norton-sub-Hamdon; in the latter church she is holding a bunch of flowers and a book (Woodforde 1946: 49, 88). The female saint in a small window in the south aisle of the church of Middlezoy may also be Saint Dorothy. She is portrayed with a chaplet about her hair and her robe girded with a chain. She holds in one hand a basket containing three flowers and in the other a large sword. As Woodforde (1946: 67) observes, it is very unusual to find Saint Dorothy represented with a sword; he suggests that the glass-painter may have misinterpreted the palm with which she is sometimes depicted (see above) and draws attention to a mistake of the same kind at Chelwood: in a window of the south aisle there is a small figure of a female saint holding a breast in a pair of pincers, the emblem proper to Saint Agatha, and a basket, Saint Dorothy's usual attribute.

Despite the fascination of artists and poets, Saint Dorothy is a patron of only few churches. In Germany, for example, she is the main patron of only one church, in Dörtelsberg. It is known, however, that in Vienna a church was dedicated to her and that on a mountain near Przelaika a chapel was dedicated to her;[74] in Danzig she had her own altar and in Regensburg a private chapel (Busse 1930: 59). In comparison with the other virgin saints, however, public testimonies of the worship of Saint Dorothy are few.

2 SAINT DOROTHY IN THE NORTH

2.0 *Her Cult and Legend in Scandinavia*

That Saint Dorothy enjoyed considerable popularity in Scandinavia is clear from the preserved Latin *cisiojani* (metrical calendars) in Denmark and Sweden, most of which include Saint Dorothy (see Odenius 1959: 149). Until the end of the fourteenth century, however, evidence for her cult is sporadic. Johansson (1950: 69-70) observes that her feast is included in a Strängnäs manuscript (UUB C 416) from around 1380, but that it is only that of a *memoria*.[75] In datings, her name appears in Swedish documents, for example, from Lödöse (*DS* II: 256 no. 1255) and Karlstorp (*DS* III: 10, no. 2044), from around 1400, but Johansson points out that even then her cult probably was not official, because 6 February (her feastday) is often not associated with her. Johansson further notes that in the *Missale Lincopense* manuscript, SKB A 97 from around 1400, she is not included (although in a fourteenth-century litany from the same diocese [UUB C 274] her name is mentioned). She is also missing in the *Breviarium Lincopense* (UUB C 435); from the same manuscript, however, it is evident that her cult was about to gain momentum, for although she is not included in the litany, six *lectiones* are devoted to her. In the *Collectarium Domini-*

---

74. To this chapel, a folktale, "Die Teufelsteine auf den Feldern um Siemianowitz," is attached. Kühnau (1910–1913: 2, 629–630, no. 1279) gives two versions of the story. (1) "Dem in Beuthener Kreise, dicht an der polnischen Grenze gelegenen Dorfe Przelaika gegenüber steht auf einem Berge ein der heiligen Dorothea geweihtes Kirchlein. Die Teufel wollten dieses Kirchlein zertrümmern und unter Felsblöcken begraben. Sie trugen die Steine dahin, doch ein Engel kämpfte gegen sie und schlug sie ihnen aus den Händen. Diese Steine liegen in der Richtung gegen Siemianowitz zu auf sieben Weilen zerstreut, und man sieht in ihnen noch die Teufelskrallen." (2) "Teufelsteine liegen auf den Feldern um Siemianowitz bei Beuthen O.-S. zerstreut. Das Volk sagt: Die höllischen Geister wären in einer Nacht durch die Luft geflogen, in der Absicht, die jenseits des Przemfaflusses auf dem Grojetzberge stehende Dorotheenkirche zu zertrümmern. Sie kamen von Westen und müssen eine weite Strecke zurückgelegt haben; denn als der Hahn zum ersten Male krähte und den Ablauf ihrer Wirkungszeit verkündete, mußten sie die Steine fallen lassen und sich in ihr Gebiet zurückziehen."

75. According to the younger printed calendars and breviaries, Saint Dorothy's feastday was celebrated as a *memoria* also in the dioceses of Skara and Uppsala, whereas in Linköping, Västerås, and Åbo in Finland, it had the rank of *simplex*, that is, with nine *lectiones*. See Maliniemi (1957: 23, 34).

canum Diocesis Aboensis (UUB C 421) from 1407, her name has been added at a later date. On the basis of this evidence, Johansson concludes that the rise of Saint Dorothy's cult in Sweden can be dated to the end of the fourteenth or the beginning of the fifteenth century.[76] In Denmark, the picture would seem to be similar, but in Norway it appears that her popularity was limited. The mention of a "Sanctę Dorotheę prębende" in a document from Oslo from 1548 (*DN* VI: 806 no. 771) and the Saint Catherine and Saint Dorothy guild (see pp. 52-53) are the only extant testimonies to her cult in Norway in the Middle Ages.

The extant books of prayers and hours show that in areas of Scandinavia, Saint Dorothy was considered one of the holy helpers (Saxtorph 1970: 52). *Anna Brade's Prayer Book* (DKB Thott 553 4to from 1497) includes a prayer, "Aff the xv nødhhielpere hwo them pakaller i syn nødh m*eth* gudelighedh tha fangher han hielp til vissæ til liiff oc siæl" (ed. Nielsen 1946–1963: 2, no. 328), which lists the following: George, Blaise, Pantaleon, Erasmus, Vitus, Christopher, Denys, Cyricus, Acacius, Magnus, Eustace, Giles, Catherine of Alexandria, Margaret of Antioch, Dorothy, and Barbara.[77] The same list of holy helpers is found also in Christiern Pedersen's *Bønnebog i at høre messe* (1514; ed. Nielsen 1946–1963: 4, no. 1174). Jørgensen (1909: 118), however, maintains that "[b]landt disse hører Dorothea til de sjældent forekommende," and indeed, the prayer "ien mygh*et* god bøn aff the xv nødhielpær" in *Johanne Nielsdatter's Book of Hours* (SKB A 42 from ca. 1480; ed. Nielsen 1946–1963: 1, no. 59) does not include Saint Dorothy among the holy helpers, and neither does the prayer of the same title in *Karen Ludvigsdatter's Book of Hours* (LUB 25 8vo from ca. 1500; ed. Nielsen 1946–1963: 1, no. 152).[78]

Despite the uncertainty concerning Saint Dorothy's status as a holy helper, a number of prayers to her are found in Danish prayer books. The longest of these is the "bøn aff ionfrw Sa*n*cta dorotea" in *Visdoms Spejl* (AM 782 4to from the beginning of the sixteenth century; ed. Nielsen 1946–1963: 3, no. 623).[79] The legend of Saint Dorothy retold in this prayer appears to be based on a source closely related to *BHL* 2325d, but

---

76. Johansson uses this date as the *terminus post quem* for the *Hemsjömanuale*, in which Saint Dorothy is included.

77. The prayer is found also in GkS 1614 4to (*Marine Issdatter's Prayer Book*). Jørgensen (1909: 118, n. 2) notes that Saint Dorothy is included also among the holy helpers on the predella of the altar in the church of Tjæreby.

78. The former prayer is found also in GkS 1613 4to (*Else Holgersdatter's Book of Hours*) and the latter also in SKB A 40 (*Ingeborg Predbjørnsdatter's Book of Hours*).

79. The prayer is found also in AM 784 4to.

with a few divergences. Thus, the prefect is called "fabrian*us*," and, as in the Middle English translations, it is said that Saint Dorothy's two sisters are sent to her ("oc then høffdi*ng* fabrian*us* han sende thil teg bode tyne søstre"). The account concludes with a plea for Saint Dorothy's intercession ("Beth for oss hellige io*m*frw Sancta dorotea at vy mote vorde verdige at faa then evige glæde m*eth* teg ewindelig, ame*n*") and a *collecta*.

A short prayer to Saint Dorothy is found in *Johanne Nielsdatter's Book of Hours* (ed. Nielsen 1946–1963: 1, no. 68), and a somewhat longer prayer is included in *Anna Brade's Prayer Book* (ed. Nielsen 1946–1963: 2, no. 297), in which she is called "*p*aradises vælluchtende rosen" and "een skyn*n*ende margarita."[80] Yet another prayer to Saint Dorothy is found in *Ingeborg Predbjørnsdatter's Book of Hours* (ed. Nielsen 1946–1963: 4, no. 915):[81]

Heel sa*n*cta Dorothea cristi fogræ brud, iech beth*er* thin mildh*et* oc thin store hellighet ath thu wilt hielpe megh i my*n* fattugdom, i hug-sæns skrøbelighet, i lego*m*mens thørff och i øgens vighelighet, oc ladh megh ey forfares i noger skadeligh sagh, ey dags tid och natter tid, och bedh so til cristu*m* for mech ath iegh skal her alt vnt ow*er* vi*n*ne oc ko*m*me til ihesu*m* cristu*m* my*n* gud, so skal iegh vere reen och gude-ligh och aff alle syndher, thet iegh ey skal frycte i døden och ey brødeligh bliffwe och effther elende skal verdæs ath see gusz søn meth alle hellige men i guddoms asiøn. O sa*n*cta Dorothea bedh for megh vsle syndher ath iegh ma [vorthe] verdugh i gusz asiøn. Ame*n*.

The same book of hours also contains "Ien annen mygh*et* god bøn aff sa*n*c-ta katerina, sa*n*cta barbare m*eth* andre io*m*fruær" (ed. Nielsen 1946–1963: 4, no. 903), which includes Saint Dorothy among the virgin saints. Finally, the prayer in AM 784 4to declares that the Virgin Mary and the virgin saints Catharine of Alexandria, Barbara, Dorothy, Margaret of Antioch, Gertrude, Agatha, Odilia, Apollonia, Clare, Cecilia, Thecla, Concordia, Petronilla, and the 11,000 virgins should be honored on Saturdays.

Om løffuerdaghen skal ma*n* tencke paa himerig*is* glede ock ere iomfrue maria m*eth* alle hellige iomfruer, sa*n*ctam Katherina*m*, sa*n*ctam Barbara*m*, sa*n*ctam Dorotea*m*, sa*n*ctam Margareta*m*, sa*n*ctam Gertrude*m*, sa*n*ctam Agata*m*, sa*n*ctam Otilia*m*, sa*n*ctam Appolonia*m*, sa*n*ctam

80. The prayer is found also in GkS 1614 4to (*Marine Issdatter's Prayer Book*) and AM 420 12mo.

81. The prayer is found also in a manuscript bound in the copy of Christiern Pedersen's *Bønnebog i at høre messe* (1514) belonging to the University of Copenhagen's Library.

Claram, sanctam Ceciliam, sanctam Teclam, sanctam Concordiam, sanctam Petronillam, the xi twsende iomfruer bede for [oss] ewindelig. Amen (Nielsen 1946–1963: 4, no. 1113a, cf. no. 1125g).

The only surviving Swedish prayer to the holy helpers is found in *Ingegärd Ambjörndotter's Prayer Book* (SKB A 43 from the beginning of the sixteenth century; ed. Geete 1907–1909: no. 166) and *Birgitta Andersdotter's Prayer Book* (SKB A 80 from around 1520), which does not refer to Saint Dorothy. Nonetheless, the *Missale Lincopense* (UUB C 427 from around 1500), includes a votive mass for the holy helpers; the *collecta* includes sixteen holy helpers, the last of which is Saint Dorothy. The same mass is found also in the *Missale Lundense* printed in 1514, where it appears as the second last among "missae speciales" in "commune sanctorum" (Lindberg 1923: 151 and 212). Kilström (1967) explains the inclusion of Saint Dorothy as follows: "eftersom Katarina, Margareta och Barbara, dvs. tre av huvudjungfrurna, hör till den ordinarie N[ödhjälpar]gruppen, har det legat nära till hands att låta även den fjärde huvudjungfrun, Dorotea, sälla sig till de övriga" (460).

Only two Swedish prayers to Saint Dorothy herself have survived, however: a shorter prayer in *Ingegärd Ambjörnsdotter's Prayer Book* (ed. Geete 1907–1909: no. 188)[82] and a longer prayer, "en ärlikin oc dyr bön aff the ärofulla jomffrunne sancta dorotea," found in MS Giessen 881 8vo from the beginning of the sixteenth century (ed. Geete 1907–1909: no. 189). The shorter prayer, according to which "Hwat människia som hedra sancta dorothea nampn mädh pater noster oc Aue maria hon skal wardha gömdh för allom dödhelikom syndom Oc dröffwilsom hedher oc äro giffwer gudh them som hona hedhra oc älska Thär maa ey diäffla äller truldom skadha göra thär henna nampn oc beläthe hedhras," focuses on the heavenly basket with roses and Theophilus's subsequent conversion. Christ, we are told, received their souls in his rose garden. The longer prayer, in which the saint is called "skinande fina pärla, oc faghersta lilia, oc renasta roos," has as its theme Saint Dorothy's virginity and her love for her heavenly spouse:

82. The shorter prayer is extant in six other manuscripts: (1) Berlin, Staatsbibliothek Cod. Berol. Theol. Lat. 71 8vo written in Vadstena in the 1470s; (2) *Christina Hansdotter's Prayer Book* (SKB A 38) from the end of the fifteenth or the beginning of the sixteenth century; (3) *Birgitta Andersdotter's Prayer Book*; (4) *Dorothea Nilsdotter's Prayer Book* (SKB A 81) written in Vadstena at the end of the fifteenth or the beginning of the sixteenth century; (5) UUB C 68 8vo written in Vadstena at the beginning of the sixteenth century, which also has an illumination of Saint Dorothy (fol. 129r); and (6) Giessen 881 8vo.

O min kärasta jomfru sancta dorathea, minz wppa thän innerlika kär-
leken, som osläkkelikin war j thino iomffrulika hiärta, til thin brud-
gomma ihesum christum Hwilkins älskogha oc kärlek swa bran j thino
renasto hiärta, at hwazske pina älla dödh kunne tik fran hans kärlek
skilia O min kärasta iomffru, thy bidher jak tik, at thu warkunna mik
wsle syndhirsko, som kald är j kärlekenom til min gud, ärna mik the
nadhena, at jak maghe han älska, owir all skapat thing, owir liff oc siäl,
oc alt thät j wärldhenne är Oc wtsläk w mino hiärta allan licamlikan
kärlek, oc alt thät mothe gudhi är.

The prayer then gives an account of Saint Dorothy's tortures. To those already known from *BHL* 2324 and 2325d a reference to how she was "drag-
hen j fula quinno hws" is added. The prayer concludes by requesting the
saint's presence at the time of death and her protection from the torments
of Hell through proper confession.

While these prayers are strictly devotional, the prayer "Een bedhe aff
sancta Dorothea" in AM 418 12mo from around 1500 (ed. Jørgensen 1909:
74; Nielsen 1946-1963: 2, no. 381) seems intended more for practical purposes: to help during difficult deliveries. In fact, Saints Margaret of Antioch
and Dorothy seem to have been the most prominent Christian helpers during childbirth (Jacobsen 1984: 105; Jón Viðar Sigurðsson 1994: 432). Here
is the text of the prayer:

Thenne hellighe jomffru sancta dorothea, som kalles at wære een roos
och een blomme aff then hellige andh Hwosom kaller hwerdagh paa
henne hellighe naffn meth een pater noster oc een Aue maria han
wordher gømder fran dieffuelen oc alle dødelighe synder Och huilket
hws henne belethe er screueth wthi Thet hws maa ey wothe ild skadhe
Oc huilken qwinnæ som meth barn pynes oc hawer hun thenne bøn
paa segh thet barn skal snarlighe føthes foruthen alt meen

Two verses "Aff sancta dorothea" and a subsequent *collecta* (ed. Nielsen
1946-1963: 2, no. 382) follow the prayer in the manuscript:

Ave gemma virtuosa
dorothea vernans rosa
vita mundi patens glosa
sis pro nobis speciosa
interuentrix gloriosa

Dorothea christo grata
afflictorum aduocata
tu adiutrix sis rogata
vt defectus et peccata
per te nobis sint ablata

Amen Pater noster och Aue maria
Bedh fore oss iomff*ru* *sanc*ta dorothea At wy maa wordhe w*er*dughe
*chris*ti nadhe

Collecta

Allemectixte eui*n*nelighe guth i hues naffn th*en* ærlighe iomff*ru* som
tholde døth fore tech dorothea owerwan manghe køns pyner Wy bethe
tich ythmyugelighe at wy mwe owerwi*n*ne w*eth* he*n*nes bøn alle vothe oc
befinde he*n*ne een snar hielperske i all wor nøttorffteligheet Amen.

The verses are identical to those printed in Mone (1853–1855: 3, 277, no.
897). The first is clearly the hymn listed as no. 1824 in Chevalier (1892–
1920: 1, 108); the second may be identified with the hymn listed as no.
36807 (1892–1920: 4, 107).

A further testimony to Saint Dorothy's popularity is the Saint Catherine and Saint Dorothy guild established in Bergen in 1397 (*DN* XVI: 34–36,
388–390): "In den nahmen Godes Amen, wittlick sy allen goden lüden, dat
na der bort Christy, unses herrn, dusenndt dreehundert søven undt vegen-
tich, do begunden frame lüde, gode tho lohne, alle godes hilligen tho ehren
unde tho einem sunderlieken lave unde tho ehren sunte Catherinen unde
Dorotheen, eine brøderschup und eine gilde tho holdende" (Nielsen 1877:
7–8). The laws of this guild, at least in their extant form, were recorded in
1502 ("Sunte Katherinen vndte sunte Dorothien gildeboek anno dm. MD
vnde twe vure geschreven"), but Nielsen (1877: 3) reckons that they do not
represent the first written document concerning the guild and believes
there must have been older records pertaining to its establishment in the
mid-fourteenth century. The laws of the guild stipulate that all "meistermans" (that is, all trade managers or masters of the German craft guilds in
Bergen) must be members of the guild,[83] and that the members of the
guild must celebrate the feastdays of the two virgin saints:

83. "Item so iss de koepman overeins geworden, dat alle meistermans in de gilde
schølen høren, de mit dem kopmanne ummegahn und ein guth knape ist: by peenen
x x ß engelsch" (Nielsen 1877: 9).

Item so schølen de gildebroder ehrlieken holden de feste sunte
Katherinen unde Dorothyen, vnde so schall men senden isslieken clos-
ter eine thune behrs: alsse Katherina virginis, dess gelieken tho sunte
Dorothien dage isslikenn kloster eine thune behrs.

Item issliken kloster tho Bergenn hebben de gilde brodere eine
ewige misse mit aller thobehøringe:

Thon grauwen mönniken ein grott verguldet kelck, misseboeck,
missewede, und alle reedschop:

Derglieken ton swarten mönken vpp sunte Dorothien altare eine
verguldede tafele, kelck und pathenen von iiij lödige m¶: missewede
unde alle redtschup, dartho thenue [sic] leuchter: vndt en Petz: [sic]
cruce: [sic] etc." (Nielsen 1877: 9–10).

That the veneration of Saint Dorothy in Scandinavia most probably
had its origins in her popularity in Germany is clear not only from the
Bergen guild, but also from the mystery play *Dorotheæ Komedie* (ed. Smith
1874: 92–143), which is preserved in DKB Thott 780 fol. from the mid-six-
teenth century, where it is entitled "Comoedia de sancta virgine Dorothea."
The work is a verse translation by Christiernus Joannis (that is, Christiern
Hansen or Jensen), principal of Vor Frue Skole in Odense,[84] of Kilian
Reuther von Melrichstadt's *Comedia gloriose parthenices et martiris Dorothee
agoniam passionemque depingens*. Nonetheless, the Danish translation,
which was made in 1531, differs in a number of ways from its source. The
play is in *knittel*, the conventional metrical form of Scandianvian poetry
during the Middle Ages. The lines are rhymed in pairs, and owing to the
need for a rhyming word, there are a number of additions to the source
text, although these are generally insignificant. The Paradise hexameters,
however, are abridged, and many of the mythological allusions have been
omitted. Moreover, the prologue has been left out, and the *argumentum*
has been rewritten as a true résumé of the contents of the play. The *argumentum* in the Danish translation has a distinctly edifying purpose,[85] and

84. "Anno mdxxxj Christiernus Joannis pedagogus iuuentutis in parrochia diue
virginis, prelato suo viuente magistro Andrea Gloeb" (143). See also Brøndum-Nielsen
(1914: 104–135) and Søholm (1972: 85–86).

85. Krogh (1940) comments: "Det er karakteristisk, at denne Prolog kaldes *Argumentum (Argumentum totius comoediæ)*, en Betegnelse der blandt andet viser, at vi be-
finder os i Nærheden af Skolekomedierne, som meget ofte indledes af to Personer: Prologus, der i de hjerteligste Vendinger bød Folk velkommen, og Argumentum's Frem-
siger, den saakaldte Argumentator, der præsenterede Personerne og forklarede Hand-
lingen. Undertiden lod man det dog – som her – være tilstrækkeligt med en Argumentator, der naturligvis ligesom Prologus havde sin Oprindelse i Mysteriernes Prelocutor

the same tendencies are noticeable also in the epilogue, "De fide et operibus breuis ad spectantes comoediam diuæ Dorotheæ contionatio" (139–143). This "føffue precken," which was added by the Danish translator for the spectators to hear before they went home, gives the play the character of an *exemplum*, of propaganda against the advancing Lutheranism.[86]

It is worth noting that while Kilian's *Comedia* was meant to be read,[87] the Danish *Dorotheæ Komedie* was clearly intended to be performed for a broad public (see, however, Søholm 1972: 89). Indeed, the legend is to a very large extent adapted to theatrical needs. Saint Dorothy is forcibly led away by Fabricius's messenger, and Fabricius alternately tempts and threatens her. She is beaten with sticks, pinched with red-hot tongs, immersed into boiling pitch, and burnt, but Saint Dorothy's body remains undamaged: "Hennes legom thet er nw saa forklaredt, / Szom legher met balsom hade thet forfaredt, / Thet er nw saa slet alt szom et eegh / Ffra hennes hoffuet oc tiil hennes leeg" (109). At Fabricius's request, she is imprisoned, but she is soon brought back before him, and, after yet another failed attempt to make her worship the idols, which she destroys with the help of the angel Paranymphus, he hands her over to his executioners. One of these, Runcardus, explains to his victim what is awaiting her: "Jeg skal nw hinge teg wed tin fod / Oc bynde teg met reff hyne stercke, / Saa tyne arme oc been skulle vercke, / Oc sette paa tin mwndt en grime, / Ther nest thiit legom tiil døde at pyne" (113). However, Saint Dorothy is not fearful, and Fabricius, resorting to his last possibility, sends for her two sisters to plead with her, but instead she restores them to the true faith, whereupon, at Runcardus's suggestion, Christen and Calisten are burnt: "Lad oss nw porre i thenne ild, / Wi viille thøm stege szom anden sild" (125). But Saint Dorothy remains firm and says to Fabricius: "Ffør wiil ieg myn hals vnder sw[erdet giffue], / Heller en ieg wiil hoss teg blif[fue]" (127). She then describes the joys that are

---

eller Herold. Man maa tænke sig, at Argumentator førte Skuespillerensemblet ind paa Spillepladsen, og – hvad Teksten viser – forestillede Hovedpersonerne en for en i følgende Orden: Dorothea, Fabritius, Theophilus og Helgenindens to Søstre, Cichriste og Caliste. Endelig var Publikum orienteret, og Spillet kunde begynde" (51–52).

86. Cf., for example, the following passage: "Hwo szom sigher, thenne historia er snac oc drømme, / Han kan Christo gud icke sømme, / Sigher helghen for tro eller gerninger icke at forhuerfue / [A]t ske ierteghen eller hymmerige at erffue / [H]an faer aff dieffuelzens indskydelsz viild, / [F]or han er aff verden oc dieffuelin sniild" (142). For a discussion of these lines, see Søholm (1972: 86–87).

87. Spengler (1898): "Der Schauplatz wechselt sehr häufig; war das Drama für die Aufführung bestimmt, was ich ... glaube, ... so könnte ich mir von der Art der Darstellung in vielen Scenen keine Vorstellung machen" (125).

awaiting her in Paradise and promises the half-convinced Theophilus that she will send him the "yrther" (130) from Paradise. But Fabricius has no more patience and gives Runcardus the following instructions: "Rwncarde, led then pighe hiid tiil stede / Oc henne pinen strax at wære redhe, / Jeg kommer strax met somme tiil hest / Oc somme tiil fod, szom the kunne best" (131). The stage instructions specify that Runcardus "extrahit gladium" and says to Saint Dorothy: "Reck frem tiit hoffwed met en ferd, / Jeg thet aff hwger, szom ieg haffuer lerd" (132). Saint Dorothy requests permission to say her last prayer ("Giiff meg en liden tiid at bede, / Szaa viil ieg strax till døden vere rede" [133]); permission is granted ("Tiil hwem tw beder, tw vist ey hort, / Skyn teg snart oc wer kort" [133]); and she thus once more confirms her belief. An angel (Paranymphus) appears, assuring her that her prayer has been heard and bringing her apples and roses: "Tin bøen hoss gwd er nw hørd, / Gwd haffwer sin nade tiil teg rørdt, / Tiil beuisning sende han teg effler oc roser, / Szom voxer inden Paredisses moszer" (133). She asks the angel to give the fruits and flowers to Theophilus and is then executed. Theophilus immediately confesses himself a Christian and is, like Saint Dorothy, tortured and killed at Fabricius's request: "... gør swerdhet oc øxerne skarpe, / Her wiil tiil ingen leeg eller harpe, / Thenne skriffuer at hugge i stycke ny, / Siw eller ote oc saa vdi ty" (138).

It is probable that the play was performed by the pupils in the school in Odense, who understood the Latin stage instructions. Smith (1874) is of the opinon that DKB Thott 780 fol., which also includes *Den utro hustru*, *Paris' dom*, and twenty-eight lines of verse of a translation of Johannes Reuchlin's play *Henno*, contains "det dramatiske Repertoire for Vor Frue Skole under Christiern Hansens Styrelse" (90). Krogh (1940), who is reluctant to classify *Dorotheæ Komedie* as a school play, nonetheless comments that it was not uncommon for pupils to perform mystery plays: "Der er altsaa i og for sig intet i Vejen for, at Skoledisciplene i Odense har kunnet honorere de Krav, som man i Almindelighed stillede til en Mysterieopførelse; man maa vel endda tænke sig, at Byen muligvis gav den Slags Foretagender økonomisk støtte" (57).

The Danish broadside ballad, *Den hellige Dorothea* (ed. Grüner-Nielsen 1912-1930: 6, 70-74), may also be based on a German original.[88] Although the earliest known printed version of the ballad is from 1642 (*En ny Dict om en Jomfru, som kaldis Dorothea, Som er affliffuet for Christi Naffns Bekiendelse skyld. Alle Gudfryctige som elske Christum til et Christeligt*

88. See Grüner-Nielsen (1912–1930: 6, 74–75).

Exempel. Prented Aar 1642), the very close copy in *Anna Gyldenstiernes Visebog* (begun in 1611) shows that older prints existed. The ballad, which is also found in Swedish translation, *Den sköna Dorothea* (ed. Sahlgren 1957-1960: 4, 93-96),[89] follows the version of the legend found in *BHL* 2324, although a number of changes have been made. Thus, Saint Dorothy's father is called "Mandieries" (stanza 2.2), and her mother's name is not mentioned.[90] Saint Dorothy's own name is explained as "Guds gaffuer god" (3.3). Her sisters, Christen and Calisten, are not mentioned, and the prefect Fabricius and the scribe Theophilus are one and the same person. Finally, the account of Saint Dorothy's tortures is reduced to only a few verse lines: "... thuinged hand hind met pinen stur / adtskelig och mange lunde; / den pine och vee, / som da mon ske, der hun var fangen och bunden" (7.3-6).

Saint Dorothy does not appear as a patron of any Scandinavian church. The reason is probably that her cult developed late, that is, after most of the churches had been built. It is known, however, that on 1 October 1487, an altar dedicated to Saints Barbara, Catherine of Alexandria, Margaret of Antioch, Dorothy, and to the 10,000 knights and the 11,000 virgins was consecrated in the Carmelite monastery church in Landskrona. It is further known that the Mariakirke in Copenhagen boasted a glass reliquary containing relics of, among others, the "quattuor virgines capitales" (Hallberg *et al.* 1967: 111, 113).

Saint Dorothy is frequently depicted in Scandinavian churches (see, for example, Rydbeck 1904: 59 and Nilsén 1986: 433). She is usually portrayed holding a basket, her attribute, as on the large pillar in the royal hall in the Vadstena monastery (Hallberg *et al.* 1967: 108, fig. 11); a bowl or cup, as in the Lund high altar (Wrangel 1915: 26-27, fig. 61 and 75),[91] may be said to be uncommon. In the church of Gørløse, Zealand, where she is frescoed in the the northern window niche, she is also holding a book (presumably the Bible); in the chapel of the Magi in Roskilde Cathedral, Zealand, where she is frescoed on the eastern wall, she is holding also a flower (Magnus-Petersen 1895: 86); and in the church of Gimlinge, Zealand, where she appears in the southern jamb of the chancel arch, she is holding also a branch (Saxtorph 1970: 76, 107, 170).

---

89. I am grateful to Tracey Sands for drawing my attention to this text.

90. The Swedish text gives the names of her parents as Dorus and Thea (2.8-9). Sahlgren (1957-1960: 4, 396) notes that he added these names from a 1770 printed edition of the ballad.

91. I am grateful to Shelly Nordtorp-Madson for this reference.

Often, Saint Dorothy is depicted in the company of other female saints, usually the three other "virgines capitales," as in, for example, the church of Tortuna, Västmanland (Cornell and Wallin 1953: 11, fig. 4), the church of Hattula in Finland (Nilsén 1986: 379, fig. 250; see also 434), or the church of Tensta, Uppland (Cornell and Wallin 1933: 79, fig. 1). She is also found together with other saints: for example, in the church of Borreby, Scania, she appears together with Saint Helena (Rydbeck 1904: 51); and in church of Kongens Lyngby, Zealand, the Trinity is surrounded by Saints Dorothy, Barbara, Ursula, and an unidentified female saint (Saxtorph 1970: 91). In the church of Gislinge, Zealand, she is in the company of Saints Bridget, Margaret of Antioch, Gertrude, Apollonia, Catherine of Alexandria, and perhaps Genevieve (Saxtorph 1970: 126; Liebgott 1982: 160); in the church of Albek, Jutland, she is in the company of Saint Catherine of Alexandria (Saxtorph 1970: 303); in the church of Nordby on Samsø, she is in the company of Saints Catherine of Alexandria and Barbara (Saxtorph 1970: 343); in the church of Råby, Jutland, she appears together with Saints Apollonia, Christina or Agatha, Catherine of Alexandria, Barbara, Gertrude, and Juliana (Saxtorph 1970: 324; illustrated in Liebgott 1982: 79); and in the church of Bunkeflo, Scania, she is found together with the Virgin Mary and Saints Catherine of Alexandria, Barbara, Margaret of Antioch, Ursula, and Mary Magdalen (Rydbeck 1904: 68).

Saint Barbara in particular seems to be a frequent companion of Saint Dorothy: the two are depicted together on the inside of one of the doors of a reliquary cabinet in the choir of the churches of Gothem, Gotland (Curman and Roosval 1959–1964: 87, fig. 107; Hallberg et al. 1967: 102, fig. 8), and Sorunda, Södermanland (Lindblom 1916: 27, fig. 16 and 17); on the altar cabinet (now lost through fire) in the church of Aspeboda, Dalarna (Hallberg et al. 1967: 127, fig. 22; see also 136); and also on the altar cabinets in the churches of Romfartuna, Västmanland (Hallberg et al. 1967: 147, fig. 29), Ekerö, Uppland, and Tierp, Uppland (Hallberg et al. 1967: 140). In the three examples just mentioned, Saints Dorothy and Barbara are depicted on each side of the Madonna; a similar arrangement appears also on the altar cabinet of the church of Valö, Uppland (Hallberg et al. 1967: 109, fig. 12), although here they are in the company of also the two other "virgines capitales" in a kind of "santa conversazione."

No church bells carrying Saint Dorothy's name are in evidence in Scandinavia; it should be noted, however, that her name appears on the rim of the Mary Magdalen bell cast in 1462 by the founder Herman for the Saint Nicolas church in Burg (Femern) (Uldall 1982: 191).

The basket, Saint Dorothy's usual attribute, is also found at 6 February on a Danish calendar stick from around 1500 (Liebgott 1982: 143–160).[92] The stick is about 120 cm. long. With a specific type of numeral sign the golden numbers are incribed according to the order of the ecclesiastical calendar. Altogether seventy-two feastdays are included. The crowns signify the Marian feasts and those of the Nordic royal saints, while initials or attributes – usually the martyrs' instruments of torture – are used to indicate the other feastdays.

The appearance of a female saint holding a basket on the seals of Michel Persøn, a parish priest in Ålborg (1452), and Thomas Buk, a canon in Haderslev (1397), leads Petersen (1886: no. 706 and 997) to identify the saint as Saint Dorothy. The basket depicted on the seal of Hans Andersøn, a parish priest in Gram (1463, 1465, 1473) may also be interpreted as an allusion to Saint Dorothy (Petersen 1886: no. 938). The identification of the female saint holding a flower and a cup on the seal of Hans Clementsøn, a vicar in the diocese of Roskilde (1487), is uncertain; it is possible that she may be Saint Dorothy (Petersen 1886: no. 303).

In Denmark, the name Dorothea first appears around 1400, but later the name or derivatives of it (e.g., Dorett, Doritt, Dorethe, Doritte) are quite common. Knudsen and Kristensen (1936–1948: 1, 201) reckon that the fact that King Christian I's and III's queens carried the name (that is, Dorothea of Brandenburg [1430–1495] and Dorothea of Sachsen-Lauenburg [1511–1571], respectively) contributed to the name's popularity. In Norway, the first occurrence of the name (that is, Dorethe [cf. *DN* V 707.2 (1499)]) is in a charter of 1476 from Bohuslän (*DN* II 669). After 1500, there are more examples; Lind (1905–1915: 201) mentions the following: "Dorethe Eloffzdotter (*NRJ* II: 81 [Romsdal 1520]), "Dorothea kyber konæ" and "Dorothe Henricks dotter" (*NRJ* II: 620 and 621 [Bergen 1521]), and "Dorethe Sebiørnsd. (*DN* III 819.23 [Romerike 1534]). The first occurrence of the name in Sweden is in 1421 (Otterbjörk 1961: 339). Finally, it should be noted that in Denmark Saint Dorothy lent her name to the flower *leucojum vernum*, in Danish called "dorothealilje" (in Swedish "snöklocka" or "klosterlilja," and in Norwegian "klosterklokke"; Lange 1968: 542–543).

2.1 *Her Cult and Legend in Iceland*
Although the legend of Saint Dorothy was told both in prose and poetry in Iceland, she figures only rarely in liturgical and historical sources, and evidence of a cult devoted to her is meagre.

---

92. See also Lithberg (1934: 91).

That the female virgin martyrs were recognized as a particular group of saints and celebrated as such is clear from the *Old Norwegian Homily Book* (ed. Indrebø 1931) dating from around 1200. The specific female virgin martyr saints are not mentioned by name, however, but simply referred to as "helgar meyjar" in connection with instructions for which saints and groups of saints are to be celebrated "in die omnium sanctorum":

> En er sia hotið halden hælgum møyum þæim er gengo í spor hæilagrar Marie drotningar. *ok* hafnaðo ollum licams munuðu*m* fyr aost guðs. *ok* vildu hældr þiona himnescu*m* bruðguma í ollu at-hæfe an saurgasc af iarðleg*r*e munuð (145).

From two Icelandic manuscripts of the *Ordo Nidrosiensis Ecclesiae*, AM 680a 4to (third quarter or last third of the thirteenth century) and AM 791 4to (second half of the fourteenth century), it is clear that Saint Dorothy was known by the middle or end of the thirteenth century;[93] in the sanctoral, both manuscripts add the following text to the mass or office for the feast of Saint Agatha:

> Jn festo sancte dorothee virginis et martyris hore nocturnales et diurnales eodem modo celebrentur quo notatum reperitur in communi suffragio de vna virgine cum illo excepto quod in secundo nocturno cantetur et legatur de sanctis confessoribus Vedasto et amando et habeatur quoque commemoratio de ipsis ad i[as] vesperas et matutinas (Gjerløw 1968: 317; see also 77).

Nonetheless, it appears that in Iceland Saint Dorothy's influence was limited. She is not mentioned in the extant Latin *cisiojani* in Iceland (ed. Beckman and Kålund 1908–1918: 2, 225–228), and her name is not included among the female saints mentioned in the fourteenth-century *Heilagra meyja drápa* (ed. Finnur Jónsson 1908–1915: 2A, 526–539 and 2B, 582–597). Apart from the two manuscripts mentioned above, the first appearance of her name in historical sources is in the wills of Teitur Þorleifsson (d. ca. 1540) and his wife, Inga Jónsdóttir, written in 1531, who both commend their sinful souls to the keeping of the almighty God, the Virgin Mary, Saint Peter, John the Baptist, Saint Anne, Saint Mary Magdalen, Saint Dorothy, Bishop Þorlákr, King Óláfr, and all saints (*DI* IX: 586, 591).

The primary testimonies to the cult of Saint Dorothy are literary and contained in the Arnamagnaean Collection, MS AM 429 12mo, an anthology, in prose and verse, of legends of exclusively women saints. Evidently,

---

93. Cormack (1994): "On the whole, the saints in whom interest is attested appear to have attained popularity before, rather than after, their feasts were adopted" (23).

specialization forms the principle of composition.[94] The collection was
probably intended for women and most likely nuns, and it is tempting to
associate it with the Benedictine convent at Kirkjubær in Síða, which was
established in 1186; as noted below (p. 65), it appears that the manuscript
was in the possession of Páll Ámundason, administrator of the convent
land from the end of the seventeenth to the beginning of the eighteenth
century.[95] The ten leaves of the manuscript that follow upon the illumination of Saint Dorothy on fol. 48v present her legend in prose and in poetry, and conclude with a Latin verse about and a prayer to Saint Dorothy.

The illumination, which takes up all of fol. 48v, is framed. The black
vertical columns are ornamented, while the horizontal lines of the frame
contain the following text" Sancta doratea ora pro nobis" (in black) and
"þetta er darateu [sic] saga meyar" (in red). Saint Dorothy herself is
depicted with long, wavy hair and wearing a crown. Her ankle-length dress
is long-sleeved and with a low neckline. A red shawl or cape is draped over
her shoulders. Her shoes are black and pointed. In her left hand, she carries
a book, and in her right a woven basket with fruits.

The prose version of the legend in MS AM 429 12mo is the *Dorotheu
saga*, which is discussed in section 3 below. The poetic version is the
Dorotheudiktur, a title given to the poem by Jón Helgason (1936–1938) in
his edition of the text (2, 359–363). Copies of the poem, in part or in full,
are found in manuscripts from the nineteenth and twentieth centuries: by

---

94. The collection is thus comparable to the German *Passienbüchlein von den vier
Hauptjungfrauen* and *Das Buch von den heiligen Mägden und Frauen*, Bokenham's
Legendys of Hooly Wummen, and in some respects to the Danish *De hellige Kvinder*,
extant in SKB K 4 from around the middle of the fifteenth century (ed. Brandt 1859).
The Danish legendary is comprised of fourteen items, representing various genres of
legends. The first two items "om joachim oc anna oc maria" and "om vorherræ fødels-
sæ" make up the *Evangelium Pseudo-Matthaei*; the third item "Aff vorherræ pyne" gives
the story of the passion based primarily on Matthew; the fourth item is *Transitus
Mariae*; and the fifth is *Visio Pauli*. These New Testament (apocryphal and canonical)
narratives are followed by legends of seven female virgin saints arranged according to
the order of the calendar: Margaret of Antioch, Christina, Cecilia, Catherine of Alexandria, Lucy, Agnes, and Sophia and her daughters. The thirteenth item is the legend
of Saint Marina. The legendary concludes fragmentarily with miracles attributed to the
Virgin Mary. According to Brandt (1859: 97), the predominance of female saints suggests that the collection was intended for women, most probably nuns. See also Gad
(1961: 188–232, esp. 189–190) and Carlé (1981: 48).

95. The other Icelandic convent was the Benedictine convent at Staður in Reynisnes (Reynistaður) in Skagafjörður, which was established in 1296.

Jón Sigurðsson in JS 399 4to (only the first stanza), by Steingrímur Thorsteinsson in AM 920 4to, and by Páll Eggert Ólason in Lbs. 2166 4to. The first stanza was printed in Jón Þorkelsson (1888: 91-92). The poem has been variously entitled "Kvæði um Dorotheu hina helgu" (Jón Sigurðsson), "Vísur af Dorotheu" (Steingrímur Thorsteinsson and Páll Eggert Ólason), and "Dorotheukvæði" (Jón Þorkelsson).

Following a preface, in which the poet appeals for divine assistance in the composition of the poem, stanzas 2-4 tell of Saint Dorothy's birth (in Rome), her many virtues, and her parents' (whose names are not mentioned) flight from Rome (their destination is not specified). The infatuation of the prefect ("grimur greifinn heidni" [5.1]) Theophilus (whose name is, however, not given until stanza 14) with Saint Dorothy and her refusal of his offer of marriage form the subject of stanzas 5 and 6. In stanzas 7-15 and 20, Saint Dorothy's sufferings are described. Stanza 7 relates that because Saint Dorothy refused to worship the heathen gods, the prefect had her imprisoned. After a digression in stanza 8, which tells of the martyrdom of Saint Dorothy's two sisters (whose names are not mentioned), the prefect's renewed attempt at having Saint Dorothy sacrifice to the heathen idols, Saint Dorothy's imprisonment, and the destruction of the idols form the subject of stanzas 9-12. Stanzas 13-15 conclude the description of Saint Dorothy's tortures by relating that she was immersed in boiling oil, that her breasts were burnt, and that, finally, she was executed. Apart from stanza 20, in which the beating of Saint Dorothy's face is related, the remaining stanzas of the poem (16-19) consists of appeals to Saint Dorothy for her intercession. The episode about the apples and roses is not included.

In Jón Helgason's (1936-1938: 359) view, the poem is recorded from oral tradition: "Digtet er uden tvivl nedskrevet efter mundtlig tradition." He bases his assumption on the garbled line "med gledinne mistu uifs" (8.9), which, through misrecollection, may have resulted from the confusion of "gud med gledina esta" (11.8) and "sua at badar mistu lifs" (8.7). He also notes that the order of the stanzas in the poem as represented by the extant manuscripts is erroneous and draws attention to the fact that stanza 11 interrupts the connection between stanzas 10 and 12, that stanza 20 should be placed earlier in the poem, and stanza 8 somewhat later. If indeed the tortures are to follow *BHL* 2324 and *Dorotheu saga*, further rearrangements would be necessary; the order of the stanzas would have to be along the lines of 7, 13, 9, 10, 12, 14, 11, 8, 20, 15. Jón Helgason comments, however, that it is uncertain if the poem ever followed the prose account accurately: "... det er meget usikkert om digtet nogensinde har fulgt prosaen nøjagtigt paa dette punkt." Other than the inclusion of both the *Dorotheudiktur* and the *Dorotheu saga* in AM 429 12mo, there is nothing to suggest a connection between the two texts.

As noted above, the *Dorotheudiktur* is followed by a Latin verse about Saint Dorothy and a fragment of a prayer to Saint Dorothy (fol. 59v). The verse is virtually identical to the first verse "Aff sancta dorothea" found in AM 418 12mo (cf. p. 51 above): "[A]ue gemma uírtuosa dorathea uernna(n)s | rosa mundí uíte patens glosa interuentrix | gracíosa sís pronobis specíosa." Apart from a number of scribal or grammatical errors in the Latin, the prayer resembles the second prayer appended to the legend of Saint Dorothy in Lambeth Palace 432 (ed. Horstmann 1880: 328; see above n. 56) and the prayer prefacing the legend as represented by *BHL* 2325d:

> [d]ífusa est gratia ín labíís tuís pro terra benedixit te dei ín eternum | cristus sempiterna deus pro cuius nomine gloriosa ma(r)tir uir | go dorathea multorum genera tormentorum superauít | te supplíciter exoramus ut eíus merítís et | precibus cuncta perícula deuíncamus íp | sam quoque ín necessitatibus nostris scelerum | ad íutrícem sencíamus Per Christum dominum nostrum Amen

That the legend of Saint Dorothy continued to be of interest in Iceland also after the Reformation is evident not only from the copies of the *Dorotheudiktur* in nineteenth- and twentieth-century manuscripts, but also from two *Dorotheukvæði*, one which is ascribed to Ólafur Jónsson (1560–1627), minister of Sandar in Dýrafjörður,[96] and another which is a paraphrase of the Danish ballad *Den hellige Dorothea*.

Ólafur Jónsson's poem is preserved in Lbs. 3170 8vo written around 1800, Lbs. 210 8vo written by Páll Pálsson (1806–1877) ca. 1860–1870,[97] and JS 510 8vo from the eighteenth or nineteenth century.[98] In fifteen stanzas (fourteen in Lbs. 201 8vo and JS 510 8vo), the poet tells a version of the legend considerably different from the one found in *BHL* 2324 and 2325d. There is no mention of Saint Dorothy's parents and sisters, and it

---

96. For biographical details about Ólafur Jónsson and a discussion of his poetry, see Páll Eggert Ólason (1919–1926: 4, 610–617) and Sigurjón Einarsson (1960).

97. The first four lines of the first stanza of *Dorotheukvæði* in this manuscript are printed in Jón Þorkelsson (1888: 92). A note preceding the poem specifies that it is copied from "Grundarbók."

98. The *Dorotheukvæði* is preceded by the following note: "Fylgjandi kvæði eru skrifað úr Grundarbók, skrifaðri árið 1832 af S. G. S."

is here the priests, who, possessed by the devil, condemn her to death because of her reluctance to give up her Christian faith.

The Icelandic paraphrase of *Den hellige Dorothea* (ed. Jón Hallur Stefánsson 1981) is preserved in seven manuscripts: (1) Lbs. 665 8vo, dated 1755 and written for the most part by the poet Árni Böðvarsson (1713–1776); (2) JS 323 8vo, written for the most part by a certain Eiríkur Jónsson in the first half of the nineteenth century; (3) JS 255 4to, written by Gunnlaugur Jónsson á Skuggabjörgum (1786–1866) in 1841; (4) JS 589 4to, also written by Gunnlaugur Jónsson in 1841; (5) Lbs. 201 8vo, written ca. 1850–1870; at the beginning of the poem, it is specified that it is copied from a manuscript by Gunnlaugur Jónsson;[99] (6) Lbs. 2166 8vo, written around 1860 by Sigmundur Matthíasson Long (1841-1924); and (7) Lbs. 2125 4to, written in 1865 or shortly after also by Sigmundur Matthíasson Long. According to Jón Hallur Stefánsson, these manuscripts fall naturally into two groups: (A) Lbs. 665 8vo, JS 323 8vo, JS 255 4to, JS 589 4to, and Lbs. 201 8vo, and (B) Lbs. 2166 8vo and Lbs. 2125 4to. He considers group A to be closer to the original than group B, which is characterized by having a number of additional stanzas (there are 35 stanzas in Lbs. 2166 and 38 in Lbs. 2125 4to as opposed to 30 in group A), none of which, however, contains factual information not found in group A.

There appears to be no connection between the two *Dorotheukvæði* and the *Dorotheu saga* or the *Dorotheudiktur*, but, as Jón Hallur Stefánsson observes, certain similarities in wording between the two *Dorotheukvæði* indicate that one poet knew the work of the other and was influenced by it. In his table of contents for Lbs. 2125 4to, Sigmundur Matthíasson Long attributes the translation to the minister Ólafur Einarsson in Kirkjubær (1573–1651); if the attribution is correct, it would seem likely that Ólafur Jónsson composed his poem under the influence of Ólafur Einarsson's translation.

Finally, it should be noted that in Iceland, a Dorothea Lafransdóttir is mentioned in a charter from the end of the sixteenth century (*DI* XV: 368, 447–448). The census of 1703 lists three women by the name of Dorothea. In 1801, four women carried the name, and in 1845 sixteen (Guðrún Kvaran and Sigurður Jónsson 1991: 184).

---

99. The first stanza of *Dorotheukvæði* in this manuscript is printed in Jón Þorkelsson (1888: 92).

3. DOROTHEU SAGA

3.0 *Transmission*

The Icelandic legend of Saint Dorothy is preserved in a single manuscript, Copenhagen, Det Arnamagnæanske Institut 429 12mo. Whether AM 429 12mo represents the original translation or a copy cannot be ascertained. Some of the errors, such as "aungum" for "ungum" (26), "eingínn" for "eigín" (39), "fíoll" for "fíell" (89), the repetition of "bren" (118), the anticipation of "af sínum" after "hana" in "frels þu hana drottínn mínn af sinum krankleika" (152–153), and the occasional omission of a word, suggest that the text is a copy. Although the evidence is only circumstantial, it should also be noted that all the other legends in AM 429 12mo appear to be copies of existing translations from Latin into Icelandic. When the original translation of the legend of Saint Dorothy was made is not known; obviously, the date of AM 429 12mo serves as a *terminus ante quem*.

3.1 *AM 429 12mo*

AM 429 12mo consists of 84 leaves. Its single-columned leaves measure 11.5 x 8.8 cm. Kålund (1889–1894: 2, 480), Jón Þorkelsson (1888: 88), and Seip (1954: 137) date the manuscript to around 1500. Unger (1877: 1, xii) dates it to the middle of the fifteenth century. His view is shared by Konráð Gíslason (1860: xi), who maintains that it is from approximately the same time as AM 621 4to, which he dates to the mid-fifteenth century. Jón Helgason (1936–1938: 2, 341), however, comments that Konráð Gíslason's dating is "næppe rigtig."

The manuscript contains the legend of Saint Margaret of Antioch (fols. 2r–13r), a Latin prayer to Saint Margaret (fol. 13v), the legend of Saint Catherine of Alexandria (fols. 15r–27r),[100] the legend of Saint Cecilia (fols. 29r–45v),[101] a so-called "Ceciliudiktur" (fols. 46r–47v; ed. Konráð Gíslason 1860: 559–560),[102] the legend of Saint Dorothy (fols. 49r–57r; ed. Unger 1877: 1, 322–328), the *Dorotheudiktur* (fols. 57r–59r; see pp. 60–61), a Latin verse about and prayer to Saint Dorothy (fol. 59v; see p. 62), the legend of Saint Agnes (fols. 61r–69r),[103] the legend of Saint

---

100. For variants from this manuscript (called C) see Unger (1877: 1, 400–421).

101. For variants from this manuscript (called C) see Unger (1877: 1, 276–294).

102. The poem was edited by Jón Helgason (1936–1938: 2, 342–346) on the basis of AM 721 4to with variants and corrections from AM 429 12mo (called B). Stanzas 1 and 31 (based on AM 429 12mo) were printed in Jón Þorkelsson (1888: 88–89).

103. For variants from this manuscript (called B) see Unger (1877: 1, 15–22).

Agatha (fols. 69r–76r), the legend of Saint Barbara (fols. 76r–80v),[104] and the legend of Fides, Spes, and Caritas (fols. 81r–84v).[105] All texts are preserved in their entirety with the exception of the legend of Fides, Spes, and Caritas, the end of which is missing.

The upper half of fol. 81r was originally blank and may have been intended for an illumination of Fides, Spes, and Caritas. Indeed, colored illuminations of Saints Margaret, Catherine, Cecilia, and Dorothy are found on fols. 1v, 14v, 28v, and 48v, respectively, and on fol. 60v, there is an illustration of Saint Agnes in black. Smaller illustrations of a similar kind appear in the text on fols. 7r, 8r, 10r, 12v, 57r, 69r (Saint Agatha, in black), and 76r (Saint Barbara, in black). Ornamental drawings appear at the bottom of fols. 35r, 52r, 52v, and 57r, and in the text of fol. 49r (the initial J). Many of the titles and initials are in red, and one initial is in blue. In some places, an open space has been left for the initials.

On fols. 59v and 81r, some lines from Hallgrímur Pétursson's *Passíusálmar* are found. The words "þetta er bok Gudrunar ad leika sier ad þui hun rifnar ei þo ostillt sie med fared" on fol. 27v suggest that the manuscript was, at least at one point, in private possession. On fols. 14r and 27v–28r, the alphabet is written in a seventeenth-century hand along with the formulaic prayer indicating the sign of the cross (in one instance referring only to the sign [of the cross]): "i nafne faudur og sonar og anda heilags amen" (27v), "Signingin*n*" (28r), and "J nafne födur og sonar og heilags Amen" (28r).

Little is known about the provenance and history of the manuscript. On a note accompanying the manuscript, Árni Magnússon records that he received it from "Páll á Flókastöðum" ("Mitt, feinged af Paale ä Flokastödum") and lists the contents of the manuscript.[106] This Páll may be the Páll Ámundason (ca. 1645–1716), who was the administrator of the convent land of Kirkjubæjarklaustur from 1681 to around 1708, and who died at Flókastaðir in Fljótshlíð, where his son-in-law, Björn Thorlacius, served as a minister.

---

104. For variants from this manuscript (called B) see Unger (1877: 1, 153–157).

105. For variants from this manuscript (called D) see Unger (1877: 1, 369–372).

106. The same information is found in Árni Magnússon's catalogue (AM 435a 4to): "Margretar Saga. de S. Catharinâ. de S. Cæciliâ, og þar i de Tiburtio et Valeriano. Carmen de S. Cæciliâ. de S. Dorotheâ. Carmen de S. Dorotheâ. de S. Agnete. de S. Agathâ. de S. Barbarâ. de S. Sophiâ, desunt nonnulla in calce. Er i 16 blada forme. feinged af Pale á Flokastòdum" (*Håndskriftfortegnelser* 1909: 17).

3.1.0 *Paleography*

Only the so-called two-storey *a* is found. The top storey is usually a closed loop as in, e.g., *Þann* (1).

In word-initial and final position, *b* is normally written with a loop, as in *blota* (4) and *dumb* (121), except in conjunction with abbreviations (e.g., *borg* [1]). Medially, it is written without a loop (e.g., *fabricius* [69]).

Only insular or round *d* is in evidence.

The *e* is always open.

Only insular *f* is in evidence. It consists of a vertical stroke with a figure 3 attached on the right. The lower loop of the 3 always ends at the descender.

The upper part of *g* is an *o;* its tail consists of either a half-circle, as in *gafu* (9), or a full circle, as in *skurdgodum* (4). The former version is the more common.

The right-hand vertical of *h* always descends below the line. It is usually written with a loop, although with some inconsistency in conjunction with abbreviations, e.g., *hann* (184), *hann* (185[1]).

The *j* is virtually identical with the tailed *r* rotunda, which is used as an abbreviation of *ed* (see below).

k is usually written with a loop; exceptions are found only in conjunction with abbreviations (e.g., *kroš* [72]). The leg of the *k* usually touches the line.

l appears with or without a loop, as in *blota* (4) and *uília* (32). When written double, it is always without a loop (e.g., *gull* [38]).

The right-hand minim of *m* and *n* does not extend below the line.

Of *r*, there are two types, minuscule *r* and *r* rotunda. *r* rotunda is used after *b, d, f, g, h, o, u, Þ,* and *y* and is in complementary distribution with minuscule *r*, except after *d, f,* and *u* where also minuscule *r* is found, e.g., *godr* (4) / *brudr* (155), *skurdgodum* (4) / *skurgod* (70), and *eílífrar* (202) / *fra* (106). A tailed *r* rotunda is found in *síalfur* (31).

Of *s*, there are two types, round or small capital *s* and long or cursive *s*. The former always sits on the line, whereas the latter extends well below the line. Small capital *s* (š) is commonly used in abbreviations of *svo* (e.g., šuo [18]) and *sér* (e.g., šer [12]) and is common also in forms of *Þessi*, especially when abbreviated (e.g., *Þeš* [14], *Þešarar* [32], *Þešum* [50], and *Þeša* [86]). In these cases, the small capital *s* probably indicates geminate *s*, and this is almost certainly also the case in *kroš* (72), *oš* (82, 202), and *mešudagur* (200), although it should be noted that š with a superscript dot is also in evidence: *Þeš́* (198). In addition, round *s* is found in the following words: *Cešaria* (12), *s(uarar)* (39, 43, 102), *s(uaradi)* (120, 173), *hanš* (124,

126, 177), *sier* (139), *serlega* (146), *hímeríkís* (167), *konungsíns* (169), *hímiríkís* (195), *fabruaríus* (198), and *mesudagur* (200).

The vertical of *t* does not normally extend above the cross-bar except in the ligature of *s + t*.

y is written with a dot. The upper part consists of a *u*; the descender veers to the left and ends in a hook.

The Tironian nota has the shape of the figure 7 with the descender forming a small hook to the right at the bottom. The stave never goes below the line, and it is always barred.

Of ligatures, *l + f* (*síalfur* [31]), *o + t* (*dottur* [20]), and *s + t* (*cristna* [3]) are in evidence. Only the ligature of *s+ t* is regularly used.

Apart from the word *amen*, which is written in capital letters (*AMEN* [203]), the following capitals are found (excluding the ornamental initials at the beginning of a chapter): *C* (*Cesaria* [12]), *E* (*En* [8, etc.]), *F* (*Fabrícius* [34, etc.]), *H* (*Heilog* [197]), *O* (*Ok* [50]), *Þ* (*Þann* [1]), and *U* (*Uar* [4]). *A*, *H*, and *N* have the shape of minuscule letters; the others appear as Roman capitals. An unusually large minuscule *a* appears in *ad* (18).

An accent is commonly found over *i* and *j* but appears to be no more than a graphic marker.

A dot below the line indicates deletion: *ḳ* (191).

3.1.1 *Abbreviations*

Superscript *a* occurs twice and stands for *ana* (*hana* [51]) and *anna* (*manna* [85]).

Superscript *c* is used in abbreviations of *mik*, *þik*, and *sik* (74, 75, 65) and is expanded *g* in accordance with forms written in full (122, 102, 13). It is also used in forms of *mikill*, e.g., *mikillí* (112; cf. *miklum* [6], *míklu* [178]).

Superscript *d* stands for *ed* (*med* [6]).

Superscript *e* stands for *re* (*drepa* [2]), *eir* (*fre⟨i⟩star* [34]) and is also used for *enn* in abbreviations of *menn* (1, etc.). In one instance, it is used for *enne* (*henne* [54]).

Superscript *ę* occurs once and stands for *ęr* (*þęr* [110]).

The *er* abbreviation is found only in *heídner* (1), *yfer* (1), and *rom-uer⟨s⟩ku* (2).

The zigzag tittle is used for *er* (*ser* [11]), *ir* (*yfir* [2]), and *r* (*er* [4]). It is also used in the abbreviation of *Dorathea*: *doratheam* (115; cf. *doratheam* [88]).

Superscript *i* stands for *id* (*uid* [57]), *il* (*til* [18]), *ir* (*uird* [156]), *ui* (*þui* [18], cf. *þuí* [71], etc.]), *ri* (*cristna* [3]), and *yrir* (*fyrir* [10], cf. *fyrir* [115]).

Superscript *i* is also used in the abbreviation of *eigi* (*e^i* [3]); it is expanded *igi*, although, when written in full, the negation is written *eígí* (15), *eckí* (42), *ecce* (46), *ecke* (48), and *ekke* (180).

Superscript *m* stands for *um* (*b*org*um* [7]).

Superscript *n* stands for *an* (*sid*an [11]) and *ann* (*þ*ann [181], cf. *þ*an*n* [12, 42], but *þa*n [67]), and in one instance *enn* (*þe*nna [184]).

Superscript *o* stands for *or* (*for*n*ír* [17]), *oru* (*f*oru [14]; cf. *f*oru [9]), *ro* (*d*rott*ni* [6]), and *uo* (*ſ*uo [128], cf. *ſ*uo [28]). It is also used in the abbreviation of *hon* (*h^o* [23]), but is expanded *h*un in accordance with the form written in full (*h*un [173]).

Superscript *r* is used for *r* (*e*r [11]), *ar* (*keis*are [2]), and *yr* (*f*yrre [49]). In one instance, it is used for *adr* (*m*adr [4]), in another for *ur* (*þurp*urakl*ędí* [160]).

The *ra* abbreviation, as in *ad*ra (19), is also used for *ar* (*gi*arna [156]) and *ur* (*sp*urd*í* [65]). It is also used in the abbreviation of *svá* (8, etc.), which is expanded *ſ*uo in accordance with forms written in full (*ſ*uo [28, etc.]).

Superscript *t* stands for *at* (*þ*at [10]), *et* (*h*et [5]), and *it* (*ſn*uit [18]).

Superscript *u* stands for *ru* (*í*umf*ru* [27]) and *ur* (*sk*urd [78]).

The superscript 2-like sign is used for *r* (*fag*urt [171]) and possibly also *ur* (*aun*ur [10]). Since no clear distinction is made between the endings -*r* and -*ur*, it is uncertain whether the sign, when it appears in terminal position, should be expanded -*r* or -*ur*. In the transcribed text, the -*ur* expansion is chosen.

The *us* abbreviation sign resembles a superscript figure 9 as in *dorath*us (15).

A tailed *r* rotunda is used for *ed* (*m*ed [11]).

An *r* rotunda with a diagonal stroke through its tail stands for *rum* (*od*rum [21]).

The Tironian nota is used for *ok* / *og*. The word is never written in full and is expanded *ok* by analogy with *ek*.

The nasal stroke proper stands for *n* (*þa*nn [1]) and *m* (*ti*ma [1]). In *hā* (= *h*ann [131]), it appears to indicate *nn*; the word is at the end of a line.

Abbreviation with suspension is uncommon. The following examples are in evidence: *.s.* = *s(uarar)* (39, 43, 102), `G´ = `G(ud)´ (52), `G´ = `G(uds)´ (80), *.s.* = *s(uaradi)* (120, 173). At 39 and 173, it is, perhaps, doubtful, if the abbreviation should be classified as a suspension, since the *s* is furnished with a superior curl or stroke.

A number of words are abbreviated in a somewhat more radical fashion with a raised horizontal stroke or a curl, e.g., *borg* (1), *byskupí* (23), *hans* (23), *herber⟨g⟩í* (23), and *konungsens* (133).

Jésús is abbreviated *ic* (44, 75), in acc. *jhm* (122), in gen. *ihc* (186, 199). The *jhu* (141) is probably a vocative form. The abbreviation *eͥ*. (6) is an isolated example.

Christr is abbreviated *xp̄r* (44, 75), in acc. *cͥsti* (122), in gen. *cͥstz* (186) or *xp̄i* (199). The *cͥsti* (141) is probably a vocative form. The abbreviation *cͥ*. (6) is an isolated example.

3.1.2 *Orthography*

VOWELS

Short and long *a* are written *a*.

u-mutation is found in two- or three-syllable forms of words with *u* in the second or third syllable.

The conjunction *eða / eðr* is written *eda* (96, etc.).

The change *vá > vo* is evident from *suo* (28, etc.), *uor* (48), *uorum* (6, 117, 118), and *uors* (199). In the abbreviation of *váru / voru* (*uᵒ* [5, etc.]) it is impossible to tell, but *voru* (*uoru*) would seem justified in the light of other evidence.

The noun *nátt / nótt* is written *nótt*: *nottína* (94), *nott⟨i⟩na* (130), *nottum* (200).

Short *e* is written *e* or, in one instance, *ie* (*hierud* [34]).

Diphthongization of *e* before *ng* is found in *einglar* (79, 194), *eínginn* (63, cf. 80-81, 129, 160, 165; see also 39 textual note), *eíngí* (182), *leingí* (116), and *leíngr* (128). Note, however, *gengu* (11). In *geingenn* (133) and *geingínn* (170) it is impossible to tell.

Note *ei* in *heilgustu* (201). The noun *greifi* is written with *ei* or *e*: *grefa* (34), *grefans* (40), *grefenn* (43), *greifenn* (87) *greifenn* (94), *greifan* (98), *greifenn* (104), *greifen* (107).

The verb *gera* appears only abbrevated. In some instances the zigzag tittle is used (*gera* [48, etc.]); in others, the word is abbreviated with a superscript *o* (*giora* [66], *gior* [117], *giortt* [145], *giort* [192]).

The endings *-ligr / -legr*, *-liga / -lega* have *e*: *trulega* (33), *diofulegt* (35), *blidlega* (37), *suíuírdlegra* (45), *akaflega* (47), *ferliga* (49), *gladlega* (86, 173), *ínnelega* (100), *efenlega* (124, 196), *serlega* (142, 146), *inne legazta* (155), *gudlegu* (157), *otalegum* (189), and *oumrędilega* (196). There is only one example of *i*: *ferliga* (49).

Long *e* is written *e* or, in a few instances, *ie*. The spelling *ie* is found once in *hér* (*hie*r [174]), in the pronoun *sér* (*sie*r [138, 139, 158, 160, 173 see textual note, 186), and in the verbal forms *sér* and *séð* (*síe*r [184], *sie*d [161]), and *fíell* (89 see textual note).

Short and long *i* are written *i*. The preposition *í* is, however, always written *j* (the only exception is *í* [186]). For accents, see above.

The preposition *fyrir* and *yfir* are written with *y*.

Short and long *o* are written *o*.

The negative prefix is *ó*: *ofridar* (9), *ouínur* (31), *otru* (45), *omak* (53), *otal* (85), *otalegum* (189), and *oumrędilega* (196).

The preposition *ór* is written *or* (9, etc.).

The fem. sing. pers. pronoun is *hun* (*hu*n [173]), but abbreviated *h°*.

Short and long *u* are written *u* and, in one instance, *v* (*audęfv*m [16]). Note, however, *o* (not *u*) in the verbal form *skolí* (37, 41).

No distinction is made between the endings -*r* and -*ur*, both are written -*r*, as in, e.g., *dętr* (10), *brudr* (155), and *lydr* (159). An exception is *nockur* (fem. nom. sing., 151). In endings, the 2-like superscript abbreviation sign is often used.

Short and long *y* are written *y*.

The noun *byskup* appears only abbreviated (23).

The noun *miskunn* is written with *y*: *myskun*nar (52), *myskun*ar (67, 203), *myskun*n (95).

The *i*-umlaut of *á* and *ó* is written *ę* (e.g., *będi* [5], *kięrleika* [6], *audęfu*m [7], *fęra* [16]) or, in a few instances, *e* (e.g., *detr* [16], *bedi* [22]). In these cases, it may be that the hook was forgotten or has faded away.

The *u*-umlaut of *a* is written *o* (*hofdu* [1]) or *au* (*aun*ur [10]).

(Older) *ø* is written *o* or *au*.

The 3rd pers. sing. pret. form of *snúa* is *snøri*: *snori* (21), *snoríz* (57), *snor`i´* (110), *snorí* (188), *snore* (191).

In unstressed, final syllables, *i* is more common than *e*, although *e* is by no means uncommon. *e* is particularly common in *henni* (*henn*e [24, 36, 38, 54, 63, 91, 94, 107, 108, 125, 139, 163, 166, 183]), in forms of the attached definite article (*manzen*s [31], *grefen*n [43], *katlenu*m [55], *stopule*n [78], *gode*t [78], *godenu* [79], *greífen*n [87, 94], *bríoste*n [91], *morgenen*n [98], *greífen*n [104], *greífe*n [107], *morgenen*n [130], *staden*n [132, 134, 164], *konungsen*s [133], *meyen*n [165), and in *ekki* (*ecce* [46], *ecke* [48], *ekke* [180]). In addition, *e* is found in the following words: *heídn*er (1), *yf*er (1), *rike* (2, 196), *keis*are (2), *storme* (9), *nafne* (26, 54), *audęfe* (45), *cristen*n (47), *fyrre* (49), *stroken*n (56), *uorde*t (60), *himne* (79), *eingen*n (80–81, 129), *uęre* (81), *unn*ed (83), *sin*ne (95, 142, 158), *orden*n (99), *talade* (100), *geingen*n (133), *mege* (145), *skap*are (149), *uisse* (165), *mínne* (175), *frosen* (182), *hínne* (185), *snore* (191). Note also *innelega* (100), *elleg*ar (119), *efenlega* (124, 196), *inne legazta* (155), *hímeríkís* (167).

As for *u* and *o*, *u* is the more common. *o* is found in the following words: *lofudo* (3), *þionudo* (6), *etludo* (13 see textual note), *mundo* (17), *marío* (44), *pino* (49, 53), *aungo* (51), *doratheo* (58), *huerso* (65), *stundo* (79), *neítudo* (111), *híno* (133, 201), *nockuro* (135).

The svarabhakti vowel is found in only three instances: *síalfur* (31), *fagurt* (171), and *kall⟨d⟩az⟨t⟩ur* (181). In other instances, -*r*/-*ur* is abbreviated with the superscript 2-like sign (see above).

CONSONANTS

b is lost in *dramskap* (135).

c is used in proper names (*kapadocia* [12], *Cesaria* [12], *Fabrícíu*s [34, etc.]) with the exception of *krist⟨i⟩na* (10) and *kalextína* (11). It is also used consistently in forms of the adjective *kristinn* (*cristna* [3, etc.]) and in *sankta* (*sancta* [28, etc.]), as well as in *Cristr* (*cristí* [122, etc.]).

Geminate *k* is written *ck* as in, e.g., *nockura* (63), with only two exceptions: *ecce* (46) and *ekke* (180). Note *ck* in *predíckadí* (187) and *c* in *ec* (73), which is elsewhere written *ek*.

d and *ð* are written *d*. *þ* for *ð* (*d*) appears once: *truþu* (3).

The infinitive marker and preposition *at* is written *at* or, in some instances, *ad*: 18, 54, 80, 81, 82, 83, 99, 107, 118. Note also *huad* (177) and *þangad* (105), but *þangat* (185) and *híngat* (199).

The noun *andlit* is written *anlit* (*anlít* [127, 129]), and *andlát* is written *anlát* (*anlatz* [201 see textual note]).

There is loss of *ð* (*d*) in *skoli þer* (41) and *hafí þer* (168).

Both *skurðgod* and *skurgoð* are in evidence: *skurdgodu*m (4), *skur goda* (22), *skurgoda* (58, 191), *skurgod* (70), *skurdgod* (76), *skurd godet* (78), *skurdgoda* (104), *skurdgoda* (106).

Note double *d* in *stundd* (185), but single *d* in *hredar* (19) and *gredí* (95). Similarly, the past participle of *leiða* is written both *leidd* (132, 164) and *leid* (134).

f before *t* is written *p*, e.g., *díupt* (69) and *eptir* (80).

g is written *g*. Length is shown by doubling, as in *hoggua* (138), or by a superscript dot, as in *hoggua* (132).

k > *g* is found throughout in *míg* (122, 156, 157), *þíg* (102, 120, 142, 148, 149), *síg* (13, 51, 115, 131, 186), and *míog* (43, 100). *ek* is written *ek* (once *ec* [73]).

Note single *g* in *begía* (25), *huorstuegía* (26 see textual note), *brugar* (35), *ligia* (62), *legía* (74, 87). In these cases, it may be that the dot was forgotten or has faded away.

The palatalization of *g* after a vowel before *i* is shown by the "backward" spellings *meygi*ar (58) and *nygi*ar (183).

h is preserved before *l* and *r*. The cluster *hn-* is not in evidence.

The noun *auðhæfi* is written without *h*: *audęfa* (44), *audęfe* (45), *audęfu*m (108).

The noun *kné* is written *hne* (71, 140).

j is normally written *i*. Apart from the preposition *í*, which is written *j*, *j* occurs in the following words: *jafn*an (31), *jh*esum (122), *jh*esu (141), *jd*ran (150).

k is written *k* or, in a few instances, *c*. Long *k* is shown by the spelling *ck*, once by the spelling *cc*, and once by *kk* (see above).

Palatal *k* is written *ki* before *æ*: *kięrleika* (6), *kięrazta* (155), *kięra* (163). Note single *k* in *dreka* (62).

l is written double before *d* (and *ð*), e.g., *ualld* (1), *uilldu* (3), *þolldu* (50), *skylld* (10), *alldri* (26), *þolldí* (53), and *holld* (90). Note, however, single *l* in *taldí* (109), *þoldí* (128), and *þoldir* (157) with original *lð*. *l* is also written double before *t* and *z*.

The assimilation of *rl* is found in *kollu*m (22) and *kallar* (144).

m is represented either by *m* or by the nasal stroke, the determining factor being almost certainly graphic convenience. Length is shown by a horizontal stroke over the *m*.

n is represented either by *n* or by the nasal stroke. As with *m*, the determining factor seems to be graphic convenience. Length is shown by a horizontal stroke over the *n*.

Distinction is normally made between the adverb *enn* and the conjunction *en*, but not consistently. In general, there seems to be a lack of consistency with regard to *n* and *nn*, e.g., *þann* (2) / *þan* (67), *henndr* (72) / *hendí* (175), *stunnd* (109) / *stund* (95), *greifen* (107) / *greifenn* (104), *stopulen* (78) / *stopulín*n (80). Note also, e.g., *stofuní* (64), *brun*ir (114), and *anad* (117), although in these cases it may be that the nasal stroke was forgotten.

Long *p* is shown by a superscript stroke, as in *up*p (81), or a dot, as in *up*p (115). In *up* (70, 133), it may be that the stroke or dot was forgotten.

For forms of *r* and their distribution, see above. Long *r* is shown by a superscript dot as in *fyr*r (169).

rs > *s* is found in *fys*tir (26).

For forms of *s* and their distribution, see above. Long *s* is shown by the small capital (s), as in *ꝥes* (14), or by doubling (ſſ), as in *uissu* (8) and *ꝥessu*m (9).

Long *t* is shown by doubling, as in *attu* (10), less frequently by a superscript dot, as in *gott* (66). There appears to be some inconsistency in the use of long and short *t*; note *reta* (109, 188, 190), *retrí* (108), but *rett*ri (106) and *retta* (150); *hiartta* (42, 52), but *hiarta* (120), *almatig* (49), and *almatígs* (67), but *almatti*gur (149) and *almattígs* (167). Short *t* is found in, e.g., *ꝥít* (65), *mẹti* (139), *uota* (195), *pretum* (187), and *seta* (198), and long *t* in *burtt* (9), *sentt* (75), *huortt* (117), *gatt* (125), *blotta* (125), *giortt* (145), *fottu*m (160), *heyrtt* (168), and *sennt*t (175).

t for *d* occurs once in the 2nd pers. plur. pres. indic.: *truít* (104).

d for *t* in the neut. of the past participle is found in *leítad* (30), *ẹtlud* (78), *unned* (83), *ꝥolad* (101), and *sed* (172).

Consonantal *u* (v) is written *u*.

The medio-passive ending is -z. Note also *ueízt* (74).

The superlative ending is -zt (*bezta* [56], *seinazta* [150], *inne legazta* [155], *kíẹrazta* [155], *kall⟨d⟩az⟨t⟩ur* [181], *síduztu* [193]), -z (*hellz* [13]), or -st (*heilgustu* [201]).

lls and *(n)ns* are written *llz* and *(n)nz*: *allzualldandí* (73), *illzku* (117), *allzuallda* (202), *allz ualldandí* (179), *a`l´zualldanda* (196), *ma*nzens (31).

The gen. ending *s* is written *z* after *t*: *cristz* (186), *tr⟨a⟩ustz* (187), *anlatz* (201 see textual note). Note also *zt* in *ꝥionuztu* (146–147).

MISCELLANEOUS
The free definite article is written with inital *h*-.

The following forms of the pronoun *engi* are found: masc. nom. sing.: *eíngín*n (63), *eingen*n (80–81), *eingen*n (129, 160), *eíngín*n (165), *eíngí* (182); masc. acc. sing.: *aungan*n (29); neut. dat. sing.: *aungo* (51) and *aungu* (84).

The following forms of *nokkurr* are in evidence: fem. nom. sing.: *nockur* (151); fem. acc. sing.: *nockura* (63); neut. dat. sing.: *nockuru* (108), *nockuro* (135); neut. nom. sing.: *nockurt* (148); neut. acc. sing.: *nockurt* (182).

The noun *stund* appears both with and without -*u* in the dat. sing.: *stundo* (79), *stundu* (85, 152), *stund* (105, 166), *stunnd* (109), *stundd* (185).

The noun *konungr* / *kóngr* is always abbreviated: *konungsens* (133), *konungsíns* (133), *konungsíns* (169), *konungsíns* (170).

As far as *-leikr* / *-leiki* forms are concerned, only the weak form is in evidence: *grimleíka* (50), *krankleíka* (97,153).

The adjective *almáttigr* appears only once in a contracted form: *almatku*m (27).

Note the strong adjectival declension in *hin*ir *fystir staf*ir (26).

The past participle of *verða* has initial *v* (*u*) in *uordet* (60).

The verb *vilja* is in the 1st pers. sing. pres. indic. *vil* (*uil ek* [44, etc.]), in the 2nd pers. *villt* (*þu uillt* [48, etc.]), and in the 3rd pers. *vill* (*hann uill* [38, etc.]).

In a few instances, the 1st pers. sing. pres. indic. ending is used in the 1st pers. sing.: *ek tru*ir (74–75), *ek fyri smar* (120), *bidr ek* (149), and *ek síer* (184).

The 1st pers. sing. pret. indic. has *-i*: *ek lofadí* (164).

The 3rd pers. plur. pres. indic. of *mega* is *mega* (66).

Of the forms *aldrigi* and *aldri*, only the shorter form is in evidence: *alldr*i (49), *alldr*i (96), *alldr*i (197).

3.2 The Sources

In his edition of *Dorotheu saga*, Unger (1877: 1, xii) maintains that the legend "stemmer temmelig nøie med Legenden i Legenda Aurea"; his view was adopted by Mogk (1904: 891), Lehmann (1937: 44), and Widding, Bekker-Nielsen, and Shook (1963: 307).

However, at the height of its popularity, the *Legenda aurea* became virtually synonymous with the genre of the legendary. As impressive as the number of manuscripts is the multiplicity of forms in which the work flourished. For a time the work was a staple of printing houses almost everywhere in Western Europe. Seybolt (1946a: 328–336) counts at least 156 editions of the *Legenda aurea* and perhaps as many as 173 published between 1470 and 1500; the more conservative figure, omitting doubtful identifications, includes 87 Latin editions and 69 vernacular ones (Seybolt 1946b: 342; Reames 1985: 4). It has been said that in the late Middle Ages the only book more widely read was the Bible.[107]

No modern critical edition of the *Legenda aurea* based on the Latin manuscripts or even a definitive listing of its thirteenth-century contents is available (Reames 1985: 243–244, n. 76). The lack of a thorough-going study of early manuscripts of the *Legenda aurea* naturally makes divergences between the Icelandic translation of the legend of Saint Dorothy and Graesse's third edition (1890), that is, *BHL* 2324, difficult to interpret. Moreover, it is difficult to know whether the text of the legend of Saint

107. See, however, Seybolt (1946b: 341).

Dorothy remained stable throughout the Middle Ages and within the *Le-genda aurea* tradition; or whether it was translated as a single legend or whether it originally formed part of a rendering of an entire legendary (or portions of it) into Icelandic.

While some sections of the Icelandic translation follow the *BHL* 2324 version closely, others do not. As in the case of the *Dorotheen passie*, the *Sunte Dorotheen passie*, the *Von sent Dorothea*, the *Erzählung vom Martyr-ium der lobesamen Jungfrau St. Dorothea*, the *Ludus de Sancta Dorothea*, and the Middle English renderings, it appears that not only have the various editors and commentators too readily postulated *BHL* 2324 as the source, but that also their hypotheses have been accepted uncritically because of the enormous popularity of the *Legenda aurea* and because of the some-what doubtful, if not misleading, authority of Graesse's edition. Indeed, in the course of more than a century of research on the various vernacular renderings of the legend of Saint Dorothy, only Willenberg (1889) voiced a certain scepticism. Nonetheless, Willenberg's rejection of *BHL* 2324 as the source of the early Middle English prose translation and Bokenham's poetic rendering of the legend finds support in the fact that a number of the details on which *BHL* 2324 and the two Middle English translations dis-agree (such as the names of Saint Dorothy's parents, the name of the bishop who baptized Saint Dorothy, and the statement that Theophilus's body was thrown to beasts and birds), are shared by some of the other vernacular renderings discussed above and the Icelandic *Dorotheu saga*. The "unknown legend," which Willenberg postulates as the source of the two Middle English translations, would thus seem to be the source of also some of the other vernacular renderings, including the *Dorotheu saga*.

Willenberg's "unknown legend" remains unknown, but certain details in *BHL* 2325d would seem to approximate some of the details in the German, Middle English, and the Icelandic texts that are either not found in *BHL* 2324 or are different. Indeed, a connection between the *BHL* 2325d version and the early Middle English and Icelandic translations is evident from the prayer prefacing the *BHL* 2325d text, which is found also at the end of the early Middle English translation (Lambeth Palace 432; see n. 56) and at the end of the *Dorotheudiktur* in AM 429 12mo. That the *BHL* 2325d version must be excluded as a direct source for the vernacular renderings is, however, obvious from certain details. The name of Saint Dorothy's tormentor is Capricius (Fabricius in *BHL* 2324 and the vernacu-lar renderings; the date provided for Saint Dorothy's martyrdom (".viii. Kal. februarij" [116] = 24 January) disagrees with the one found the vernacular renderings; and the statement that sick people were healed by the fragrance of the roses ("Tanta erat fragrantia rosa*rum*, ut multi debiles infirmi, p*a*ralitici *et* leprosi ex ea*rum* odore sunt refocilati at*que* curati" [112–114]) is found in only one of the vernacular texts, the *Erzählung vom Martyrium der lobesamen Jungfrau St. Dorothea* ("von den rossen dye vm do gesant hett Dorothea / do von gye so gutter gemach / wer krankch oder syech lag / wer chrvmp oder vor vergicht lag / vil schir er do genas" [42, 44]). The source of the *Dorotheu saga*, as well as the *Dorotheen passie*, the *Sunte Dorotheen passie*, the *Von sent Dorothea*, the *Erzählung vom Martyrium der lobesamen Jungfrau St. Dorothea*, the *Ludus de Sancta Dorothea*, and the Middle English renderings must have been a text which was in the main identical with *BHL* 2324, but which differed in regard to certain details, some of which are now found in *BHL* 2325d. Whether or not *BHL* 2325d should be viewed as a *Legenda aurea* text cannot be ascertained, for, as noted above, it is not known if the text of the legend of Saint Dorothy remained stable within the *Legenda aurea* tradition.

In the edition below, the text of *BHL* 2324 edited by Graesse faces the text of the *Dorotheu saga*. The text of *BHL* 2325d appears in the appendix.

3.3 The Translation

The *Dorotheu saga* opens in a somewhat more leisurely fashion than both the *BHL* 2324 and 2325d versions. Omitting the introductory phrase ("Gloriosa virgo et martir Dorothea ex patre Doro et matre Thea fuit progenita ex nobili sanguine senatorum" [*BHL* 2324, 1–2]; "TEmporib*us* Capricij prefecti gloriosa uirgo *et* m*a*rtyr dorothea ex patre dorotheo, matre u*er*o theódora ex nobili senato*rum* s*an*guine *est* orta" [*BHL* 2325d, 9–10]), the translator begins with an account of the persecution of Christians in Rome as a means of setting the stage for the ensuing events: "J Þan*n* tima sem heídn*er* m*en*n hofdu ualld yf*er* roma borg *ok* ollu ro*muer*(s)ku rike *ok* þan*n* sem þa u*ar* keis*ar*e yf*ir* þeim let pina *ok* drepa alla c*ri*stna m*en*n þa sem a gud tru*þu ok* ha*n*s nafn lofudo *ok ei*gi uilldu blota skurdgodu*m* ..." (1–4). He then introduces Saint Dorothy's parents and sisters at length, rearranging the material in the Latin text and adding a few details:

Vn*de* dorotheus uir bonus *et* iustus jdola sperne*n*s roma*m* relinque*n*s cu*m* possessionib*us*, agris, uineis, castris domib*us* ac uniu*er*sis diuitijs suis tra*n*sfretauit cu*m* uxore sua theodora et cu*m* duab*us* filiab*us* cristen, *et* calisten, *et* perrexit i*n* regnu*m* Capadocię, *et* peruenit i*n* ciuitate*m* Cesaream ibi*que* habitauit (*BHL* 2325d, 12–16) > ... Uar j fyr nef*n*dri ro*m*a borg einn godr m*a*dr sa er dorathus e*r* nef*n*dr ha*n*s kona het theodera þau u*oru* be̜di vel c*ri*stin *ok* þionudo drottni u*orum ihesu* crist með miklum kíęrleika. rik uoru þau at audęfum będi at borgum ok ste`i´nhusum uingordum gullí ok silfri ok gimsteinum suo at ⟨þau⟩ uissu eigi aura sínna tal En suo sem þau uoru uafin j þessum ofridar storme þa foru þau j burtt or þeim herudum ok yfir gafu allt þat er þau attu fyrir guds skylld tuęr dętr attu þau het aunur krist(i)na en aunur kalextína þau hofdu þęr með ser sidan gengu þau j þat herad er kapadocia heitir j þann stad ⟨er⟩ CeSaria heitir ok fengu Ser þar herbergi sem þau ętludo síg hellz með nadum uera mega (4–13).

Whereas *BHL* 2324 and 2325d then proceed to relate the birth of Saint Dorothy and her baptism, the Icelandic text pauses and devotes a passage to Saint Dorothy's two sisters' renegade actions. During an outbreak of persecution in Caesarea, certain "blótmenn" (14) came to the house at a time when Dorathus (Dorotheus) was away. They captured the sisters, and, promising them wealth if they would worship the pagan gods and torture if they refused, forced them to apostatize. With what appears to be a practical concern for coherence and order in the narrative, the lacuna in the original, in which the sisters are neglected until Saint Dorothy converts them from their apostasy, is thus filled, although since this arrangement is found also in the *Dorotheen passie*, the *Erzählung vom Martyrium der lobesamen Jungfrau St. Dorothea*, and the *Ludus de Sancta Dorothea*, it is doubtful if this deviation from the Latin reflects the skills of the translator; it seems more likely that it was contained in the original Latin source. A similar display of narrative scruple (in fact, one which may be ascribed to the translator) is found when Saint Dorothy is brought to her sisters, who at this point are reintroduced into the story; here the translator adds that these are the sisters "sem fyrr segir fra at snunar uoru fra rettri tru ok til skurgoda uíllu" (105–106).

Similar types of cross-referencing are found elsewhere in the translation. Thus, when Saint Dorothy instructs the angel to bring the basket to Theophilus, the translator adds – perhaps as a means of referring to a previous episode – that she had promised to send apples, roses, and, according to the translator, herbs (cf. *Dorotheæ Komedie*, see p. 55) to Theophilus the day before: "þui at ek lofadí honum þui j giar þa er ek uar leidd fyrir stadenn" (164). A "reminder" of the same kind is found in the angel's speech when giving Theophilus the basket: "has rosas cum pomis mittit tibi soror mea Dorothea de paradiso sponsi sui" (*BHL* 2324, 70–71) > "tak hier uid þeim eplum ok rosum sem ek hefí j mínne hendí er dorathea systir min hefir ydr senntt eptir þui sem hun sagdíz hafa lofat ydr" (174–176). Finally, when Theophilus is reintroduced into the story after

Saint Dorothy's execution, the translator adds that "[N]u er at segía fra konungsíns skrifara theopholo sem fyrr uar getit" (169–170).

In the account of the birth and baptism of Saint Dorothy in the Icelandic translation the names of Saint Dorothy's parents correspond to those found in *BHL* 2325d rather than *BHL* 2324, but the details are elaborated variously. For example, we are told that the child was not only named after her parents, but also that that the name was drawn from the first letters of each of their names ("hinir fystir stafir or huorstuegía þeira nafne" [26]). Moreover, the child was given her name at the request of her parents ("fadir henar ok modir uílldu at þat uęri dregit af begía þeira nofnum" [24–25]); this information is not found in *BHL* 2324 or 2325d. Like *BHL* 2324, but unlike *BHL* 2325d (and the *Sunte Dorotheen passie*, the *Erzählung vom Martyrium der lobesamen Jungfrau St. Dorothea*, the Middle English translations, and the prayer in *Visdoms Spejl*), the name of the bishop who secretly baptized Saint Dorothy is not given.

This tendency to elaborate and amplify is found throughout *Dorotheu saga*. It is especially conspicuous in the more emotionally charged episodes, as is evident in the following example, which describes Fabricius's infatuation with Saint Dorothy:

> Quod invidus serpens inimicus castitatis dyabolus non sustinens Fabricium terrae praefectum in amorem virginis Dorotheae stimulans, ut ipsam carnali concupiscentia appeteret (*BHL* 2324, 11–14; cf. *BHL* 2325d, 21–23) > [N]u suo sem manzens ouínur díofullínn síalfur sem jafnan er uanr um `at´ sítía at suíkía þann er gud elskar ok hann ser god uílía þesarar meyiar til síns skapara ok trulega þionustu ok stoduga honum ueítandí þui fre(i)star hann þes grefa er yfir þau híerud uar settr hann het Fabrícius fiandínn brugar diofulegt eítr med honum ok kueíktí lostasemis girnd til þesarar meyiar (31–36).

The concern for dramatic effect is found mostly in the encounters and clashes of the martyr with her persecutor. It is in the depiction of Saint Dorothy's sufferings and tortures that the translation achieves its greatest dramatic effects: an abundance of visual detail, violent physical actions, the contrast between bodily mutilation and spiritual calm, between the fury of the persecutor and the quiet confidence of the saint. Thus, the account of Fabricius's torture of Saint Dorothy after the destruction of the idol, although related "med stuttum ordum ok skiotu mali" (92–93), is considerably amplified. The translation omits mention of the fact that Saint Dorothy was placed on a gibbet "pedibus elevatis" (*BHL* 2324, 35; *BHL* 2325d, 50–51), but adds that she was beaten "uęgdarlaust suo at blod fíell

u*m* allan*n* hen*ar* likama" (89). The torches with which her breasts are
burnt are not, as in the Latin, small ("faculae" [*BHL* 2324, 36; *BHL* 2325d,
53]), but large ("st*or* blys" [91]). And whereas Fabricius in the Latin
"infremuit" (*BHL* 2324, 49; *BHL* 2325d, 70), in the Icelandic text we are
told "han*s* lif allt [bran*n*] af gri*m*d *ok* re*í*d*í*" (126).

Although the scenes of torture of Saint Dorothy provides the most
poignant illustration, the dramatization of the legend in the translation is
not limited to her martyrdom only. Where *BHL* 2324 and 2325d merely
report that the two sisters were burnt back-to-back at Fabricius's command, the translation is emphatic in its addition: he "geck e*í* fyr if*ra* e*n*
þe*i*ra likam*ir* uor*u* all*í*r brun*ir* up*p* at kolu*m*" (114–115).[108] And whereas
BHL 2324 merely says that Theophilus's body was hacked into pieces "et
ad manducandum projicitur" (78), the translation adds that they were
thrown to birds and beasts ("f*yrir* fugla *ok* u*í*ll*í* dyr" [194]). (It should be
noted, however, that since this phrase is found also in the *Dorotheen passie,*
the *Erzählung vom Martyrium der lobesamen Jungfrau St. Dorothea,* and the
Middle English translations, it is questionable if it should be attributed to
the translator of *Dorotheu saga.*)[109]

Much of this dramatization is achieved by using descriptive adjectives
and adverbs, e.g., "rosas cum pomis" (*BHL* 2324, 48; *BHL* 2325d, 69) >
"lystug epl*í* *ok* m*a*rgar ros*ir*" (123) and "dicens" (*BHL* 2324, 70) > "s(uaradi) hon*u*m gladlega m*ed* fogr*um* ordum" (173–174). In this connection,
mention must also be made of the doublet renderings, which are quite

---

108. In *Dorotheu saga,* as in *BHL* 2324 and 2325d, Saint Dorothy is sent to her
sisters; by contrast, in both the Middle English translations and the prayer in *Visdoms
Spejl* (as noted above) the sisters are sent to Saint Dorothy.

109. Cf. Vitz (1991: 98–99): "Latin works were commonly written by religious or
clerics primarily for purposes of inspiration. Such works were generally performed –
read aloud from a lectionary, occasionally sung – in a sedate fashion in a liturgical or
semiliturgical setting: in the Mass itself; more commonly, in the Liturgy of the Hours
(matins especially); or in the refectory or chapter. By contrast, vernacular works were
generally composed for nonreligious, nonliterates, and commonly performed by jon-
gleurs. The requirement that a story about a saint be entertaining – that it be a 'good
story' – is markedly greater for vernacular works than for those in Latin, though in fact
many Latin works are quite entertaining and were surely intended at least in part as an
innocent, interesting and pleasurable way to fill leisure time. ... But laymen are not a
captive audience like monks and nuns, and if they do not appreciate the way a story
is told, or what is told, they may well just walk away, or fail to pay the performer.
Thus, while Latin sources are sometimes a bit dry or undramatic, vernacular composi-
tions reliably liven up the story: they give the characters names, provide dramatic details and vivid dialogue, and so on."

common, e.g., "magicis artibus" (*BHL* 2324, 21; *BHL* 2325d, 32) > "af
golldr*um* ok fíolkyngí" (61), "columnam" (*BHL* 2324, 30; "colu*m*nas" [*BHL*
2325, 40]) > "eí*n*a stora sulu eda tr*e*stolpa" (69), "devastas" (*BHL* 2324, 33;
BHL 2325d, 48) > "hefi*r* ... hrakt *ok* yfi*r* un*n*ed *ok* eytt" (82–83), "malefica" (*BHL* 2324, 45; *BHL* 2325d, 65) > "hin ílla *ok* hí*n* heí(m)ska m*ę*r"
(116), "illusorie" (*BHL* 2324, 54; "derisorie" [*BHL* 2325d, 75]) > "*m*ed
nockuro spottí eda dr*a*mskap" (135), "electa mea" (*BHL* 2324, 61; "dilecta
mea" [*BHL* 2325, 93]) > "hí*n* in*n*e legazta *ok* hi*n* kí*ę*rasta brudr" (155).
Note also "amoena" (*BHL* 2324, 39; *BHL* 2325d, 58) > " hín fagr*a* ... *ok*
hi*n* ín*n*elega" (100).

A similar tendency is found in the rendering of miracles. Thus, whereas the Latin simply states that Saint Dorothy "adjutorio Christi illaesa
manens, ac si balsamo ungeretur" (*BHL* 2324, 19–20; "adiuto*r*io illessa
p*e*rmane*n*s *et* no*n* adusta s*ed* uncta oleo ac si Balsamo ung*e*retu*r*" [*BHL*
2325d, 29–30]) after having been cast into a vessel of burning oil, the translation, through use of alliteration and similes, offers a much fuller description: "h*u*n bad `G(ud)´ ser myskun*n*ar af ollu hi*a*rtta heyrdí h*a*nn *ok* hen*a*r
b*e*n *ok* sa hen*a*r píno *ok* omak e*r* h*u*n þolldí fyr*i*r hans nafne *ok* híalpadí
hen*n*e suo ad þa e*r* kvalar(ar)n*i*r letu af at síoda hana þa ste h*u*n ut af
katlenu*m* suo kat *ok* glod s*e*m h*u*n hefdi set*it* j kalld*r*i daugg *ok* suo ⟨uar⟩
hen*a*r lika*m*r s*e*m h*u*n hefdi uer*it* strokenn *m*ed hit bezta balsamu*m*"
(52–57). A similar example is the account of the destruction by angels of
Fabricius's pillar with his god on top of it. The account in the translation is
amplified, especially in comparison with *BHL* 2324 (29–33), which does not
include Saint Dorothy's prayer, but also in comparison with *BHL* 2325d:

Beata dorothea i*n* terra*m* p*r*ostrata eleuatis*que* oculis i*n* c*ę*lum, orauit
domi*n*um, ut ost*e*nderet om*n*ipotentia*m* sua*m* subiu*n*gensque qu*a*re tu
`es´ deus solus *et* no*n* alius preter te. ET ecce multitudo angelor*um*
cu*m* impetu ue*n*ie*n*tes et ita jdolu*m* conc*u*sserunt, *quod* n*e*c p*a*rticul*ę*
etiam minutissim*ę* colum*n*ę aut idoli reperirentur. In sup*e*r audiens
uoces demo*n*um p*e*r aera clamantiu*m* *et* dice*n*tiu*m* dorothea cur nos sic
deuastas (*BHL* 2325d, 42–48) > heilog doratea fell þa oll t*il* íard*a*r *ok*
lagdí bad*a*r henn*d*r sín*a*r j kro*s* *ok* bad t*il* guds med þe*s*u*m* ordu*m*
styrktu m*i*g drottin*n* mín*n* allzualldandí suo at ec þola vel allar þ*ę*r
pín*u*r sem þeir uílía a m*i*g legía fyr*i*r þítt naf*n* *ok* þeir spari m*i*g eckí
þu*i*at þu ueízt at ek tru*i*r a þ*i*g mín*n* signadí skaparí ih*e*sus crist*r* *ok*
sentt mer þi*n*a híalp suo at ek gaufga e*i*gi sk*u*rdgod þeira blind *ok* dauf.
[E]n er fab*r*ic*ius* heyrdí hu*e*rsu ⟨hun⟩ badz fyr*i*r þa uar lokít at bua u*m*

stopulen e*r* sk*ur*d godet stod a *ok* ętlud at leida h*an*a þangat t*il* at
gaufga *ok* luta godenu a þeirí so*m*u stundo komu guds ei*n*gl*ar* af hi*m*ne
ept*ir* bodi `G(uds)´ *ok* h*an*s uílía *ok* brutu stopulí*n*n *ok* god*it* suo ad
ei*n*ge*n*n sa þar s*u*o m*i*k⟨it⟩ af ad ei*n* flís eda span*n* uęre ept*ir*. up*p* j
lopt*it* heyrdu men*n* ad díoflarnír greníudu *ok* sogdu s*u*o heilog dorathea þu hef*ir* oS alla hrakt *ok* yf*ir* un*n*ed *ok* eytt ollu*m* u*orum* uílía s*u*o
ad u*er* kom*um* au*n*gu fr*am* fyr*ir* þínu*m* bęnu*m* (71–84).

Yet another example is the account of Saint Dorothy's rejection of Fabricius's offer of marriage:

Audiens hoc dulcis Dorothea quasi lutum terrae despiciens terrenas divitias et intrepida se Christo desponsatam fatebatur (*BHL* 2324, 16–17;
BHL 2325d, 25–27) > heilog dorathea S(uarar) s*u*o malí grefa*n*s herra
sagdí h*un* yd⟨r⟩ar b*or*gír *ok* kastala gull *ok* gí*m*steína skoli þer bíoda
þe*i*m er þ*at* uilía hafa *ok* þeiri sem ydr fr*u* uill uera e*n* eckí mer þui at
ek a m*er* an*an* bidil þan*n* er ek an*n* af aullu hi*ar*tta grefe*n*n sp*ur*dí hu*ar*
sa bídíl uęri er h*un* elskadi s*u*o míog h*un* S(uarar) sa bidill e*r* ihes*us*
*cris*tr so*n* íu⟨m⟩fr*u* marío *ok* h*an*s audęfa uil ek níota en ek fyr*ir* lit oll
i*ar*dnesk audęfe *ok* alla uillu *ok* otr*u* suíuírdlegr*a* goda ydara (39–45).

As evident from the last example, direct speech is introduced in the
adaptation.[110] This use of enlivening dialogue and of scenes where the
source has indirect speech or unremarkable third-person narrative, is very
characteristic of the Icelandic text. In *BHL* 2324 and 2325d, Fabricius's only
comment after the torture of Saint Dorothy is that she has suffered enough
("satis namque castigata es" [*BHL* 2324, 39–40; *BHL* 2325d, 58–59]); in the
translation, he adds that if she were wise, she would follow his advice,
worship his gods, and become wealthy ("fylg min*um* radu*m* *ok* uílía, ef þu
ert klok þui at þu hef*ir* noga pi*n*u þolad sk*al* ek g*er*a þíg ríka m*ed* m*er* ef
þu uillt elska god u*or*" [100–102]).[111] Moreover, the translation also includes Saint Dorothy's response, which has no equivalent in *BHL* 2324 and
2325d: "drottín*n* mínn uíl ⟨ek⟩ elska *ok* h*an*s sígnudu mod*ur*. *en* ek neíta
dioflu*m* ydru*m* *ok* allrí sk*ur*dgoda uíllu þeirí sem þer heidn*ir* men*n*. truít

---

110. It should be noted that the same conversation is found also in the *Erzählung
vom Martyrium der lobesamen Jungfrau St. Dorothea* (12).

111. Cf. the *Erzählung vom Martyrium der lobesamen Jungfrau St. Dorothea*: "dw
pist gemartert genvg vil / gedenkch an deyner jugent czil / las dich nymer nötten /
weder marteren noch töten / o mynichleichew magt / wye pist dw so gor verczagt /
daz dw dich nicht wild vorcheren / dein marter mvzz sich meren / nvn cher wyder durch
deyner jugent / dein leyb hat marter genvg / er hyes dye magt füren hynczwe" (24, 26).

a" (102–104). Similar examples are found in the description of Fabricius's wrath and in the account of Theophilus's conversion:

> Quod audiens Fabricius furore succensus mox eam in dolium plenum ferventis olei mitti jussit (*BHL* 2324, 17–19; *Quod audiens capricius furore succensus et ut uerba non protrahamus. Primo est in Cathastam missa oleo feruenti plenam* (*BHL* 2325d, 27–28]) > [E]n þa er Fabricius heyrdi at hun uilldí ecce hlyda fortaulum hans ok at hun uar cristenn ok stodug j guds þionustu þui uard hann akaflega reidr ok sagdi Suo medan þu uillt ecke gera minn uilia ok trua a god uor almatig þa skalltu þola suo ferliga pino ok naud at alldri fyrre þinir frendur þolldu slíka pínu. Ok j þesum grimleíka let hann taka meyna suo at hun kom aungo ordi fyrir síg ok let sioda hana j eínum katlí storum fullum af oleum (46–52).

> Tunc Theophilus prorupit in voces laudando et glorificando Christum Deum Dorotheae, qui mense Februario, dum magna frigora terram cogebant nec aliquod virgultum frondibus vestitur, rosas et poma, quibus vult, mittere potens est, cujus nomen sit benedictum (*BHL* 2324, 72–75; *Theophilus hęc uidens litteram, quam scribebat, in terram iactauit, et dimissis manibus uelut amens effectus unum dominum ihesum christum dei filium publice confessus proclamauit* [*BHL* 2325d, 116–119]) > [E]n Suo `sem´ theophelus sa þesa míklu iarteígn þa kalladi `hann´ harí roddu ok sagdi Suo. eínn er gud allz ualldandí sa er dorathea truir a ok bodar en uor gud er ekke utan díofuls spott ok hans daraskapur. En hun hefir þat af sínum gudí at j þann tíma sem ueturínn er kall⟨d⟩az⟨t⟩ur ok oll iordínn frosen ok eíngí uidur hefir lauf nockurt eda grodur. þa gefur hann henne nygiar rosir ok epli Suo ⟨at⟩ hun ma þat gefa hueríum sem hun uíll. ok upp a þenna gud uíl ek trua þui at ek síer at hann hefir ualld yfir alla adra guda (178–185).[112]

---

112. Cf. the *Erzählung vom Martyrium der lobesamen Jungfrau St. Dorothea*: "Do das wunder geschach / Theophilus offenleich sprach / in des chvniges sal / das man es hört vberall besvnder / das got yeczvnd macht rossen / vnd ephphellen wol gemach / wen dye czeyt ist yeczvnd als chald / von zzne vnd von eys also gestalt / ym ist nichcz so vil czw machen / an endes czil der apgot Appollo ist so swach / des er nicht gemachen mag / pluvnd vnd chlaynes reys / Jesus gewaltig ist / vnd ways daz dye svnne / lawfft noch irrer art / der man hat auch seyn rechte vart / der svmer vnd auch der wyntter lankch / dye sübem planetten habent auch uren gankch / als in ist gesaczt auff / chayner chvmt nicht aws seynen lauff / dornoch vnd er geordnet ist / wan ir wolt Jesum Christ / von dem dye rayn magt / Dorothea hat gesagt / ir schult fürwar gelawben / daz dye sternen nicht tawgen / czw helffen noch der svnne got / wer dem abgot dyentt der wird czw spot" (44).

The translator also enlivens the narrative by drawing the audience in. When relating the execution of Saint Dorothy, the translator renders "Et decollata et ad Christum suum sponsum feliciter collocata est" (*BHL* 2324, 66; Quę statim ex tunc decollata est et anima eius perrexit ad christum [*BHL* 2325d, 115–116]) as "en heilog dorathea uar þa hogguín j samri stund ok for med þeSum píslar sigri `til' almattígs guds j eilífa hímeríkíS fagnadí sem nu hafí þer heyrtt fra sagt" (166–168). And when at the end of the legend the information about the date of Saint Dorothy's death and her feastday is presented,[113] the translator, with what appears to be almost a pastoral concern, exhorts his audience to honor and worship Saint Dorothy: "nu heidrum ok dyrkum híno heilgustu mey sancta doratheam ok beidum þeS at hun arní oS uid allzuallda gud eílífrar híalpar ok myskunar będi þeSa heims ok annars at eílífu utan enda" (201–203). Note that in the Icelandic text, the date of Saint Dorothy's martyrdom is given as 6 February 387 ("hínn seta dag manadar þeS er heítír fabruaríuS þa uar lidit fra híngat burdí uors herra ihesu cristi þríu hund`r´ud atta tigir ok síau ar" [198–199]), not 13 February 287 as in *BHL* 2324 ("anno domini CCLXXXVII Idus Februarias" [67–68]) or 24 January as in *BHL* 2325d (".viii. Kal. februarij" [116]).[114] While it seems natural to give 6 February (her feastday) as the date of her execution, the year 387 for 287 in *Dorotheu saga* is most likely the result of a misreading, as is almost certainly the statement that Saint Dorothy was starved in prison for seven days (".uíí. daga" [62]) instead of nine ("novem diebus" [*BHL* 2324, 22; *BHL* 2325d, 36]), although, interestingly, the *Dorotheen passie* also has seven days ("Siben tage" [138]).

The *Dorotheu saga* emphasizes the religious aspect of the legend. Thus, according to the translation, the conception and birth of Saint Dorothy took place through divine intervention to console her parents and others and to convert many pagans to Christianity ("... attu þau enn dottur sín amillum þa sem gud gaf þeim til hugganar ok morgum odrum Suo at hun snori morgum heidnum monnum bedi konum ok kollum til rettrar truar fra skur goda uíllu" [20–23]).[115] And after Saint Dorothy's first miracle, it is said in the translation that many people praised God in heaven ("lofudu gud j hímíríkí sem uerdugt uar" [59]), which has no equivalent in *BHL* 2324 and 2325d.

113. *Dorotheu saga* and the *Dorotheen passie* present the information about the date of Saint Dorothy's martyrdom at the end of the legend.

114. Cf. n. 33 concerning the *Dorotheen passie* where also a misreading appears to have taken place.

115. Cf. the *Erzählung vom Martyrium der lobesamen Jungfrau St. Dorothea*: "dez frewt vater vnd myter sich / daz got ein chind so lobleich / in czw trost het geben" (6, 8).

In the process of adapting the Latin legend to a simple, unlettered, audience, what is only implicit in the Latin original is made explicit in the translation. Thus, in *BHL* 2324 and 2325d, it is only implied that Saint Dorothy was healed through divine intervention after having been hung upside down on a gibbet, lacerated with hooks, scourged, and had her breasts burnt: "De mane producta nec ulla macula nec ulla laesio apparuit" (*BHL* 2324, 37-38); "MAne uero sancto producta est gloriosa uirgo et martyr dorothea, nec ulla macula seu lesio in ea apparuit" (*BHL* 2325d, 55-56). The translation underlines the work of providence: "En um nottína hafdí hun þar skamma stund uer⟨it⟩ adr enn gud síalfr med sinne myskunn grędí oll henar sar sem hun hafdi fengit a sínum likama suo sem hun hefdí alldri sar fengit eda anann krankleíka" (94-97).[116] Similarly, *BHL* 2324 and 2325d nowhere specify that Fabricius became angry when Saint Dorothy converted her sisters (although his irate response is evident from the context); again the Icelandic version emphasizes the point: "fabricius ... ęrdíz ... af mikílli grimd ok reídí" (112-113).[117] One last detail: the translator not only states that after bringing the basket to Theophilus, the angel disappeared, but also that no one knew what became of it ("huarf meyenn j burt suo at eingínn uisse huad af henne uard" [165-166]).

The *Dorotheu saga* also appears to eschew vague or abstract narrative details. Thus, about the many heathens who convert to Christianity after the miraculous destruction of Fabricius's idol, the Latin says simply they "martirii palmam ingressi sunt" (*BHL* 2324, 34; "palmam martyrij attigerunt [*BHL* 2325d, 49]); the translation is more concrete and says that they "þolldu gladlega allar þęr pínur ok kualír sem greifenn uílldí a þa legia fyrir guds nafn. let hann suma pina en ⟨suma⟩ drepa" (86-88). About Saint Dorothy's conversion of her sisters it is said that she addressed them gently, "auferens ab iis caecitatem cordis et eas ad Christum convertit" (*BHL* 2324, 43; "auferens ab eis cęcitatem cordis ipsas denuo ad christum conuertit" [*BHL* 2325d, 62-63]); in the Icelandic translation she "taldí ... fyrir þeim reta tru ok suo kom at þęr logdu allt a henar ualld snor`i´ hun þeim fra allri uíllu ok uann tru. suo at þęr neítudo díoflum en íatudu gudí sínum skapara" (109-111).

Despite what appears to be a concerted effort on the part of the translator to expand and amplify, certain episodes or pieces of information have been simplified or omitted. The angel's garment ornamented with stars ("in

---

116. Cf. the *Erzählung vom Martyrium der lobesamen Jungfrau St. Dorothea*, according to which the Savior himself appears (see p. 25).

117. Interestingly, the same addition is found in the *Sunte Dorotheen passie* (see p. 23).

cujus veste stellae fuerunt" [*BHL* 2324, 63-64; "*in* qua stellę aureæ texta resple*n*dueru*n*t" [*BHL* 2325d, 97]), or the curly hair of the angel ("crispo capite" [*BHL* 2324, 63; "crispato crine" *BHL* 2325d [98]) who, incidentally, in the Icelandic is a little beautiful girl ("eína litla fag*ra* mey" [159]), and not a boy as in *BHL* 2324 and 2325d, all go unremarked. These omissions appear to be accidental, since they seem to contradict the translator's efforts to explain, interpret, and amplify. The claim that when starved in prison Saint Dorothy was sustained by the heavenly consolation of angels and emerged more beautiful than ever ("Quae nutrita a sanctis angelis dum producitur ad tribunal, pulchrior, quam nunquam visa fuerit, apparuit cunctique mirabantur, quod tot diebus absque cibo tam formosa videretur" [*BHL* 2324, 22-25]), which is not found in the translation, is not included in *BHL* 2325d and may thus not have been included in the source text.

The translation is embellished with a number of rhetorical devices. The description of the conversion of Saint Dorothy's two sisters, who "neítudo díoflu*m* en íatudu gudí sínu*m* skap*ara*" (111), is marked by antithesis. Dorothy's miraculous healing is described with a simile: "ste h*un* ut af katlenu*m* s*u*o kat *ok* glod se*m* h*un* hefdi set*it* j kalld*ri* daugg *ok* s*u*o ⟨uar⟩ hen*ar* lika*m*r se*m* h*un* hefdi uer*it* strokenn m*ed* hit bezta balsamu*m*" (55-57). As this last example shows, alliteration is often used, although it appears to be restricted primarily to dramatic episodes, such as the torture of Saint Dorothy's two sisters ("h*ann* ... bad taka syst*ur* hen*ar* bad*ar ok* bínda sam*an* at bokunu*m ok* kasta j elld b*re*nanda" [112-114]), where the heightening of the style is evident, and, in particular, to direct speech, as evident from the following examples:

þu hin ílla *ok* hín heí(m)ska męr hu*er*su lei*n*gí uilltu halldaz j þi*n*u hardlyndí *ok* illzku (116-117).

ek fyri smar þíg *ok* þin god du*m*b *ok* dauf *ok* alla þina sęmd *ok* hego*m*a en ek uíl þola fy*ri*r mín*n* sígnada skap*ara* jhes*u*m c*ri*stí allar þęr pín*ur* se*m* þu uíllt a míg leggía þuí at j h*ans* gardí ma ek lesa lystug eplí *ok* m*ar*gar ros*ir* a þe*s*um tíma *ok* m*ed* honu*m* uil ek glediaz ęfenlega *ok* han*S* helgu*m* mon*nu*m a hi*m*num (120-124).

kom hín in*n*e legazta *ok* hin kíęrazta brudr allt þat *er* þu hef*ir* bedít mig `þat´ skal ek gi*ar*na ueita þer *ok* ertu uel ui*r*d af m*er* fyr*ir* þa míklu pi*n*u er þu þold*ir* fyr*ir* míg (155-157).

Alliteration also marks the concluding, collective appeal to Saint Dorothy and for her assistance and intervention with the Almighty:

nu heidru*m ok* dyrku*m* híno heilgustu mey *sanct*a doratheam *ok* beid-
u*m* þe*s* at hu*n* arní o*s* u*id* allzuallda gud eílífrar híalp*ar ok* myskuna*r*
bẹdi þe*s*a hei*m*s *ok* an*n*ars at eílífu utan enda AMEN (201–203).

Read aloud, the rhythm and word-music created by the alliteration com-
bine to convey that "choyce celestiall musicke, equall to / The motion of
the spheres" (5.2.133–134) that was to be so masterfully invoked by Dekker
and Massinger centuries later.

THE TEXT

A NOTE ON THE PRESENT EDITION
This diplomatic edition of *Dorotheu saga* reproduces the text of AM 429 12mo, fols. 49r–57r as closely as possible. Accordingly, both the punctuation and the distribution of upper and lower case letters in the manuscript are retained.

Abbreviations are expanded in accordance with the normal spelling of the scribe. The expansions of abbreviations by means of a supralinear symbol or letter are given in italics, as are instances of abbreviation by contraction. In cases of abbreviation by suspension, the expansion is placed in parentheses.

Obvious misspellings have been corrected and marked with an asterisk, the original being provided in the apparatus. Letters or words assumed to have been accidentally omitted by the scribe are added in angle brackets. Words or letters now illegible are printed in square brackets. Words or letters added above or below the line, are presented in ` ´ and ´ `, respectively.

The Latin text of *De sancta Dorothea* from *BHL* 2324 = *Jacobi a Voragine: Legenda Aurea Vulgo Historia Lombardica Dicta*, ed. Th. Graesse (3rd ed.; Dresden and Leipzig, 1890; rpt. Osnabrück: Otto Zeller Verlag, 1969) is reprinted on facing pages.

De sancta Dorothea

Gloriosa virgo et martir Dorothea ex patre Doro et matre Thea fuit
progenita ex nobili sanguine senatorum. Illis temporibus viguit persecutio
christianorum in terra Romanorum. Unde ipse Dorus spernens ydola,
Romana derelinquins praedia cum possessionibus, agris, vineis, castris ac
domibus transfretavit cum uxore sua et duabus filiabus Christen et
Calisten, perrexit in regnum Cappadociae venitque in civitatem Caesaream
ibique habitans genuit filiam, de cujus vita nunc intendimus loqui. Et ipsa
genita secundum morem christianorum occulte baptizata est a quodam episcopo sancto, qui nomen ei imposuit ex patre et matre compositum. Doro-

[I] **[49r]** J Þann tima sem heídner menn hofdu ualld yfer roma borg ok ollu
romuer(s)ku rike ok þann sem þa uar keisare yfir þeim let pina ok drepa
alla cristna menn þa sem a gud truþu ok hans nafn lofudo ok eigi uilldu
blota skurdgodum. Uar j fyr nefndri roma borg einn godr madr sa er
5   dorathus er nefndr hans kona het theodera þau uoru bẹdi uel cristin ok
þionudo drottni uorum *ihesu crist med miklum kíẹrleika. rik uoru þau at
audẹfum bẹdi at borgum ok ste`i´nhusum uingordum gullí ok silfri ok gim-
steínum suo at ⟨þau⟩ uissu eigi aura sínna tal En suo sem þau uoru uafin j
þessum ofridar storme þa foru þau j burtt or þeim herudum ok yfir gafu
10   allt þat er þau attu fyrir guds skylld tuẹr dẹtr attu þau het aunur krist(i)na
en aunur kalextína þau hofdu þẹr med ser sidan gengu þau j þat herad er
[49v] kapadocia heítir j þann stad ⟨er⟩ CeSaria heitir ok fengu Ser þar
herbergi sem þau *ẹtludo síg hellz med nadum uera mega

[II]   [E]n þegar þat frettu blotmenn þeS sama stadar þa foru þeir til husa
15   þeira sem dorathus hafdí ser herbergi tekit ok uar hann þa eígi heima en
detr hans badar toku þeir ok hetu þeim audẹfvm ef þẹr uilldu blota ok fẹra
forním godunum en at audrum kostí sogduz þeir mundo pina þẹr morgum
pislum ok gatu þeir Suo snuit þeim til blota ok heidíns *atrunadar þui ad
þẹr uoru hrẹdar fyrir píslum þeim er lagdar uoru a adra cristna menn

20   [III]   [E]n litlum tima her eptir attu þau enn dottur sín amillum þa sem
gud gaf þeim til hugganar ok morgum odrum Suo at hun snori morgum
heidnum monnum bedi konum ok kollum til rettrar truar fra skur goda
uíllu hun uar skird af eínum byskupí j hans herber(g)í ok þat nafn gefit at
[50r] hun skylldí heíta. dorathea uar henne af þui þat nafn gefit at fadir
25   henar ok modir uílldu at þat uẹrí dregit af begía þeira nofnum ok hafdir
hinir fystir stafir or *huorstuegía þeira nafne. þegar a *ungum alldri uar

---

2 þa] + *open space for a word which is now erased.*   5 het] + *open space for a word
which is now erased.*   6 ihesu crist] *abbreviated* e^i. c^i.   13 ẹtludo] ẹlltudo.   18 atru-
nadar] aturnadar.   26 huorstuegía] horustegía.   26 ungum] aungum.

10   thea autem ipsa puella repleta est spiritu sancto, virtutibus et omni pacis disciplina imbuta, formosa valde super omnes puellas regionis illius. Quod invidus serpens inimicus castitatis dyabolus non sustinens Fabricium terrae praefectum in amorem virginis Dorotheae stimulans, ut ipsam carnali concupiscentia appeteret. Qui mittens pro ea, spondens thesaurum et res

15   absque compoti determinatione pro dote prodere ipsam legitimo toro producendam. Audiens hoc dulcis Dorothea quasi lutum terrae despiciens terrenas divitias et intrepida se Christo desponsatam fatebatur. Quod audiens Fabricius furore succensus mox eam in dolium plenum ferventis olei mitti jussit, ipsaque adjutorio Christi illaesa manens, ac si balsamo

hun full af helgum annda ok þionadí gudí almatkum ok hans modur íumfru
sancta maríu um fram alla hluti hun uar suo fogr ok frid skopud af gudí
at aungann fann henar líka huorkí mey ne konu j þui landi ok þo at uidar
30 uęrí leítad

[IV]   [N]u Suo sem manzens ouínur díofullínn síalfur sem jáfnan er uanr
um `at´ sítía at suíkía þann er gud elskar ok hann Ser god uílía þeSarar
meyiar til síns skapara ok trulega þionustu ok stoduga honum ueítandí þui
fre(i)star hann þeS grefa er yfir þau híerud uar settr hann het Fabrícius
35 fiandínn brugar diofulegt eítr med honum ok kueíktí lostasemis girnd til
þeSarar meyiar ok let hann senda eptir henne en þegar sem hun kemr fyrir
hann talar hann blidlega til henar at hun skolí [50v] fylgia hans uilía ok
*bydr henne borgir ok kastala gull ok gimsteina ok at hann uill fa henar Ser
til *eigín konu ef hun uill hans radum fram fara heilog dorathea S(uarar)
40 suo malí grefans herra sagdí hun yd(r)ar borgír ok *kastala gull ok *gím-
steína skoli þer bíoda þeim er þat uilía hafa ok þeiri sem ydr fru uill uera
en eckí mer þui at ek a mer anan bidil þann er ek ann af aullu hiartta
grefenn spurdí huar sa bídíl uęri er hun elskadi suo míog hun S(uarar) sa
bidill er ihesus cristr son íu(m)fru marío ok hans audęfa uil ek níota en ek
45 fyrir lit oll iardnesk audęfe ok alla uillu ok otru suíuírdlegra goda ydara.

[V]   [E]n þa er Fabricius heyrdi at hun uilldí ecce hlyda fortaulum hans
ok at hun uar cristenn ok stodug j guds þionustu þui uard hann akaflega
reidr ok sagdi Suo medan þu uillt ecke gera minn uilia ok *trua a god uor
almatig þa skalltu þola suo ferliga pino ok naud at alldri fyrre [51r] þinir
50 fręndur þolldu slíka pínu. Ok j þeSum grimleíka let hann taka meyna suo
at hun kom aungo ordi fyrir síg ok let sioda hana j einum *katlí storum
*fullum af oleum en hun bad `G(ud)´ ser myskunnar af ollu hiartta heyrdí
hann ok henar bęn ok sa henar píno ok omak er hun þolldí fyrir hans
nafne ok híalpadí henne suo ad þa er kualar(ar)nir letu af at síoda hana þa
55 ste hun ut af katlenum suo kat ok glod sem hun hefdi setit j kalldri daugg
ok suo (uar) henar likamr sem hun hefdi uerit strokenn med hit bezta

38 bydr] bidr.   39 eigín] eingínn.   40 kastala] kastalar.   40-41 gimsteina] gímsteínar.
48 trua] tura.   51 katlí] kaltlí.   52 fullum] fullan.

20   ungeretur. Multi autem paganorum videntes hoc miraculum intra se ad
      Christum convertuntur, Fabricius vero credens hoc magicis artibus fieri,
      ipsam in carcerem reclusit novem diebus absque ciborum alimentis. Quae
      nutrita a sanctis angelis dum producitur ad tribunal, pulchrior, quam
      nunquam visa fuerit, apparuit cunctique mirabantur, quod tot diebus
25   absque cibo tam formosa videretur. Fabricius vero dixit: nisi Deos in
      praesente adores, equulei poenas non evades. Dorothea respondit: Deum
      adoro, non daemonem; Dii enim tui daemones sunt. Et prostrata in terram
      elevatisque in coelum oculis oravit ad dominum, ut ostenderet omnipoten-
      tiam suam, et quod ipse sit solus Deus et non alius praeter eum. Erexerat
30   namque Fabricius columnam et desuper ydolum. Et ecce multitudo angel-
      orum cum impetu veniens conterit ydolum, quod nec particula columnae
      inveniretur. Et audita est vox daemonum per aëra clamantium: Dorothea,

balsamum þar uar mart heidit folk uid ok `sa´ a þeSa íarteígn ok snoríz til
rettra⟨r⟩ truar fra skurgoda uíllu fyrir fortolur heilagra⟨r⟩ doratheo meygiar
ok lofudu gud j hímíríkí sem uerdugt uar.

60 [VI]   En sem fabricius sa þeSa íarteígn þa sagdí hann at þetta uerí uordet
af golldrum ok fíolkyngí henar ok let taka meyna ok kasta j myrkua stofu
ok let hana þar ligia .uíí. daga ok at hun hafdí huerkí at eta ne dreka ok
eínginn skylldi til henar koma at ueita henne nockura híalp ok er þeSi
'uika` uar lidín þa let hann taka hana [51v] or myrkua stofuní ok leída
65 fyrir sig hann spurdí hana huerso hefir þu nu hugsat þít mal e⟨t⟩lar þu nu
at bídía til goda uorra liknar ok lu`t´a þeim er þeir mega allt gott giora hun
suarar til almatígs guds uíl ek bídía myskunar þan er mer ueítir gott ok
ollum þeim er hans leíta en eigi díoflar þeir er þer truít a.

[VII]   [Þ]a let fabricius tak⟨a⟩ eína stora sulu eda trestolpa ok grafa díupt
70 nídr j iord ok let þar up a setía eítt stort skurgod þui at hann uílldí at hun
felle a hne fyrir þui ok gau⟨f⟩ga þat. heilog doratea fell þa oll til íardar ok
lagdí badar henndr sínar j kroS ok bad til guds med þeSum ordum styrktu
mig drottinn mínn allzualldandí suo at ec þola uel allar þer pínur sem þeir
uílía a mig legía fyrir þítt nafn ok þeir spari mig eckí þuiat þu ueízt at ek
75 truir a þig mínn signadí skaparí ihesus cristr ok sentt mer þina híalp suo at
ek gaufga eigi skurdgod þeira blind ok dauf. [52r]

[VIII]   [E]n er fabricius heyrdí huersu ⟨hun⟩ badz fyrir þa uar lokít at bua
um stopulen er skurd godet stod a ok etlud at leida hana þangat til at
gaufga ok luta godenu a þeirí somu stundo komu guds einglar af himne
80 eptir bodi `G(uds)´ ok hans uílía ok brutu stopulínn ok godit suo ad ein-
genn sa þar suo mik⟨it⟩ af ad ein flís eda spann uere eptir. upp j loptit heyrdu menn ad *díoflarnír greníudu ok sogdu suo heilog dorathea þu hefir oS
alla hrakt ok yfir unned ok eytt ollum uorum uílía suo ad uer komum
aungu fram fyrir þínum benum.

82 díoflarnír] díofdlarnír.

cur nos sic devastas? Et multa millia paganorum ad Christum manifeste convertebantur, qui etiam martirii palmam ingressi sunt. Ipsa autem Doro-
35 thea equuleo est suspensa pedibus elevatis, uncis laceratur corpus ejus, virgis castigatur, flagellis flagellatur, deinde ad mammillas virginis faculae ardentes applicatae sunt et ipsa semimortua usque ad crastinum reclusa est. De mane producta nec ulla macula nec ulla laesio apparuit. De quo etiam cum ipse praeses miraretur, dixit ei: adhuc revertaris amoena puella, satis namque
40 castigata es. Et misit eam ad duas sorores suas, Christen et Calisten, quae metu mortis a Christo recesserant, ut ipsae Dorotheam sororem suam a Christo avellerent. Dorothea autem leniter alloquens praedictas sorores, auferens ab iis caecitatem cordis et eas ad Christum convertit. Quod

85 [IX] [A] þeirí stundu snoruz *til* rett(r)*ar* tru*ar* otal heídín*na* m*anna* *ok*
lofudu gud fyrir þeSa *íarteígn se*m* uerdugt u*ar* *ok* þolldu gladlega allar þ*er*
pín*ur* *ok* kualír se*m* greífenn uílldí a þa legia fyrir guds naf*n*. let h*ann* suma
pína e*n* ⟨suma⟩ drepa e*n* *heilag`a´ mey doratheam let h*ann* taka *ok* ber'ia
med suípu*m* u*e*gd*ar*laust s*u*o at blod *fíell u*m* allan*n* hen*ar* likama *ok* med
90 íarnkombu*m* let h*ann* slíta holld af beínu*m* hen*ar*. en eptir þetta allt sam*an*
let h*ann* taka stor blys logandí *ok* brenna af h*en*ne bríosten [52v] e*n* þa er
þeir hofdu lokít at pína hana þeSu*m* píslum se*m* nu hefir uerit fra sagt med
stuttu*m* ordu*m* *ok* skiotu mali þa u*ar* hun þo en*n* eí alþíngís daud. let þa
greífenn kasta h*en*ne j myrkua stofu. En u*m* nottína hafdí h*un* þ*ar* skamm*a*
95 stund *uer⟨it⟩ adr en*n* gud síalfr med sin*n*e myskun*n* gr*e*dí aull hen*ar* sar
se*m* h*un* hafdi fengi*t* a sínu*m* likama s*u*o se*m* h*un* hefdí alld*r*i sar fengi*t* eda
anan*n* kra*n*kleíka.

[X] [U]m m*o*rgenen*n* snemm*a* u*ar* h*un* leídd fyrir greifan *ok* se*m* h*ann*
sa han*a* ad h*un* u*ar* heílbrigd orden*n* allra sín*n*a sara þa undradíz h*ann*
100 míog *ok* talade s*u*o *til* hen*ar* þu hín fagr*a* mey *ok* hin ín*n*elega fylg minu*m*
radu*m* *ok* uílía ef þu ert klok þui at þu hefir noga pínu þolad sk*al* ek g*e*ra
þíg ríka med m*er* ef þu uillt elska god u*or*. En heílog m*er* S⟨uarar⟩ drottín*n*
mín*n* uíl ⟨ek⟩ elska *ok* h*an*s sígnudu mod*ur*. en ek neíta dioflu*m* ydru*m* *ok*
allrí sk*ur*dgoda uíllu þeirí se*m* þer heidn*ir* men*n*. truít a. þa let gr*e*ífenn taka
105 hana j samr*i* stund *ok* f*e*ra þangad se*m* h*ann* fann syst*ur* hen*ar* þ*er* se*m* fyrr
segir fra at snun*ar* u*o*ru [53r] fra rettr*i* tru *ok* *til* sk*ur*dgoda uíllu *ok* *e*tladí
þ*er* s*u*o geta talat fyrir h*en*ne ad h*un* blotadi med þeim *ok* greífen het þeim
mik*l*um aud*e*fu*m* *til* ef þ*er* g*e*ti snu*it* h*en*ne fra retr*í* tru med nock*u*ru radí
En þeg*ar* j samr*i* stun*n*d er h*un* sa syst*ur* sin*ar* þa taldí h*un* fyrir þeim reta
110 tru *ok* s*u*o kom at þ*er* logdu allt a hen*ar* ualld snor`i´ h*un* þeim fra allr*i*
uíllu *ok* uan*n* tru. s*u*o at þ*er* neítudo díoflu*m* en íatudu gudí sínu*m* skap*ar*a

86 íarteígn] íarteíngn.   88 en] *written in margin with insertion marks in the text.*
88 heilag`a´] heílog`a´.   89 fíell] fíoll.   95 uer⟨it⟩] uer *with a zigzag tittle between*
e *and* r.   106 *e*tladí] + ad.

audiens Fabricius ambas sorores dorso ad dorsum ligari fecit et in ignem
45   projici et cremari. Et dixit Dorotheae: quousque, malefica, nos protrahis?
aut sacrifica et vives, aut sententia capitali plecteris. Illa laeto vultu respondit: quicquid vis, passura sum pro Christo domino et sponso meo, in
cujus horto deliciae, et rosas cum pomis colligam et laetabor cum ipso in
aeternum. Hoc audiens tyrannus in se ipsum infremuit praecepitque, ut
50   pulchritudo ejus et facies ejus baculis et fustibus caederetur, et ut tortores
fatigarentur et quod nec vestigia faciei in ipsa apparerent, et in carcere
servata in crastinum. De mane vero producitur illaesa a salvatore nostro
curata, sententia capitali judicatur, et dum extra muros ducitur, videns eam
Theophilus protonotarius regni quasi illusorie rosas de viridario sponsi sui
55   petens sibi mitti, quod illa promisit. Cum autem venit ad locum decollationis, rogavit dominum pro omnibus, qui ad honorem sui nominis suae me-

[XI]   [E]n þegar fabricius uard þessa uarr þa ęrdíz hann af mikílli grimd
ok reídí ok bad taka systur henar badar ok bínda saman at bokunum ok
kasta j elld brenanda ok geck eí *fyr ifra en þeira likamir uoru allír brunir
115   upp at kolum. sidan let hann kalla helga doratheam fyrir síg ok taladí til
henar mikillí reidí þu hin ílla ok hín heí(m)ska męr huersu leingí uilltu
halldaz j þínu hardlyndí ok illzku j motí godum uorum ok gior anad huortt
skíott ef þu uillt lífa ad *ofra godum uorum ok [53v] bren *reykelsi fyrir
þeim ellegar dęmi ek þig til dauda ok til *hardari pisla en þu hefir adr haft.
120   heilog dorath`e´a S(uaradi) þa med stodugu híarta. ek fyri smar þíg ok þin
god dumb ok dauf ok alla þina sęmd ok hegoma en ek uíl þola fyrir mínn
sígnada skapara jhesum cristí allar þęr pínur sem þu uíllt a míg leggía þui
at j hans gardí ma ek lesa lystug eplí ok margar rosir a þeSum tíma ok med
honum uil ek glediaz ęfenlega ok hanS helgum monnum a himnum

125   [XII]   [E]n þegar fabricius heyrdí at hann gatt eigi snuit henne til blotta
þa brann hanS lif allt af grimd ok reídí ok let kualara sla hana med morgum
hoggum storum będi henar signada anlít ok likama þar til er ⟨þeir⟩ uoru
Suo modir at þeir þoldí eigi leíngr fyrir mędí ok Suo hofdu þeir slegit henar
anlit ok likama at eingenn kendí hana fyrir sarum ok blod ras. sidan let
130   hann taka hana ok geyma um nott(í)na en um morgenenn let [54r] hann
leída hana fyrir síg ok dęma til dauda sidan ⟨let⟩ hann leída hana til þeS
stadar sem hana skylldi hoggua ok er hun uar leidd fyrir stadenn þa uar
konungsens skrífarí geingenn up j konungsíns pallaz j híno hęstu turna
borgarínar ok sa at heilog męr doratea uar leid fyrir stadenn þa kalladí
135   hann a h⟨an⟩a suo sem med nockuro spottí eda dramskap ok bad at hun
skylldí senda Ser af þeim eplum ok íurtum ok rosum sem hun sagdí at yxí
j gardí unnanda síns en hun lofadí honum þui ok sagdiz þat skylldu gera.
ok þa er hun kom j þann stad er hana skylldi hoggua þa bad hun sier orlofs
Suo at hun męti bídía fyrir Sier til guds ok þat uar henne ueítt þa fell hun
140   a sín hne ok bad til guds med þessum ordum

114 fyr ifra] fyri fra.   118 ofra] opra   118 bren] + bren.   118 reykelsi] reykelski.
119 hardari] hardara.

moriam passionis peragerent, ut in omnibus salvarentur tribulationibus et
praecipue a verecundia, paupertate et a falso crimine liberarentur et in fine
vitae contritionem et remissionem omnium peccatorum obtinerent, muli-

60   eres vero parientes nomen ejus invocantes celerem sentiant in doloribus
profectum. Et ecce vox de coelo audita est: veni, electa mea, omnia, quae
petiisti, impetrasti. Dorothea vero inclinata ad ictum spiculatoris apparuit
puer purpura indutus, discalceatus, crispo capite, in cujus veste stellae
fuerunt, ferens in manu orarium, id est sportulam cum tribus rosis et tot

65   malis. Cui Dorothea: obsecro te, domine mihi feras, eas Theophilo scribae.
Et decollata et ad Christum suum sponsum feliciter collocata est. Passa est
autem gloriosa virgo et martir Dorothea anno domini CCLXXXVII Idus
Februarias Fabricio praeside sub Dyocletiano et Maximiano imperatoribus

[XIII] [H]ínn signadí *skapari drottinn jhesu cristí styrktu alla cristna menn huernn j sinne stet ok serlega þa sem kalla a mítt nafn fyrir þig og minar [54v] pinu mínníz med godum ordum eda uerkum huort sem þat eru kallar eda konur gef þeim uilía til at bęta þat sem þeir eda þer hafa þer j

145 moti giortt Suo at eptir lifit mege þeir audlaz inngongu hímíríkís med þer ok þinum uolldum monnum a doms degí ok Serlega geym þu alla mína þion-uztu menn fra ollum uondum uerkum ok uilía drottínn mínn enn meira uil ek bídía þíg a huern sem nockurt fals uerdr logit ok a *mítt nafn kallar frels þu þa þar af en bidr ek þíg almattigur gud mínn skapare at þu gefír ollum

150 cristnum monnum retta jdran ok aflat sinna synda a seinazta tíma síns lífs ok ef nockur kona kuelz j barn burd ok kallar hun a mítt nafn a huerrí stundu sem þat er þa frels þu hana drottínn mínn af sinum krankleika.

[XIV] [Þ]egar hun hafdí talat þessi ord þa uar heyrd rodd af hímnum suo męlandí kom hín inne legazta ok hin kięrazta brudr allt þat er þu he[55r]-

155 fír bedít mig `þat' skal ek giarna ueita þer ok ertu uel uird af mer fyrir þa míklu pinu er þu þoldir fyrir míg ok sem allír hofdu heyrt þesa gudlegu rodd ok heílog męr dorathea reís upp af bęn sínne þa sa hun standa nęr síer eína litla fagra mey ok allr lydr sa sem uid uar hana hun uar berfętt sinum fottum en yfir sier hafdi hun eitt purpuraklędi Suo at eingenn þottiz hafa

160 sied anat þuilikt fyr hafdi hun j sinum hondum eína lítla korf med þrimur *eplum ok morgum rosum ok baud heilagri *dorateu þesa korf hun suaradí henne Suo ber hana mín kięra systír j borg(i)na til konungsíns skrifara teopholo þuí at ek lofadí honum þui j giar þa er ek uar leidd fyrir stadenn þegar hun hafdi þetta mǽllt þa huarf meyenn j burt suo at eínginn uisse

165 huad af henne uard. en heilog dorathea uar þa hogguín j samri stund [55v] ok for med þesum píslar sigri `til' almattígs guds j eilífa hímeríkís fagnadí sem nu hafí þer heyrtt fra sagt

141 skapari] skafari.   148 mítt] mínnt.   150 jdran] n corrected from a.   152 hana] + af sínum.   162 eplum] eptlum.   162 dorateu] doratea.

Romanorum. Theophilus autem stans in palatio praesidis et ecce puer
70   apparuit circa eum et sustulit eum in partem dicens: has rosas cum pomis
mittit tibi soror mea Dorothea de paradiso sponsi sui. Puer vero disparuit.
Tunc Theophilus prorupit in voces laudando et glorificando Christum
Deum Dorotheae, qui mense Februario, dum magna frigora terram coge-
bant nec aliquod virgultum frondibus vestitur, rosas et poma, quibus vult,
75   mittere potens est, cujus nomen sit benedictum. Et illius affirmatione et
praedicatione fere tota terra convertitur. Videns hoc tyrannus pluribus
generibus tormentorum, quam Dorotheam cruciavit, ultimum vero in particulas minunas succidi jussit et ad manducandum projicitur. Theophilus
vero sacro baptismate mystico corpore et sanguine Christi communicatus
80   est, perrexit ad Christum, qui glorificat sanctos suos, et glorificatur ipse in

[XV]   [N]u er at segía fra konungsíns skrifara theopholo sem fyrr uar
170 getit at hann uar geingínn upp j konungsíns turna ok suo sem hann hafdí
setit þar eina lítla stund kom þar ínn eitt fagurt mey barn ganganda ok
hafdí j sínum hondum eina lítla kórf hann þottíz ei hafa sed annad þuilikt
fyr. theopholus bad hana sítía nęr *síer en hun s(uaradi) honum gladlega
med fogrum ordum ok sagdi suo tak hier uid þeim eplum ok rosum sem ek
175 hefí j mínne hendí er dorathea systir min hefir ydr senntt eptir þui sem
hun sagdíz hafa lofat ydr ok þegar hun hafdí þetta talat þa huarf hun fra
hans auglíti suo at hann uíss(i) eigi huad af henní uard [56r]

[XVI]   [E]n suo `sem´ theophelus sa þesa míklu iarteígn þa kalladi `hann´
harí roddu ok sagdi suo. eínn er gud allz ualldandí sa er dorathea truir a ok
180 bodar en uor gud er ekke utan díofuls spott ok hans daraskapur. En hun
hefir þat af sínum gudí at j þann tíma sem ueturínn er kall(d)az(t)ur ok oll
iordínn frosen ok eíngí uidur hefir lauf nockurt eda grodur. þa gefur hann
henne nygiar rosir ok epli suo ⟨at⟩ hun ma þat gefa hueríum sem hun uíll.
ok upp a þenna gud uíl ek trua þui at ek síer at hann hefir ualld yfir alla
185 adra guda. ok a hínne somu stundd for hann þangat er hann fann crístna
menn ok let skíra sig í nafní ihesu cristz ok bad gefa síer guds likama til
híalpar ok tr(a)ustz j motí fiandans uelum ok pretum ok predíckadí sidan
guds erendí ok reta tru fyrir ollum þeim sem honum uílldu hlyda ok snorí
otalegum lyd til guds ok fra [56v] skurgoda uíllu ok raungum atrunadí.

190 [XVII]   [Þ]egar Fabrícíus spurdí at theopholus hafdí tekit reta tru ok at
hann snore suo morgum lyd til guds fra skurgoda uíllu þa let hann taka
hann ok pína morgum pislum ⟨j⟩ senn suo sem hann hafdí adr giort uid
heílaga mey *doratheam ok at síduztu let hann hauggua hann j sundr j sma
styckí ok kasta ut fyrir fugla ok uíllí dyr. en eínglar guds toku sal hans ok
195 fluttu til hímíríkís dyrdar. suo sem allra annara guds píslar uota j
oumrędilega dyrd med gudí a`l´zualldanda j þat ríke sem ęfenlega stenndr

173 síer] seír.   182 eíngí] written in margin with insertion mark in the text.   190
Fabrícíus] Fabírcíus.   191 taka] + k.   193 mey] corrected from meñ.   193 dora-
theam] toratheam.   194 fugla] g corrected from l.

his, qui patri sanctoque spiritui consubstantialis et coaeternus vivit et regnat Deus in saecula saeculorum. Amen.

med gledí *ok* fagnadí *ok* alldri uerdr endir a. Heilog mer dorathea uar hals
hogguin hínn seta dag manadar þes er heitír fabruaríus þa uar lidit fra
híngat burdí uors herra ihesu cristi þríu hund`r´ud atta tigir *ok* síau ar. *ok*
200 er henar meSudagur .íííí. nottum eptir [57r] kerta messu halldínn j mínníng
henar píslar *ok* *anlatz. nu heidrum *ok* dyrkum híno heilgustu mey sancta
doratheam *ok* beidum þeS at hun arní oS uid allzuallda gud eilífrar híalpar
ok myskunar bedi þeSa heims *ok* *annars at eilífu utan enda AMEN

APPENDIX

BOLOGNA, BIBLIOTECA UNIVERSITARIA COD. 2800

Codex 2800 in the Bologna University Library consists of 92 leaves measuring approximately 185 x 125 cm. (Frati 1909: 109). The manuscript, which may be dated to the mid-fifteenth century, was written by a certain Johannes Mundinus, whose name appears on fols. 64v ("Ego Johannes mundenus bononiensis civis transcripsi feliciter"), 66v ("Ego Johannes mundenus transcripsi. anno domini. 1449. die. xii decembris"), and 92 ("Ego Johannes mundenus bononiensis transcripsi manu propria"). According to Poncelet (1924), the manuscript was "olim monasterii Sancti Salvatoris in quo signatus erat 56" (360). The manuscript contains three works: "S. Ambrosius. De officiis" (fols. 1–64v), the legend of Saint Dorothy (= *BHL* 2325d; fols. 65r–66v), and the "Liber Enchiridion editus ab Augustine Laurentii Rogatu" (fols. 67r–92). The text of the legend of Saint Dorothy is edited below.

[65r]   Oratio gloriosissimę uirgines `et martyris´ sanctę dorotheę.

OMnipote*n*s mitissime deus, in cui*us* nom*in*e gloriosa uirgo et martyr dorothea tormento*rum* suo*rum* g(e)nera superauit, te supplicite*r* exoram*us*, ut eius meritis *et* precib*us* cuncta pericula deuitem*us*, *et* ipsam celer*em*

5   adiutrice*m* in n*os*tris necessitatib*us* sentiam*us*. P*er* d*omi*num n*os*trum ihes*um* christum fili*um* tuum q*ue*sim*us*.

Gloriosissimę ac beatissimę virg`i´nis *et* martyris Dorotheæ Vita feliciter Incipit.

[I] TEmporib*us* Capricij prefecti gloriosa uirgo *et* ma*r*tyr dorothea ex

10   patre dorotheo, matre u*er*o theódora ex nobili senato*rum* sanguine *est* orta. Jllis na*m*que dieb*us* uiguit p*er*secut*io* christianorum in terra romano*rum*. V*n*de dorotheus uir bonus *et* iustus jdola sperne*n*s roma*m* relingue*n*s cum possessionib*us*, agris, uineis, castris domib*us* ac uniu*er*sis diuitijs suis transfretauit cu*m* uxore sua theodora et cu*m* duab*us* filiab*us* cristen, *et* calisten, *et*

15   p*er*rexit i*n* regnum Capadocię, *et* peruenit i*n* ciuitatem Cesaream ibique habitauit, *et* genuit tertiam filiam, *que* á beato appollinari episcopo *est* occulte baptizata, *et* i*n* fide p*ar*entum, q*ui* christiani era*n*t dilige*n*ter i*n*structa *et* á sa*n*cto appollinari ep*iscop*o dorothea ex p*at*re *et* m*at*re nom*in*ata.

[II] CRescente *ergo* puella *impleta est spiritu* sancto uirtutis *et omni* pacis
20 disciplina imbuta ac *omnium* oculis graciosa formosa ualde *super omnes*
mulieres regionis illius. Quod uidens antiquus castitatis inimicus serpens
diabolus et non substinens capricium prefectum regni capodocię in amore
gloriosę uirginis dorotheæ stimulans, ut ipsam carnali concupiscentia
appeteret. Qui mittens pro ea spondens thesaurum et res absque computi
25 *detrectratione pro dote ipsam legitimo thoro ducendam. Audiens hoc dulcis dorotheæ diuitias eius quasi lutum terrę despiciens et intrepida se christo
desponsatam fatebatur. Quod audiens capricius furore succensus et ut uerba
non protrahamus. Primo est in Cathastam missa oleo feruenti plenam.
Sancta uirgo sacratissima dei adiutorio illessa permanens et non adusta sed
30 uncta oleo ac si Balsamo ungeretur, ad quod miraculum paganorum multitudo stupefacta ad fidem christi conuersa est.

[III]   CApricius uero credens hoc magicis artibus fieri ipsam carcere reclu-
sit nouem diebus absque cibo et potu. ubi uirgo deo deuota est á sanctis
angelis opulente [65v] nutrita ut dum *producetur ante tribu`n´al, pul-
35 chrior quam unquam fuit apparuit, de quo cuncti, qui aderant mirabantur,
quam sic delicata puella nouem diebus absque omni humano uictu tam formosa appareret. Tunc capricius litem dorotheę dixit. Nisi deos in presenti
adores, aculei pęnas non euades. Cui virgo gratiosa respondit. Deum uerum
adorabo non demones, nam dij tui demonia pessima sunt, et jdola muta, qui
40 nec sibi nec alijs prodesse possunt. Tunc Capricius columnas erexit, et
desuper idolum poni precepit, et uirginem deo sacratam ad sacrificia
deorum compellere nitebatur. Beata dorothea in terram prostrata eleuatisque
oculis in cęlum, orauit dominum, ut ostenderet omnipotentiam suam sub-
iungensque quare tu `es´ deus solus et non alius preter te.

45 [IV]   ET ecce multitudo angelorum cum impetu uenientes et ita jdolum
concusserunt, quod nec particulę etiam minutissimę columnę aut idoli
reperirentur. In super audiens uoces demonum per aera clamantium et
dicentium dorothea cur nos sic deuastas, ex quo multa paganorum milia ad
christum conuersa sunt, qui etiam palmam martyrij attigerunt. Tunc
50 nephandus iudex virginem dorotheam iussit in aculeo suspendi pedibus
eleuatis et corpus eius precepit ericijs pellibus lacerari. Virgis immanibus
cedi et flagellis acerrimis cruciari ita, quod cedentes deficerentur. Deinde ad
mamillas virginales faculę ardentes apposite sunt et sic diutissime castigata
tandem semimortua usque in crastinum in carcere reclusa est.

24–25 detrectratione] *uncertain.*   33 potu] u *corrected from* o.   34 producetur]
producentur.   39 jdola] j *in margin.* 48 dorothea] *superscript* o *above* o^2.   51 Virgis]
V *in margin.*   52 Deinde] D *in margin.*

55   [V] MAne uero sancto producta est gloriosa uirgo et martyr dorothea, nec
      ulla macula seu lesio in ea apparuit, de quo etiam ipse preses mirabatur
      cogitansque citius blandis uerbis, quam duris, uinceretur, dixit ad puellam.
      Adhuc reuertaris Amena puella et tui ipsius miserearis, satis namque
      castigata es. Et cum nec sic proficere posset, misit eam ad duas sorores suas
60   cristen et calisten, quę metu mortis á christo recesserant, ut sororem suam
      dorotheam si fas esset á christo euellerent. Dorothea autem leniter alloquens
      sorores suas auferens ab eis cęcitatem cordis ipsas denuo ad christum
      conuertit. Quod audiens prefes ambas sorores dorso ad dorsum ligatas in
      ignem copiosum proici iussit concremari sorore ipsorum astante et uidente,
65   cui dixit preses. Quousque tu malefica nos protrahis aut sacrifica dijs, et
      uiues aut sententia capitali punieris.

      [VI]   DOrothea uero leto uultu ac ilari uoce respondit dicens. Quicquid
      uis parata sum [66r] pro christo domino et sponso meo, in cuius paradiso
      rosas cum pomis colligam et letabor cum ipso in eternum. Audiens hoc
70   tyrannus in se ipsum fremuit, quod nec blandis nec asperis eam uincere
      posset. Tunc precepit impiissimus iudex, ut pulchra facies uirginis fustibus
      cederetur, ut tortores fatigarentur, et quod nec uestigia faciei apparerent.
      Demum lassatis tortoribus *uirgo in carcere recluditur, in quo uisitatione
      diuina consolatur et perfectissime sanatur. Et cum de mane producitur
75   uidens eam scolasticus cesareæ theophilus nomine eam derisorie alloquitur
      dicens. Dorothea quo duceris modo, ubi est modo sponsus tuus, quę ei
      angelico uultu et tota iucunda dixit. Ad uiridiarium sponsi mei, ubi hodie
      leta reficiar. At ille. mitte nobis de rosis que crescunt in hoc uiridario. Quę
      respondit ei. Si dignus inuentus fueris apud sponsum meum fiet utique, quod
80   petitisti, et hoc tibi signum do. Si rosas receperis, ad palmam martyrij non
      dubites te uocatum.

      [VII]   CVm autem deuenit ad locum decollationis, rogauit dominum pro
      omnibus, qui memoriam suę passionis peragerent, ut in omnibus suis tribula-
      tionibus seu angustijs et necessitatibus ipsarum aduocatam perciperent et per-
85   sonam. Et precipue quicumque assidua inuocatione ipsam imploraverit ab
      omni uerecundia prorsus capitali nec non á paupertate et falso crimine
      liberentur et nihilominus in extremis contritionem `ac´ ueram confessio-
      nem at omnium suorum peccatorum plenam remissionem obtineant Viatico
      corporis et sanguinis domini nostri ihesu christi non priuentur. Mulieres eti-
90   am parturientes nomen eius inuocantes celerem sentiant in doloribus suis

58 Amena] A *in margin.*   61 dorotheam] *in margin with insertion marks in the text.*
73 uirgo] *uncertain.*   78 At] A *in margin.*   80 Si] S *in margin.*   87 ac] *underneath
is written* et, *which the scribe presumably forgot to cross out.*

profectum. Et in qua domo eius imago depicta fuerit, ibi non furtum notabile nec homicidium continget, ibi etiam mors subitanea non nocebit. Qua oratione facta audita est uox de cęlo dicens. Veni dilecta mea, ueni columba formosa mea, quod postulas impetrasti. Qui memoriam tuę pas-
95   sionis peregerint, petitionis suę salutarem á domino consequentur effectum.

[VIII]   VIrgo autem sacratissima ad ictum speculatoris ilariter inclinata apparuit puer indutus purpura, in qua stellę aureæ texta resplenduerunt crispato crine et discalciatus incedebat aspectu quidem iuuenilis sed uerbis et moribus senilis ferens in manibus sportulam plenam rosis et tria mala
100   punica et Virginem dorotheam sic blande alloquitur aggreditur dicens. Accipe Virgo deo cara munusculum, quod mittit tibi sponsus tuus. Cui Virgo dorothea obsecro domine [66v] mi feras eas theophilo et dicas. Theophile hoc mittit tibi dorothea et ego attuli huc de paradiso sponsi sui. Vide an uelis cum ipsa pro eius nomine presentem uanitatem deferere, qui
105   suis fidelibus talia munuscula in eterno conuiuio non desunt propinare. his dictis inclinauit virgo benedicta collum iugulo et accepto uno ictu reddidit spiritum domino. Theophilus uero sedit scribendo priuilegium in palatio presidis et ecce puer apparuit coram eo portans sportulam cum rosis pariter et pomis offerens theophilo, sicut commisit ei virgo dorothea.

110   [IX]   Theophilus uero et omnes astantes pariter et uidentes stupefacti et super prudentia pueri et euidentia miraculi. Nam puer qui apparuit uix biennis uidebatur sed ut octogenarius loquebatur. Tanta erat fragrantia rosarum, ut multi debiles infirmi, paralitici et leprosi ex earum odore sunt refocilati atque curati. Tunc rumor et tumor inuasit uniuersos quo modo in
115   medio hyemis rosę ita essent recentes. Quę statim ex tunc decollata est et anima eius perrexit ad christum .viii. Kal. februarij. Theophilus hęc uidens litteram, quam scribebat, in terram iactauit, et dimissis manibus uelut amens effectus unum dominum ihesum christum dei filium publice confessus proclamauit. Ex tunc Theophilus totam illam terram ad fidem conuertit,
120   qui Vltimo post multa tormentorum genera corpus eius in particulas minutas Incisum perrexit ad christum. AMEN.
     Finis. Deo gratias. Laus deo.
  Gloriosissimę et constantissimę uirginis et martyris Beatę dorotheę uita feliciter explicit. Ego Johannes mundenus transcripsi. anno domini. 1449.
125   die. xii decembris.

100 Virginem] V corrected from o.   103 Theophile] superscript o over o.

BIBLIOGRAPHY

Acta Sanctorum. Februarii Tomus Primus. Ed. Joannes Bollandus and Godefridus Henschenius. Paris: Victor Palmé, 1863; rpt. Brussels, 1966.

Aldhelm. "De Laudibus Virginitatis sive De Virginitate Sanctorum." In *Octavi Sæculi Ecclesiastici Scriptores Maxima ex Parte Recensentur quorum Opera Omnia Nova et, quod antea prorsus in auditum fuit.* Ed. J.-P. Migne. Patrologia Cursus Completus, Series Latina 89. Paris: [n. p.], 1850. Cols. 103–162.

Arne Magnussons i AM. 435A-B, 4to indeholdte håndskriftfortegnelser med to tillæg. [Ed. Kr. Kålund.] Copenhagen: Gyldendal, 1909.

Arnim, Achim von; and Clemens Brentano, ed. *Des Knaben Wunderhorn. Alte deutsche Lieder.* 3 vols. Ed. Heinz Rölleke. Heidelberg: Mohr and Zimmer, 1806–1808; rpt. Stuttgart: Reclam, 1987.

Atkinson, Clarissa W. *Mystic and Pilgrim: The Book and the World of Margery Kempe.* Ithaca and London: Cornell University Press, 1983.

Bahlmann, P. *Die lateinischen Dramen von Wimphelings Stylpho bis zur Mitte des sechzehnten Jahrhunderts, 1480–1550.* Münster: Regensberg, 1893.

Banasik, A. "Gottfried Keller's Adaptation of Medieval Legends for the XIXth C. Audience." In Legenda aurea: *Sept Siècles de Diffusion. Actes du colloque international sur la* Legenda aurea: *texte latin et branches vernaculaires à l'Université du Québec à Montréal 11–12 mai 1983.* Ed. Brenda Dunn-Lardeau. Cahiers d'études médiévales. Cahier spécial 2. Montreal: Éditions Bellarmin, 1986. Pp. 283–288.

Beckman, N.; and Kr. Kålund, ed. *Alfrœði íslenzk.* 3 vols. Samfund til udgivelse af gammel nordisk litteratur 37, 41, 45. Copenhagen: Møller, 1908–1918.

Bede. "Martyrologium de natalitiis sanctorum; cum auctario Flori et aliorum." In *Venerabilis Bedæ Opera quæ supersunt omnia, nunc primum in anglia, ope codicum manuscriptorum, editionumque optimarum.* 12 vols. Ed. J.A. Giles. London: Whittaker and Co., 1843–1844. Vol. 4, pp. 16–72.

BHL = Bibliotheca Hagiographica Latina Antiquae et Mediae Aetatis. Subsidia hagiographica 6. Brussels: Société des Bollandistes, 1898–1899; rpt. 1992. *Supplementum.* Subsidia hagiographica 12. Brussels: Société des Bollandistes, 1911. *Novum Supplementum.* Subsidia hagiographica 70. Brussels: Société des Bollandistes, 1986.

Bode, Karl. *Die Bearbeitung der Vorlagen in Des Knaben Wunderhorn.* Palaestra 76. Berlin: Mayer & Müller, 1909.

Bowers, Fredson, ed. *The Dramatic Works of Thomas Dekker.* 4 vols. Cambridge: Cambridge University Press, 1953–1961.

Brandt, C.J., ed. *De hellige Kvinder, en Legende-samling.* Copenhagen: Gad, 1859.

Braun, Joseph. *Tracht und Attribute der Heiligen in der deutschen Kunst.* Stuttgart: J.B. Metzler, 1943.

Brentano, Clemens. *Gesammelte Schriften.* Ed. Christian Brentano. 9 vols. Frankfurt am Main: J. D. Sauerländers Verlag, 1852–1855.

Breslauer, Martin. *Das deutsche Lied geistlich und weltlich bis zum 18. Jahrhundert.* Berlin, 1908; rpt. Hildesheim: Georg Olms Verlag, 1966.

Brownlee, Kevin. "Martyrdom and the Female Voice: Saint Christine in the *Cité des dames.*" In *Images of Sainthood in Medieval Europe.* Ed. Renate Blumenfeld-Kosinski and Timea Szell. Ithaca and London: Cornell University Press, 1991. Pp. 115–135.

Brun, J. Le. "Martyrologies." In *New Catholic Encyclopedia* 9. New York: McGraw-Hill, 1967. Pp. 317–318.

Brøndum-Nielsen, Johs. *Sproglig forfatterbestemmelse. Studier over dansk sprog i det 16. århundredes begyndelse.* Copenhagen and Kristiania [Oslo]: Gyldendal, 1914.

Bugge, John. *Virginitas: An Essay in the History of a Medieval Ideal.* International Archives of the History of Ideas, Series Minor 17. The Hague: Nijhoff, 1975.

Bump, Jerome. *Gerard Manley Hopkins.* Twayne's English Authors Series. Boston: Twayne Publishers, 1982.

Busse, Lotte. *Die Legende der heiligen Dorothea im deutschen Mittelalter.* Greifswald: [n. p.], 1930.

Butler, Pierce. *Legenda Aurea—Légende Dorée—Golden Legend. A Study of Caxton's Golden Legend with Special Reference to Its Relations to the Earlier English Prose Translation.* Baltimore: John Myrphy Company, 1899.

Byrne, Sister Mary of the Incarnation. *The Tradition of the Nun in Medieval England.* Washington D. C.: Catholic University of America, 1932.

Carlé, Birte. "Structural Patterns in the Legends of the Holy Women of Christianity." In *Aspects of Female Existence. Proceedings from The St. Gertrud Symposium "Women in the Middle Ages" Copenhagen, September, 1978.* Ed. Birte Carlé *et al.* Copenhagen: Gyldendal, 1980. Pp. 79–86.

—. *Skøger og jomfruer i den kristne fortællekunst. Den skandinaviske tradition og dens rødder i middelhavslandene.* Odense University Studies in Languages and Literatures 20. Odense: Odense University Press, 1981.

—. *Jomfru-fortællingen. Et bidrag til genrehistorien.* Odense University Studies in Scandinavian Languages and Literatures, 12. Odense: Odense University Press, 1985.

—. "Men and women in the saints' sagas of *Stock. 2. fol.*" In *Structure and Meaning in Old Norse Literature: New Approaches to Textual Analysis and Literary Criticism.* Ed. John Lindow *et al.* The Viking Collection 3. Odense: Odense University Press, 1986. Pp. 317–346.

Caxton, William. *The Golden Legend.* Ed. F.S. Ellis. 7 vols. London: Dent, 1900.

Cazelles, Brigitte. *The Lady as Saint: A Collection of French Hagiographic Romances of the Thirteenth Century.* Philadelphia: University of Pennsylvania Press, 1991.

Chevalier, Ulysse. *Repertorium hymnologicum. Catalogue des chants, hymnes, proses, séquences, tropes, en usage dans l'Église latine depuis les origines jusqu'à nos jours.* 6 vols. Louvain: Imprimerie Lefever, 1892–1920.

Christine de Pizan. *The Book of the City of Ladies.* Trans. Earl Jeffrey Richards. New York: Persea Books, 1982.

Cormack, Margaret. *The Saints in Iceland. Their Veneration from the Conversion to 1400.* Subsidia Hagiographica 78. Brussels: Société des Bollandistes, 1994.

Cornell, Henrik; and Sigurd Wallin. *Uppsvenska målarskolor på 14-talet.* Stockholm: Almqvist & Wiksell, 1933.

—. *Uppsvenska kyrkomålningar på 1500-talet.* Stockholm: Humanistiska Sällskapet, 1953.

Craig, Hardin. *English Religious Drama of the Middle Ages.* Oxford: Clarendon, 1955.

Crecelius, W. "Zu des Knaben Wunderhorn." *Alemannia* 12 (1884): 59–79.

Creizenach, Wilhelm. *Geschichte des neueren Dramas.* 3 vols. 2nd. rev. ed. Halle, 1911–1923; rpt. New York: Benjamin Blom, 1965.

Curman, Sigurd; and Johnny Roosval. *Sveriges kyrkor. Konsthistoriskt inventarium. Gotland.* 4:1. Stockholm: Generalstabens litografiska anstalts förlag, 1959–1964.

Curnow, Maureen Cheney. "The Boke of the Cyte of Ladyes." *Les Bonnes Feuilles* 3 (1974): 116–137.

—. "The *Livre de la Cité des Dames* of Christine de Pisan: A Critical Edition." Diss. Vanderbilt University, 1975.

Daae, Ludvig. *Norges helgener.* Christiania [Oslo]: Malling, 1879.

Delany, Sheila, trans. *A Legend of Holy Women: Osbern Bokenham,* Legends of Holy Women. Notre Dame and London: University of Notre Dame Press, 1992.

Delehaye, Hippolyte. *Les légendes hagiographiques.* 3rd rev. ed. Subsidia Hagiographica 18. Brussels: Société des Bollandistes, 1927.

—. *Les passions des martyrs et les genres littéraires.* 2nd rev. ed. Subsidia Hagiographica 13B. Brussels: Société des Bollandistes, 1966.

D'Evelyn, Charlotte; and Anna J. Mill, ed. *The South English Legendary.* 3 vols. Early English Text Society 235, 236, 244. London: Oxford University Press, 1956–1959.

DI= Diplomatarium Islandicum. Íslenzkt fornbréfasafn. 16 vols. Copenhagen and Reykjavík: Möller and Hið íslenzka bókmentafélag, 1857–1952.

DN= Diplomatarium Norvegicum. Oldbreve til Kundskab om Norges indre og ydre Forhold, Sprog, Slægter, Sæder, Lovgivning og Rettergang i Middelalderen. Ed. Chr. C.A. Lange and C.R. Unger. 22 vols. Christiania [Oslo]: Malling, 1852; Oslo: Kommisjonen for Diplomatarium Norvegicum, 1992.

DS = Diplomatarium Suecanum. Svenskt diplomatarium. Ed. J.G. Liljegren, *et al.* Stockholm: Norstedt, 1829.

Dubois, Jacques, ed. *Le Martyrologe d'Usuard. Texte et commentaire.* Subsidia Hagiographica 40. Brussels: Société des Bollandistes, 1965.

—. *Les martyrologes du moyen âge latin.* Typologie des sources du moyen âge occidental 26. Brepols: Turnhout, 1978.

—; and Geneviève Renaud, ed. *Edition pratique des martyrologes de Béde, de l'anonyme Lyonnais et de Florus.* Paris: Éditions du Centre National de la Recherche Scientifique, 1976.

—, ed. *Le Martyrologe d'Adon: Ses deux familles, ses trois recensions. Texte et commentaire.* Sources d'histoire médiévale. Paris: Éditions du Centre National de la Recherche Scientifique, 1984.

Dümmler, Ernst, ed. *Poetae Latini Aevi Carolini 2. Monvmenta Germaniae Historica.* Ed. Societas Aperiendis Fontibvs Rervm Germanicarvm Medii Aevi. Berlin: Weidmannische Verlagsbuchhandlung, 1884; rpt. Munich: Monumenta Germaniae Historica, 1978.

Ehrenberg, Hermann. *Deutsche Malerei und Plastik von 1350–1450.* Bonn and Leipzig: Schroeder, 1920.

Eis, Gerhard. "Zu Schades Dorotheen Passie." *Zeitschrift für deutsches Altertum und deutsche Literatur* 72 (1935): 92–94.

Erk, Ludwig. *Deutscher Liederhort.* Rev. by Franz M. Böhme. 3 vols. Leipzig, 1893–1894; rpt. Hildesheim: Georg Olms Verlag, 1963.

Falk, Franz. *Die Druckkunst im Dienste der Kirche zunächst in Deutschland bis zum Jahre 1520.* Cologne: J. P. Bachem, 1879.

Feifalik, Julius, ed. *Volksschauspiele aus Mähren.* Olmüz: Eduard Hölzel, 1864.

Finnur Jónsson, ed. *Den norsk-islandske Skjaldedigtning.* IA–IIA (tekst efter håndskrifterne) and IB–IIB (rettet tekst). Copenhagen: Gyldendal, 1908–1915.

Fleith, Barbara. *Studien zur Überlieferungsgeschichte der lateinischen Legenda aurea.* Subsidia Hagiographica 72. Brussels: Société des Bollandistes, 1991.

Franz, Adolph. *Die Messe im deutschen Mittelalter. Beiträge zur Geschichte der Liturgie und des Religiösen Volkslebens.* Freiburg im Breisgau: Herdersche Verlagshandlung, 1902.

Frati, Lodovico. "Indice dei codici latini conservati nella R. Biblioteca Universitaria di Bologna." *Studi Italiani di Filologia Classica* 17 (1909): 1–171.

Gad, Tue. *Legenden i dansk middelalder.* Copenhagen: Dansk videnskabs forlag, 1961.

—. *Helgener. Legender fortalt i Norden.* Copenhagen: Rhodos, 1971.

Gaiffier, B. "Bulletin des publications hagiographiques." *Analecta Bollandiana* 76 (1958): 469–470.

Gardner, W.H.; and N.H. Mackenzie, ed. *The Poems of Gerard Manley Hopkins.* 4th ed. London: Oxford University Press, 1967.

Geete, Robert, ed. *Svenska böner från medeltiden.* Samlingar utgifna af svenska fornskrift-sälskapet 131, 133, 135. Stockholm: Norstedt & Söner, 1907–1909.

Gerould, Gordon Hall. Rev. of Joseph Martin Peterson, *The Dorothea Legend: Its Earliest Records, Middle English Versions, and Influence on Massinger's "Virgin Martyr"* (1910). *Englische Studien* 44 (1912): 257–260.

—. *Saints' Legends*. Boston and New York: Houghton Mifflin Company, 1916.

Gjerløw, Lilli, ed. *Ordo Nidrosiensis Ecclesiae*. Libri Liturgici Provinciae Nidrosiensis Medii Aevi 2. Oslo: Norsk Historisk Kjeldeskrift-Institutt, 1968.

Goodwin, K.L. "An Unpublished Tale from *The Earthly Paradise*." *Victorian Poetry* 13:3–4 (1975): 91–102.

Gosse, Edmund; and Thomas James Wise, ed. *The Complete Works of Algernon Charles Swinburne*. 20 vols. London: William Heinemann, 1925–1927; rpt. New York: Russell & Russell, 1968.

Gradl, H. "Deutsche Volksaufführungen. Beiträge aus dem Egerlande zur Geschichte des Spiels und Theaters." *Mittheilungen des Vereins für Geschichte der Deutschen in Böhmen* 33 (1895): 121–152, 217–241, 315–336.

Grüner-Nielsen, H., ed. *Danske Viser fra Adelsvisebøger og Flyveblade 1530–1630*. Med Ordbog af Marius Kristensen og nye Tillæg af Nils Schiørring og Iørn Piø. 7 vols. Copenhagen: Reitzel, 1978–1979.

Guðrún Kvaran and Sigurður Jónsson frá Arnarvatni. *Nöfn Íslendinga*. Reykjavík: Heimskringla, 1991.

Günter, Heinrich. *Psychologie der Legende. Studien zu einer wissenschaftlichen Heiligen-Geschichte*. Freiburg: Herder, 1949.

Gärtner, Kurt. "Ein mittelniederdeutsches Fragment der Dorothealegende in der Stadtbibliothek zu Braunschweig." In *Litterae Ignotae. Beiträge zur Textgeschichte des deutschen Mittelalters: Neufunde und Neuinterpretationen*. Ed. Ulrich Müller. Göppinger Beiträge zur Textgeschichte 50. Göppingen: Kümmerle Verlag, 1977. Pp. 61–63.

Görlach, Manfred. *The* South English Legendary, Gilte Legende *and* Golden Legend. Braunschweiger Anglistische Arbeiten 3. Braunschweig: Technische Universität Carolo-Wilhelmina zu Braunschweig, Institut für Anglistik und Amerikanistik, 1972.

—. "The *Legenda aurea* and the Early History of *The South English Legendary*." In *Legenda aurea: Sept Siècles de Diffusion. Actes du colloque international sur la Legenda aurea: texte latin et branches vernaculaires à l'Université du Québec à Montréal 11–12 mai 1983*. Ed. Brenda Dunn-Lardeau. Cahiers d'études médiévales. Cahier spécial 2. Montreal: Éditions Bellarmin, 1986. Pp. 301–316.

Hallberg, Svante; Rune Norberg; and Oloph Odenius. "Den heliga Barbara i svensk kult och konst under medeltiden." *Med hammara och fackla* 25 (1967): 83–191.

Hamer, Richard, ed. *Three Lives from the Gilte Legende ed. from MS B.L. Egerton 876*. Heidelberg: Carl Winter Universitätsverlag, 1978.

Heffernan, Thomas J. *Sacred Biography. Saints and Their Biographers in the Middle Ages*. Oxford: Oxford University Press, 1988.

Heinzelmann, Martin. "Sanctitas und Tugendadel. Zu Konzeptionen von 'Heiligkeit' im 5. und 10. Jahrhundert." *Francia* 5 (1977): 741–752.

Horstmann, Carl. "Prosalegenden." *Anglia* 3 (1880): 293–360.

—, ed. *Sammlung altenglischer Legenden.* Heilbronn: Verlag von Gebr. Henninger, 1878; rpt. Hildesheim: Georg Olms Verlag, 1969.

—, ed. *Altenglische Legenden. Neue Folge. Mit Einleitung und Anmerkungen.* Heilbronn: Verlag von Gebr. Henninger, 1881; rpt. Hildesheim: Georg Olms Verlag, 1969.

—, ed. *The Early South-English Legendary or Lives of Saints.* Early English Text Society 57, 59. London: Trübner & Co., 1887.

Hunt, Mary Leland. *Thomas Dekker: A Study.* New York: Columbia University Press, 1911.

Indrebø, Gustav, ed. *Gamal norsk homiliebok. Cod. AM 619 4⁰.* Oslo: Dybwad, 1931.

Jacobi a Voragine: Legenda Aurea Vulgo Historia Lombardica Dicta. Ed. Th. Graesse. 3rd ed. Dresden and Leipzig, 1890; rpt. Osnabrück: Otto Zeller Verlag, 1969.

Jacobsen, Grethe. "Pregnancy and Childbirth in the Medieval North: A Topology of Sources and a Preliminary Study." *Scandinavian Journal of History* 9 (1984): 91–111.

Jefferis, Sibylle; and Konrad Kunze. "Passienbüchlein von den vier Hauptjungfrauen." In *Die deutsche Literatur des Mittelalters. Verfasserlexikon 7.* Ed. Kurt Ruh. 2nd rev. ed. Berlin and New York: Walter de Gruyter, 1989. Cols. 325–328.

Johansson, Hilding, ed. *Hemsjömanualet. En liturgi-historisk studie.* Samlingar och studier till svenska kyrkans historia 24. Stockholm: Svenska kyrkans diakonistyrelses bokförlag, 1950.

Johnsen, Oscar Albert. "Gildevæsenet i Norge i middelalderen." *Historisk tidsskrift* ser. 5, vol. 5:2 (1921): 73–101.

Jón Hallur Stefánsson. "Dórótheukvæði, uppruni þess og afdrif. Tvær uppskriftir að Dórótheukvæði, auk umfjöllunar þar um." (Unpublished manuscript, 1981.)

Jón Helgason, ed. *Íslenzk miðaldakvæði. Islandske digte fra senmiddelalderen.* I.2. Copenhagen: Levin & Munksgaard and Munksgaard, 1936; II. Copenhagen: Munksgaard, 1938.

Jón Þorkelsson. *Om Digtningen på Island i det 15. og 16. Århundrede.* Copenhagen: Høst, 1888.

Jón Viðar Sigurðsson. "Utenlandske kvinnehelgener på Island i høymiddelalderen." In *Samtíðarsögur: The Contemporary Sagas. Níunda alþjóðlega fornsagnaþingið, Akureyri 31.7–6.8. 1994. Forprent.* 2 vols. Akureyri: [n. p.], 1994. Vol. 1, pp. 423–434.

Jørgensen, Ellen. *Helgendyrkelse i Danmark. Studier over kirkekultur og kirkeligt liv fra det 11te aarhundredes midte til reformationen.* Copenhagen: Hagerup, 1909.

Keller, Gottfried. *Sieben Legenden.* Ed. Hugh W. Puckett. Storm Library of German Texts. New York: Storm Publishers, [n. d.].

Kilström, Bengt Ingmar. " Nödhjälparna." *Kulturhistorisk Leksikon for nordisk middelalder* 12. Copenhagen: Rosenkilde and Bagger, 1967. Cols. 458–466.

Kirschbaum, Engelbert; and Günter Bandmann, *et al.*, ed. *Lexikon der christlichen Ikonographie.* 8 vols. Rome: Herder, 1968–1976.

Klenke, Sister M. Amelia, ed. *Three Saints' Lives by Nicholas Bozon.* St. Bonaventure, NY: The Franciscan Institute, 1947.

—, ed. *Seven More Poems by Nicholas Bozon.* St. Bonaventure, N. Y.: The Franciscan Institute, 1951.

Knudsen, Gunnar; and Marius Kristensen. *Danmarks gamle Personnavne. I. Fornavne.* 2 vols. Copenhagen: Gad, 1936–1948.

Koeppel, Emil. *Quellen-Studien zu den Dramen George Chapman's, Philip Massinger's und John Ford's.* Quellen und Forschungen zur Sprach- und Culturgeschichte der germanischen Völker 82. Strassburg: Karl J. Trübner, 1897.

Konráð Gíslason, ed. *Fire og fyrretyve for en stor deel forhen utrykte prøver af oldnordisk sprog og literatur.* Copenhagen: Gyldendal, 1860.

Krogh, Torben. *Ældre dansk teater. En teaterhistorisk Undersøgelse.* Copenhagen: Munksgaard, 1940.

Kunze, Konrad. "Alemannische Legendare (I)." *Alemannisches Jahrbuch* 1971/72 (1973): 20–45.

Kühnau, Richard. *Schlesische Sagen.* Schlesiens volkstümliche Überlieferungen. Sammlungen und Studien der Schlesischen Gesellschaft für Volkskunde. 4 vols. Leipzig: Teubner, 1910–1913.

Künstle, Karl. *Ikonographie der christlichen Kunst.* 2 vols. Freiburg im Breisgau: Herder & Co., 1926–1928.

Kålund, Kr. *Katalog over Den arnamagnæanske Håndskriftsamling.* 2 vols. Copenhagen: Gyldendal, 1889–1894.

Lafourcade, Georges. *La jeunesse de Swinburne (1837–1867).* 2 vols. Publications de la Faculté des Lettres de l'Université de Strasbourg 44–45. Paris: Les belles Lettres; London: Oxford University Press, 1928.

Lang, Cecil Y., ed. *The Swinburne Letters.* 6 vols. New Haven: Yale University Press, 1959–1962.

Lange, Johan. "Prydplanter." *Kulturhistorisk Leksikon for nordisk middelalder* 13. Copenhagen: Rosenkilde and Bagger, 1968. Cols. 541–545.

Lapidge, Michael; and Michael Herren, trans. *Aldhelm: The Prose Works.* Cambridge: Brewer, 1979.

Lehmann, Paul. *Skandinaviens Anteil an der lateinischen Literatur und Wissenschaft des Mittelalters. 2. Stück.* Sitzungsberichte der Bayerischen Akademie der Wissenschaften. Philosophisch-historische Abteilung Jahrgang 1937, Heft 7. Munich: Verlag der Bayerischen Akademie der Wissenschaften, 1937.

Liebgott, Niels-Knud. *Hellige mænd og kvinder.* [Århus]: Wormianum, 1982.

Lievens, Robrecht. "Kerstine van Pizen." *Spiegel der Letteren* 3 (1959): 1–16.

Lind, E. H. *Norsk-isländska dopnamn ock fingerade namn från medeltiden.* Uppsala: Almqvist & Wiksell, 1905–1915.

Lindberg, Gustaf. *Die Schwedischen Missalien des Mittelalters. Ein Beitrag zur vergleichenden Liturgik. I. Kalendarium, Proprium de tempore, Proprium de sanctis, Commune sanctorum.* Uppsala: Almqvist & Wiksell, 1923.

Lindblom, Andreas. *Nordtysk skulptur och måleri i Sverige från den senare medeltiden.* Kongl. Vitterhets Historie och Antikvitets Akademien. Stockholm: Cederquist, 1916.

Linke, Hansjürgen. "Das volkssprachige Drama und Theater im deutschen und niederländischen Sprachbereich." In *Europäisches Spätmittelalter.* Ed. Willi Erzgräber. Neues Handbuch der Literaturwissenschaft 8. Wiesbaden: Akademische Verlagsgesellschaft Athenaion, 1978. Pp. 733–763.

Lithberg, Nils. "Kalendariska hjälpmedel." In *Tideräkningen.* Ed. Martin P:n Nilsson. Nordisk kultur 21. Stockholm: Bonnier, Oslo: Aschehoug & Co., Copenhagen: Schultz, 1934. Pp. 77–94.

Ludwig, V.O. *Die heilige Dorothea.* Kleine historische Monographien. No. 13b. 1. Reihe: Heiligenleben. Vienna: Reinhold Buch- und Kunst-Verlag, 1928.

Magnus-Petersen, J. *Beskrivelse og Afbildninger af Kalkmalerier i danske Kirker.* Copenhagen: Reitzel, 1895.

Maliniemi, Aarno, ed. *Zur Kenntnis des Breviarium Aboense. Cod. Holm. A 56.* Academia Scientiarum Fennica 9. Helsinki: Suomalaisen Kirjallisuuden Kirjapaino, 1957.

Maltzahn, Wendelin von. *Deutscher Bücherschatz des 16., 17. und 18. bis um die Mitte des 19. Jahrhunderts.* Jena, 1875; rpt. Hildesheim: Georg Olms Verlag, 1966.

Mariani, Paul L. *A Commentary on the Complete Poems of Gerard Manley Hopkins.* Ithaca and London: Cornell University Press, 1970.

Martyrologium Romanum. In *Propylaeum ad Acta Sanctorum Decembris.* Ed. Hippolyte Delehaye *et al.* Brussels: Société des Bollandistes, 1940.

Mayer, August L. *Geschichte der Spanischen Malerei.* Leipzig: Klinkhardt & Biermann, 1922.

McLaughlin, Eleanor Commo. "Equality of Souls, Inequality of Sexes: Woman in Medieval Theology." In *Religion and Sexism: Images of Woman in the Jewish and Christian Traditions.* Ed. Rosemary Radford Ruether. New York: Simon and Schuster, 1974. Pp. 213–266.

McLuskie, Kathleen. "The Plays and the Playwrights: 1613–42." In *The* Revels *History of Drama in English* 4. Ed. Louis Potter. London and New York: Methuen, 1981. Pp. 127–260.

Melchers, Erna; and Hans Melchers. *Das Jahr der Heiligen. Geschichte und Legende.* Munich: Südwest, 1965.

Menhardt, Hermann. Review of Lotte Busse, *Die Legende der heiligen Dorothea im deutschen Mittelalter. Zeitschrift für deutsche Philologie* 55 (1930): 447–448.

Mogk, Eugen. *Geschichte der norwegisch-isländischen Literatur.* 2nd rev. ed. Strassburg: Trübner, 1904.

Mone, F.J., ed. *Lateinische Hymnen des Mittelalters.* 3 vols. Freiburg im Breisgau: Herder'sche Verlagshandlung, 1853-1855.

Nielsen, Karl Martin, ed. *Middelalderens danske bønnebøger.* 4 vols. Copenhagen: Gyldendal, 1946-1963.

Nielsen, Yngvar. *St. Catharinas og St. Dorotheas Gilde i Bergen.* Christiania Vidensk.-Selsk. Forhandl. no. 2. Christiania [Oslo]: [n.p.], 1877.

Niewöhner, Heinrich, ed. *Die Gedichte Heinrichs des Teichners.* 3 vols. Deutsche Texte des Mittelalters. Berlin: Akademie-Verlag, 1953-1956.

Nilsén, Anna. *Program och funktion i senmedeltida kalkmåleri. Kyrkmålningar i Mälarlandskapen och Finland 1400-1534.* Stockholm: Kungl. Vitterhets Historie och Antikvitets Akademien, 1986.

Notker Balbulus. "Martyrologium." In *Remigii Monachi S. Germani Antissiodorensis, Beati Notkeri Balbuli S. Galli Monachi, Opera Omnia.* Ed. J.-P. Migne. Patrologia Cursus Completus, Series Latina 131. Paris: Garnier, 1884. Cols. 1025-1164.

NRJ = *Norske Regnskaber og Jordebøger fra det 16de Aarhundrede.* Ed. H. J. Huitfeldt- Kaas and Arne Odd Johnsen. Norsk Historisk Kjeldeskrift-Institutt. 5 vols. Christiania [Oslo]: Gundersen; Oslo: Styret for Kjeldeskriftfondtet, 1887-1966.

Odenius, Oloph. "Cisiojani Latini. Neue Beiträge zur Bibliographie der metrischen Kalendarien des Mittelalters." *Arv* 15 (1959): 61-154.

Otterbjörk, Roland. "Helgener: Sverige." *Kulturhistorisk Leksikon for nordisk middelalder* 6. Copenhagen: Rosenkilde and Bagger, 1961. Cols. 338-339.

Pailler, Wilhelm. *Religiöse Schauspiele für Mädchen. Mit einer musikalischen Beilage von Bernhard Deubler.* 4th ed. Linz: Verlag der F.J. Ebenhöch'schen Buchhandlung, 1899.

Páll Eggert Ólason. *Menn og menntir siðskiptaaldarinnar á Íslandi.* 4 vols. Reykjavík: Gutenberg, 1919-1926.

Petersen, Henry. *Danske gejstlige Sigiller fra Middelalderen.* Copenhagen: Reitzel, 1886.

Peterson, Joseph Martin. *The Dorothea Legend: Its Earliest Records, Middle English Versions, and Influence on Massinger's "Virgin Martyr."* Heidelberg: Rößler & Herbert, 1910.

Poncelet, Albertus. "Catalogus Codicum Hagiographicorum Latinorum Bibliothecae Universitatis Bononiensis." *Analecta Bollandiana* 41 (1924): 320-370.

Priebsch, R. "Aus deutschen Handschriften der Königlichen Bibliothek zu Brüssel." *Zeitschrift für deutsche Philologie* 36 (1904): 371-387.

Quentin, Henri. *Les martyrologes historiques du moyen âge. Étude sur la formation du Martyrologe Romain.* Paris, 1908; rpt. Darmstadt: Scientia Verlag Aalen, 1969.

Rabanus Maurus. "Martyrologivm." In *Corpvs Christianorvm Continuatio Mediæualis* 44. Ed. John McCulloh. Turnholt: Brepols, 1979. Pp. 1-161.

Reames, Sherry L. *The* Legenda aurea: *A Reexamination of Its Paradoxical History.* Madison: University of Wisconsin Press, 1985.

Reinach, Salomon. *Répertoire de peintures du Moyen Age et de la Renaissance (1280–1580).* 6 vols. Paris, 1905–1923; rpt. Nendeln/Liechtenstein: Kraus Reprint, 1978.

Rieser, Ferdinand. *"Des Knaben Wunderhorn" und seine Quellen. Ein Beitrag zur Geschichte des deutschen Volksliedes und der Romantik.* Dortmund: F.W. Ruhfus, 1908; rpt. Hildesheim: Georg Olms Verlag, 1983.

Robertson, Elizabeth. "The Corporeality of Female Sanctity in *The Life of Saint Margaret.*" In *Images of Sainthood in Medieval Europe.* Ed. Renate Blumenfeld-Kosinski and Timea Szell. Ithaca and London: Cornell University Press, 1991. Pp. 268–287.

Rossetti, William Michael, ed. *The Poetical Works of Christina Georgina Rossetti.* London: Macmillan, 1906; rpt. Hildesheim: Georg Olms Verlag, 1970.

Rossi, J.B. de; and L. Duchesne, ed. *Martyrologium Hieronymianum.* Brussels: Société des Bollandistes, 1894. [Excerpt of *Acta Sanctorum,* Nov. t. II, pars prior.]

Ruether, Rosemary Radford. "Misogynism and Virginal Feminism in the Fathers of the Church." In *Religion and Sexism: Images of Woman in the Jewish and Christian Traditions.* Ed. Rosemary Radford Ruether. New York: Simon and Schuster, 1974. Pp. 150–183.

Rydbeck, Otto. *Medeltida kalkmålningar i Skånes kyrkor.* Lund: Berling, 1904.

Sahlgren, Jöran, ed. *Svenska folkvisor.* 4 vols. Uppsala: Kungl. Gustav Adolfs Akademien, 1957–1960.

Salisbury, Joyce E. "Fruitful in singleness." *Journal of Medieval History* 8 (1982): 97–106.

Saxtorph, Niels M. *Jeg ser på kalkmalerier. En gennemgang af alle kalkmalerier i danske kirker.* 2nd rev. ed. Copenhagen: Politikens forlag, 1970.

Schachner, Heinrich. "Das Dorotheaspiel." *Zeitschrift für deutsche Philologie* 35 (1903): 157–196.

Schade, Oskar, ed. *Geistliche Gedichte des XIV. und XV. Jarhunderts vom Niderrhein.* Hannover: Carl Rümpler, 1854; rpt. Amsterdam: Rodopi, 1968.

Schanze, Frieder. "Schrade, Michel." In *Die deutsche Literatur des Mittelalters. Verfasserlexikon* 8. Ed. Kurt Ruh. 2nd rev. ed. Berlin and New York: Walter de Gruyter, 1992. Col. 841.

Schreiber. W.L. *Holzschnitte mit Darstellungen der männlichen und weiblichen Heiligen. Handbuch der Holz- und Metallschnitte des XV. Jahrhunderts* 3. Leipzig: Karl W. Hiersemann, 1927.

Schreiner, Klaus. "'Discrimen veri ac falsi.'" *Archiv für Kulturgeschichte* 48 (1966): 1–53.

Schulenburg, Jane Tibbetts. "The Heroics of Virginity: Brides of Christ and Sacrificial Mutilation." In *Women in the Middle Ages and the Renaissance: Literary and Historical Perspectives.* Ed. Mary Beth Rose. Syracuse: Syracuse University Press, 1986. Pp. 29–72.

Seip, Didrik Arup. *Palæografi. B: Norge og Island.* Ed. Johs. Brøndum-Nielsen. Nordisk kultur 28:B. Stockholm: Bonnier; Oslo: Aschehoug; Copenhagen: Schultz, 1954.

Serjeantson, Mary S., ed. *Legendys of Hooly Wummen by Osbern Bokenham.* Early English Text Society, Original Series No. 206. London: Humphrey Milford, Oxford University Press, 1938.

Seybolt, Robert Francis. "Fifteenth Century Editions of the *Legenda aurea.*" *Speculum* 21 (1946a): 327–338.

—. "The *Legenda aurea,* Bible, and *Historia scholastica.*" *Speculum* 21 (1946b): 339–342.

Sharp, William. *Dante Gabriel Rossetti. A Record and a Study.* London: Macmillan, 1982; rpt. New York: AMS Press, 1970.

Sigurjón Einarsson. "Séra Ólafur á Söndum." *Skírnir* 134 (1960): 74–128.

Smith, S. Birket. *De tre ældste danske Skuespil.* Copenhagen: Klein, 1874.

Spengler, Franz. "Kilian Reuther von Melrichstadt." In *Forschungen zur neueren Litteraturgeschichte. Festgabe für Richard Heinzel.* Weimar: Emil Felber, 1898. Pp. 121–129.

Sprenger, R. "Kleine Bemerkungen. 2. Zu Philipp Massinger's 'The Virgin Martyr.'" *Englische Studien* 22 (1896): 146–148.

Stadler, J.E.; and Franz Joseph Hein. *Heiligen-Lexikon oder Lebensgeschichten aller Heiligen.* 5 vols. Augsburg: Schmid, 1858–1861.

Stammler, Wolfgang. *Mittelniederdeutsches Lesebuch.* Hamburg: Paul Hartung Verlag, 1921.

—. *Prosa der deutschen Gotik. Eine Stilgeschichte in Texten.* Literarhistorische Bibliothek 7. Berlin: Junker and Dünnhaupt Verlag, 1933.

Surtees, Virginia. *The Paintings and Drawings of Dante Gabriel Rossetti (1828–1882): A Catalogue Raisonné.* Oxford: Clarendon Press, 1971.

Swinburne, Algernon Charles. *Poems and Ballads.* London: Edward Moxon & Co., 1866.

Søholm, Ejgil, ed. *Dorotheæ komedie.* Tidlig dansk dramatik. Copenhagen: Munksgaard, 1972.

Thiébaux, Marcelle. *The Writings of Medieval Women.* Garland Library of Medieval Literature B:14. New York and London: Garland Publishing, 1987.

Toldberg, Helge. "Dorothæa komedie." *Kulturhistorisk Leksikon for nordisk middelalder* 3. Copenhagen: Rosenkilde and Bagger, 1958. Cols. 253–254.

Tönnies, Eduard. *Leben und Werke des Würzburger Bildschnitzers Tilmann Riemenschneider 1468-1531.* Studien zur deutschen Kunstgeschichte 22. Strassburg: Heitz, 1900.

Ukena, Elke. *Die deutschen Mirakelspiele des Spätmittelalters. Studien und Texte.* 2 vols. Europäische Hochschulschriften I. Deutsche Literatur und Germanistik 115. Frankfurt: Lang, 1975.

Uldall, F. *Danmarks middelalderlige Kirkeklokker.* Copenhagen: Lehmann & Stage, 1906; 2nd ed. [n.p.]: Hikuin, 1982.

Unger, C.R., ed. *Heilagra manna søgur. Fortællinger og legender om hellige mænd og kvinder.* 2 vols. Christiania [Oslo]: Bentzen, 1877.

Venturi, A. *Storia dell'arte italiana. V: La pittura del trecento e le sue origini.* Milan: Ulrico Hoepli, 1907; rpt. Nendeln: Kraus Reprint, 1967.

Vincent of Beauvais. *Bibliotheca Mvndi sev Specvli Maioris Vincentii Bvrgvndi præsvlis Bellovacensis, ordinis prædicatorvm, theologi ac doctoris Eximii, tomvs qvartvs, qvi Specvlvm Historiale inscribitvr.* Dvaci: Ex Officina Typographica Baltazaris Belleri sub Circino aureo, 1624; rpt. Graz: Akademische Druck- und Verlagsanstalt, 1965.

Vitz, Evelyn Birge. "From the Oral to the Written in Medieval and Renaissance Saints' Lives." In *Images of Sainthood in Medieval Europe.* Ed. Renate Blumenfeld-Kosinski and Timea Szell. Ithaca and London: Cornell University Press, 1991. Pp. 97–114.

Vogelsang, Willem. *Die Holzskulptur in den Niederlanden. I. Das erzbischöfliche Museum zu Utrecht.* Utrecht: A. Oosthoek, 1911.

Wegener, Philipp. *Drei mittelniederdeutsche gedichte des 15. jarhunderts mit kritischen bemerkungen. Jahrbuch des Pädagogiums zum Kloster Unser Lieben Frauen in Magdeburg.* Magdeburg: Carl Friese, [1878].

Widding, Ole; Hans Bekker-Nielsen; and L. K. Shook. "The Lives of the Saints in Old Norse Prose. A Handlist." *Mediaeval Studies* 25 (1936): 294–337.

Willard, Charity Cannon. "The Franco-Italian Professional Writer: Christine de Pizan." In *Medieval Women Writers.* Ed. Katharina M. Wilson. Athens: University of Georgia Press, 1984. Pp. 333–363.

Willenberg, Gotthelf. "Die Quellen von Osbern Bokenham's Legenden." *Englische Studien* 12 (1889): 1–37.

Williams-Krapp, W. "Dorothea." *Die deutsche Literatur des Mittelalters. Verfasserlexikon 2.* Ed. Kurt Ruh. 2nd rev. ed. Berlin and New York: Walter de Gruyter, 1980. Cols. 211–216.

—. "German and Dutch Translations of the *Legenda aurea.*" In Legenda aurea: *Sept Siècles de Diffusion. Actes du colloque international sur la* Legenda aurea: *texte latin et branches vernaculaires à l'Université du Québec à Montréal 11–12 mai 1983.* Ed. Brenda Dunn-Lardeau. Cahiers d'études médiévales. Cahier spécial 2. Montreal: Éditions Bellarmin, 1986a. Pp. 227–232.

—. *Die deutschen und niederländischen Legendare des Mittelalters. Studien zu ihrer Überlieferungs-, Text- und Wirkungsgeschichte.* Tübingen: Max Niemeyer Verlag, 1968b.

Wimmer, E.; and G. Binding. "Dorothea." *Lexikon des Mittelalters* 3. Munich and Zürich: Artemis, 1985. Cols. 1318–1319.

Wimmer, Otto. *Handbuch der Namen und Heiligen*. 3rd rev. ed. Innsbruck: Tyrolia, 1966.

Wolpers, Theodor. *Die englische Heiligenlegende des Mittelalters*. Tübingen: Max Niemeyer, 1964.

Woodforde, Christopher. *Stained Glass in Somerset 1250–1830*. London: Oxford University Press, 1946.

Wrangel, E. *Det medeltida bildskåpet från Lunds Domkyrkas högaltare*. Lunds Universitets Årsskrift. N. F. Afd. 1. Vol. 11, no. 3. Lund: Gleerup; Leipzig: Harrassowitz, 1915

Åmark, Mats. *Sveriges medeltida kyrkklockor*. Stockholm: Almqvist & Wiksell, 1960.

INDEX OF MANUSCRIPTS

*The Arnamagnaean Collection
(Det arnamagnæanske Institut, Co-
penhagen; Stofnun Árna Magnús-
sonar, Reykjavík)*
  AM 418 12mo: 39, 51
  AM 420 12mo: 49
  AM 429 12mo: 38, 59, 60,
    63–87, 89, 91, 93, 95, 97, 99,
    101, 103
  AM 435a 4to: 65
  AM 621 4to: 64
  AM 680a 4to: 59
  AM 721 4to: 64
  AM 782 4to: 48
  AM 784 4to: 48, 49
  AM 791 4to: 59
  AM 920 4to: 61
*Berlin, Staatsbibliothek Preussischer
Kulturbesitz*
  Cod. Berol. Theol. Lat.
    71 8vo: 50
Bologna, Biblioteca Universitaria
  Cod. 2800: 21, 104-107
Braunschweig, Stadtbibliothek
  Fr. 87: 20
Brussels, Koninklijke Bibliotheek
  F II: 21
Cambridge, Corpus Christi College
  Corpus Christi 145: 34
Copenhagen, Det kongelige Bibliotek
  DKB Thott 553 4to: 48
  DKB Thott 780 fol.: 53, 55
  GkS 1613 4to: 48
  GkS 1614 4to: 48, 49
*Dessau, Zweigstelle der Universitäts-
und Landesbibliothek Sachsen-Anhalt*
  Cod. Georg. 24 8vo: 20

Dresden, Sächsische Landesbibliothek
  Cod. M 249: 26
Dublin, Trinity College
  Trinity College 319: 36, 37
*Giessen, Universitätsbibliothek der
Justus Liebig-Universität*
  Giessen 881 8vo: 50
*Hannover, Niedersächsische Landes-
bibliothek*
  Cod. 84a: 20
Heidelberg, Universitätsbibliothek
  Cod. Pal. Germ. 392: 25
Karlsruhe, Badische Landesbibliothek
  Cod. Licht. 69: 18
  Cod. Licht. 70: 18
Klagenfurt, Landesarchiv
  Cod. 6/30: 23
Klosterneuburg, Stiftsbibliothek
  Cod. 1079: 25
Kremsmünster, Stiftsbibliothek
  CC 81: 27
London, British Library
  BL Addit. 11565: 34-36
  BL Addit. 35298: 34-36
  BL Addit. 36963: 37
  BL Arundel 168: 34, 40
  BL Arundel 327: 37
  BL Harley 2277: 34
  BL Harley 5272: 34, 40
  BL Royal 2. A. xviii: 34, 35, 40
London, Lambeth Palace Library
  Lambeth Palace 72: 34-36
  Lambeth Palace 432: 34, 35,
    39, 40, 62, 75
Lund, Universitetsbiblioteket
  LUB 25 8vo: 48

Manchester, Chetham's Library
  Chetham 8009: 34–35, 40
Munich, Bayerische Staatsbibliothek
  Cod. Germ. 478: 20
  Cod. Lat. Mun. 22309: 24
*Nürnberg, Germanisches National-
museum*
  Cod. 8601: 23
Oxford, Bodleian Library
  Laud Misc. 108: 34
Paris, Bibliothèque Nationale
  BN Nouv. acq. lat. 3075: 34
  BN Lat. 3879: 4
*Praha, Narodní Knihovna České
Republiky*
  Cod. IV D: 20
Reykjavík, Landsbókasafn
  JS 255 4to: 63
  JS 323 8vo: 63
  JS 399 4to: 61
  JS 510 8vo: 62
  JS 589 4to: 63
  Lbs. 201 8vo: 62, 63
  Lbs. 665 8vo: 63
  Lbs. 2125 4to: 63
  Lbs. 2166 4to: 61
  Lbs. 2166 8vo: 63
  Lbs. 3170 8vo: 62
Southwell, Southwell Cathedral
  Southwell Cathedral VII: 34

St. Gall, Stifsbibliothek
  Cod. 1006: 24
Stockholm, Kungliga Biblioteket
  SKB A 38: 50
  SKB A 40: 48
  SKB A 42: 48
  SKB A 43: 50
  SKB A 80: 50
  SKB A 81: 50
  SKB A 97: 47
  SKB K 4: 60
Uppsala, Universitetsbiblioteket
  UUB C 68: 50
  UUB C 274: 47
  UUB C 416: 47
  UUB C 421: 48
  UUB C 427: 50
  UUB C 435: 47
  UUB C 497: 20
*Vienna, Österreichische Nationalbib-
liothek*
  Poem. Germ. 2819: 26
  Poem. Germ. 2848: 26
  Poem. Germ. 2901: 26
*Wolfenbüttel, Herzog-August-Biblio-
thek*
  Cod. 1231 Helmst.: 26

INDEX OF NAMES

Acacius, Saint 18, 48

Acta Sanctorum 1, 9, 19, 27

Ado 4, 5, 6; *Martyrologium* 4

Agatha, Saint 12–16, 33, 37, 38, 46, 49, 57, 59, 64, 65

Agnes, Saint 7, 12, 13, 33, 37, 38, 43, 60, 64, 65

Albek 57

Aldhelm, Saint 2–4, 8, 34, 38; *De laudibus virginitatis* 2, 38

Alemannia 24

Alphege, Saint 34

Ambrose, Saint: *De institutione virginis; De virginibus ad marcellinam; De virginitate; Exhortatio virginitatis* 2

Amphitruo: see Plautus, Titus Maccius

Anastasia, Saint 13, 15

Andersøn, Hans 58

Anna Brade's Prayer Book 48, 49

Anna Gyldenstiernes Visebog 56

Anne, Saint 37, 59

Anslay, Bryan 33

Antony, Saint 18

Apollonia, Saint 49, 57

Apuleius: *Metamorphoses* 29

Aristotle 11

Árni Böðvarsson 63

Árni Magnússon 65

Arnim, Achim von 30

Aspeboda 57

Atkinson, Clarissa W. 16

Augsburg 25, 46

Augustine, Saint 2, 11, 32; *De civitate Dei* 32; *De sancta virginitate* 2

Augustine of Canterbury, Saint 34

Augustinians 37, 40

Austria 25, 27

Auxerre 2

Baden 45

Banasik, A. 30

Bandmann, Günter 45

Baptista Mantuanus Carmelita Theologus 29; *De Beata virgine* 29

Barbara, Saint 1, 9, 15, 18, 20, 48–50, 56, 57, 65

Barking Abbey 2, 3

Baronius 6

Bautzen 26

Bavaria 23–25

Bebenhauser Legendar 18

Beckman, N. 59

Bede, the Venerable 3, 4, 6; *Martyrologium* 3

Bekker-Nielsen, Hans 74

Benedict XIV, Pope 6

Benedictines 5, 25, 29, 60

Bergen 52, 53, 58

BHL 2323 19, 27, 41

BHL 2324 8, 9, 11, 12, 14, 18–21, 23, 24, 26–30, 35, 38–41, 51, 56, 61, 62, 74–85, 87, 88, 90, 92, 94, 96, 98, 100, 102

BHL 2325d 21, 23–26, 28, 38, 39, 48, 51, 62, 75–85, 104–107

Bible 19, 24, 60, 74
Binding, G 9, 27
Birgitta Andersdotter's Prayer Book
    50
Björn Thorlacius 65
Blaise, Saint 9, 18, 48
Boccaccio *De casibus virorum il-*
    lustrium; *De mulieribus claris*;
    Decameron 32, 33
Bode, Karl 30
Bohemia 27
Bohuslän 58
Boke of the Cyte of Ladyes 33
Bokenham, Osbern 37–40, 43, 60,
    75; *Legendys of Hooly Wum-*
    men 37, 60
Bollandists 1, 7
Bologna 1
Borreby 57
Bower, Fredson 41
Bozon, Nicole 38
Brandt, C.J. 60
Braun, Joseph 45
Brendan, Saint 34
Brentano, Clemens: *Die monate* 30
Breslauer, Martin 30
Breviarium Lincopense 47
Bridget, Saint 34, 57
Brixen 9
Brun, J. Le 2
Brøndum-Nielsen, Johs. 53
Buch von den heiligen Mägden und
    Frauen, Das 18, 38, 60
Bump, Jerome 44, 45
Buk, Thomas 58
Bunkeflo 57
Burg 57
Burgh, Thomas 37
Burne-Jones, Edward: "St. Theo-
    philus and the Angel" 43
Busse, Lotte 7, 8, 11, 19–21, 23–
    25, 39, 47

Butler, Pierce 35
Butzbach 27
Caesarea 1–3, 10, 23, 29, 36, 38,
    41, 44
Calendar of Antioch 2
Calista (*alias* Calisten) 4
Calisten (*alias* Calista) 10, 25, 54,
    56
Capgrave, John 40
Cambridge 37, 40
Cappadocia 1, 2, 10
Capricius (*alias* Fabricius, Sabri-
    cius) 76
Caritas, Saint 16, 64
Carlé, Birte 7, 12, 16, 60
Carmelites 20, 56
Catherine of Alexandria, Saint 1,
    9, 18, 37, 46, 48–50, 52, 56,
    57, 60, 64
Caxton, William: *Golden Legend*
    34–36, 38, 39, 43
Cazelles, Brigitte 12, 13
Cecilia, Saint 20, 33, 37, 43, 49,
    60, 64
"Ceciliudiktur" 64
Chad, Saint 34
Chaucer, Geoffrey: *Legend of*
    Good Women 37, 38
Chelwood 46
Chevalier, Ulysse 6, 41, 52
Chiliani Equitis Mellerstatine: *see*
    Reuther, Kilian, von Melrich-
    stadt
Christ: *see* Jesus Christ
Christa (*alias* Christen) 4
Christen (*alias* Christa) 10, 54, 56
Christian I, King 58
Christian III, King 58
Christina, Saint 14–15, 20, 37, 38,
    60
Christina Hansdotter's Prayer Book
    50

Christine de Pizan: *Le livre de la cité des dames* 32, 33, 38
Christopher, Saint 18, 48
Chronographer of 354 2
Clare, Saint 20, 49
Clare Priory, Suffolk 37
Clement X, Pope 6
Clementsøn, Hans 58
Clichtove, Josse: *Elucidatorium ecclesiasticum* 6
Codex Bernensis 2
Codex Epternacensis 2
Codex Wissenburgensis 2
Collectarium Dominicanum Diocesis Aboensis 47–48
Cologne, 1, 20, 21, 41
Concordia, Saint 49
Copenhagen 56
Cormack, Margaret 59
Cornell, Henrik 57
Craig, Hardin 41
Crecelius, W. 30
Creizenach, Wilhelm 27–29
Curman, Sigurd 57
Curnow, Maureen Cheney 32, 33
Cuthbert, Saint 34
Cyprian, Saint: *De habitu virginum* 2
Cyricus, Saint 18, 48

Dalarna 57
Danzig 45, 47
Darmstädter Legendar 18
De Dorothea 24–25, 39
Dekker, Thomas 41, 42, 86; *The Virgin Martyr* 41–44
Delany, Sheila 37, 38
Delehaye, Hippolyte 7, 8, 13, 14, 16, 17
Denmark 47, 48, 58
Denys, Saint 18, 48
Depositio episcoporum 2

Depositio martyrum 2
D'Evelyn, Charlotte 34
Diocletian 1, 7, 9, 42
Dominicans 34
Dorothea of Brandenburg, Queen 58
Dorothea of Sachsen-Lauenburg, Queen 58
Dorothea Lafransdóttir 63
Dorothea Nilsdotter's Prayer Book 50
Dorothea und Theophilus 30
Dorotheas Blumenkörbchen; see *Sieben Legenden*
Dorotheen passie 19, 20, 23, 27, 75–77, 79, 83
Dorotheu saga 60–87, 89, 91, 93, 95, 97, 99, 101, 103
Dorotheudiktur 60–64, 75
Dorotheukvæði 62, 63
"Dorotheukvæði" (*alias Dorotheudiktur*) 61
Dorotheus (*alias* Dorus) 20, 21, 23, 27, 38, 40, 77
Dorotheæ Komedie: see Joannis, Christiernus
Dorus (*alias* Dorotheus) 9, 20, 21, 56
Dresden 27
Dubois, Jacques 4, 5
Duchesne, L. 1, 2
Dunstan, Saint 34
Dümmler, Ernst 4
Dýrafjörður 62
Dörtelsberg 46

Edmund, Saint and King 34
Edmund of Abingdon, Saint 34
Edward, Saint 34
Eger 27
Ehrenberg, Hermann 45
Eiríkur Jónsson 62

Eis, Gerhard 20, 21
Ekerö 57
Elizabeth of Hungary, Saint 38
Elizabeth of Thüringen, Saint 37
Elsässische Legenda aurea, Die 18
Else Holgersdatter's Book of Hours 48
England 2, 34–35, 37, 41, 46
Erasmus, Saint 18, 48
Erk, Ludwig 30
Erzählung vom Martyrium der lobesamen Jungfrau St. Dorothea, Die 25, 27, 38, 75–79, 81–84
Essex 2
Eusebius of Caesarea: *Ecclesiastical History* 3–4
Eustace, Saint 18, 48
Evangelium Pseudo-Matthaei 60
Exeter Ordinale 34

Fabricius (*alias* Capridius, Sabricius) 10, 23–25, 28, 29, 41, 44, 54–56, 78–82, 84
Falk, Franz 20
Feifalik, Julius 27
Femern 57
Fides, Saint 16, 34, 37, 65
Finland 47, 57
Finnur Jónsson 59
Fleith, Barbara 18
Fljótshlíð 65
Flókastaðir 65
Florus of Lyons 4–6; *Martyrologium* 4
France, 17, 32, 41
Franciscans 38
Franz, Adolph 18
Frati, Lodovico 104
Frideswide, Saint 34

Gad, Tue 8, 11, 12, 14, 16, 60

Gaiffier, B. 8
Gandersheim 29
Gardner, W.H. 44
Gärtner, Kurt 20
Geete, Robert 50
Gelenius: *De admiranda sacra* 20
Genevieve, Saint 57
Genoa 8
George, Saint 18, 48
Germany 17–19, 26, 46, 53
Gerould, Gordon Hall 36, 40
Gertrude, Saint 49, 57
Giles, Saint 18, 48
Gilte Legende 34–39
Gimlinge 56
Gislinge 57
Gjerløv, Lilli 59
Gloucester 34
Godding, Robert SJ 1
Goodwin, K.L. 43
Golden Legend: see Caxton, William
Gothem 57
Gotland 57
Gradl, H. 27
Graesse, Th. 8, 35, 40, 42, 75, 76, 87
Gram 58
Greff, Joachim 28
Gregory XIII, Pope: *Emendatio* 6
Gregory the Great: *Dialogues* 4
Gregory of Tours 4
Grey, Georg 33
Grüner-Nielsen, H. 55
Guðrún Kvaran 63
Gunnlaugur Jónsson 63
Günter, Heinrich, 7, 14
Görlach, Manfred 34–37
Gørløse 56

Haderslev 58
Hallberg, Svante 56, 57

Hallgrímur Pétursson: *Passíu-sálmar* 65
Hamer, Richard 37
Hansen, Christiern: *see* Joannis, Christiernus
Harburger Legenda aurea I 18
Hattula 57
Heffernan, Thomas J. 14, 17
Heilagra meyja drápa 59
Heiligen Leben, Der 18, 25
Heiligen Leben (Redaktion), Der 18
Heiligenleben Hermanns von Fritz-lar, Der 18
Hein, Franz Joseph 7
Heinrich der Teichner 26
Heinrich von Nuyß 20
Heinzelmann, Martin 13
Helena, Saint 57
Hellige Dorothea, Den 55, 62, 63
Hellige Kvinder, De 38, 60
Hemsjömanualet 48
Herimannus Contractus: *Martyro-logium* 5
Herman, Founder 57
Hermann, Nikolaus: *Ein schön new geistlich Lied von S. Dorothea* 30
Herren, Michael 3
Hildelitha, Abbess 2
Holbein the Older 45
Hopkins, Gerard Manley 43–45
Horstmann, Carl 34, 35, 39–41, 62
Hrotswitha: *Dulcitius; Sapientia* 29
Hungary 17

Iceland 58, 59, 62, 63
Indrebø, Gustav 59
Inga Jónsdóttir 59
Ingeborg Predbjørnsdatter's Book of Hours 48, 49

Ingegärd Ambjörndotter's Prayer Book 50
Italy 2, 5, 17, 46

Jacobsen, Grethe 51
Jacobus de Voragine 8, 9, 17, 87; *Legenda aurea* 8, 9, 17, 18, 21, 30, 33–35, 38, 41, 74–76, 87
Jan de Baenst 33
Jean de Vignay: *Légende Dorée* 33, 35
Jeanne de Bourgogne 33
Jefferis, Sibylle 20
Jensen, Christiern: *see* Joannis, Christiernus
Jerome, Saint 2, 11
Jesus Christ 7, 10–17, 24, 25, 45, 46, 50, 60
Joannis, Christiernus: *Dorotheæ Komedie* 53–55, 77
Johanne Nielsdatter's Book of Hours 48, 49
Johansson, Hilding 47, 48
John the Baptist 59
Jón Hallur Stefánsson 63
Jón Helgason 60, 61, 64
Jón Sigurðsson 61
Jón Þorkelsson 61, 62–64
Jón Viðar Sigurðsson 51
Juliana, Saint 15, 38, 57
Justina of Tergeste, Saint 7, 13, 15
Jutland 57
Jørgensen, Ellen 48, 51

Karen Ludvigsdatter's Book of Hours 48
Karlstorp 47
Karweyß 20
Kenelm, Saint 34
Keller, Gottfried: *Sieben Legenden* 30, 31

Kilström, Bengt Ingmar 50
Kirkjubær 60, 63
Kirkjubæjarklaustur 60, 65
Kirschbaum, Engelbert 45
Klosterneuburg 25, 45
Knudsen, Gunnar 58
Kristensen, Marius 58
Koelhoff 20
Koeppel, Emil 41
Kongens Lyngby 57
Konrad von Soest 45
Konráð Gíslason 64
Konrad von Würzburg 23
Kosegarten, Ludwig: *Legenden* 30
Krogh, Torben 27, 53, 55
Kulm 27
Kunze, Konrad 18, 20
Kühnau, Richard 47
Künstle, Karl 17, 45
"Kvæði um Dorotheu hina helgu"
    (*alias Dorotheudiktur*) 61
Kålund, Kr. 59, 64

Lahier, François: *Le grande Meno-
    loge des saintes* 27
Lambach 27
Landskrona 56
Lang, Cecil Y. 44
Lange, Johan 58
Langport 46
Lapidge, Michael 3
Legenda aurea: see Jacobus de
    Voragine
Légende Dorée: see Jean de Vignay
Leger, Saint 34
Lehmann, Paul 74
Leonard, Saint 18
Liber pontificalis 4
Liden der hilger Machabeen, Dat
    20
Liebgott, Niels-Knud 18, 57
Lievens, Robrecht 33

Lind, E.H. 58
Lindberg, Gustaf 20, 50
Lindblom, Andreas 57
Linke, Hansjürgen 27
Linköping 47
Lithberg, Nils 58
Lochner, Stephan 45
Lorenzetti, Ambrogio 46
Lucy, Saint 37, 38, 60
Ludus de Sancta Dorothea 27, 28,
    75–77
Ludwig, V.O. 25
Lund 56
Luxeuil 2
Lyons 4, 6
Lödöse 47

Mackenzie, N.H. 44
Magdeburg 20
Magnus, Saint 48
Magnus-Petersen, J. 56
Mainz 4
Maliniemi, Aarno 47
Maltzahn, Wendelin von 30
Margaret of Antioch, Saint 1, 9,
    13, 15, 18, 20, 37, 38, 48–51,
    56, 57, 60, 64
Mariani, Paul L 45
Marienburg 20
Marina, Saint 60
Marine Issdatter's Prayer Book 48,
    49
Mark 46
Martha, Saint 38
Martyrologium Fuldense 4
Martyrologium Hieronymianum
    1–3
Martyrologium Romanum 6
Mary, the Virgin 25, 45, 46, 49,
    57, 59, 60
Mary Magdalen, Saint 24, 37, 38,
    57, 59

Massinger, Philip: see: Dekker, Thomas
Maximian 9
Mayer, August L. 46
McLaughlin, Eleanor Commo 12
McLuskie, Kathleen 42
Menhardt, Hermann 25
Mentzer, Simon 20
Mergentheim 27
Michael, Saint 34
Middlezoy 46
Mill, Anna J. 34
Missale Lincopense 47, 50
Missale Lundense 50
Mittelfränkische Heiligenpredikt 18
Mogk, Eugen 74
Mone, F.J. 52
Morris, William 43, 44
Muggensturm 45

Netherlands, The 18, 27
Nicholas of Cusa 9, 17
Nicolas, Saint 18
Niederdeutsche Legenda aurea, Die 18
Nielsen, Karl Martin 48–51
Nielsen, Yngvar 52, 53
Niewöhner, Heinrich 26
Nilsén, Anna 57
Nimwegen 27
Nordby 57
Norton-sub-Hamdon 46
Nordtorp-Madson, Shelly 56
Norway 48, 58
Notker Balbulus: Martyrologium 5
Nürnberg, 20, 45

Odenius, Oloph 47
Odense, 53, 55
Odilia, Saint 45, 49
Ólafur Einarsson 63
Ólafur Jónsson: Dorotheukvædi 62, 63

Óláfr Haraldsson, Saint 59
Old Norwegian Homily Book 59
Ordo Nidrosiensis Ecclesiae 59
Origen 17
Oslo 48
Ostfalen 21
Oswald, Saint 34
Otterbjörk, Roland 58
Ovid 42
Oxford 34

Pailler, Wilhelm: S. Dorothea: Legende in Zwei Aufzügen 30
Páll Ámundason 60, 65
Páll Eggert Ólason 61, 62
Páll Pálsson 62
Pantaleon, Saint 18, 48
Paris 5
Paris' dom 55
Passienbüchlein von den vier Hauptjungfrauen 20, 38, 60
Passional 30
Pedersen, Christiern: Bønnebog i at høre messe 48, 49
Pepwell, Henry 33
Persøn, Michel 58
Peschia 1, 46
Peter, Saint 24, 59
Petersen, Henry 58
Peterson, Joseph Martin 35, 41–43
Petronilla, Saint 49
Philippe VI de Valois 33
Phillip the Good 33
Pius IX, Pope 1
Plato 11
Plautus, Titus Maccius: Amphitruo; Aulularia 28, 29
Poncelet, Albertus 104
Pre-Raphaelites 43
Priebsch, R. 21
Przelaika 46
Pseudo-Jerome 6

Pulsiano, Phillip 36

Quentin, Henri 4, 5
Quintianus 12

Rabanus Maurus: *Martyrologium*
    4, 5
Ravenna 5
Reames, Sherry L. 9, 74
Red Bull Theater 41
Regensburg 47
Reichenau 5
Reinach, Salomon 45
Renaud, Genevieve 4, 5
Reuchlin, Johannes: *Henno* 55
Reuther, Kilian, von
Melrichstadt: *Comedia gloriose
    parthenices et martiris Doro-
    thee agoniarn passionemque
    depingens* 28, 29, 53, 54
Reynisnes 60
Reynistaður 60
Rieser, Ferdinand 30
Rhineland 17
Robertson, Elizabeth 15
Roch, Saint 18
Rome, 1, 11, 19, 23, 36, 44, 61,
    76
Romerike 58
Romfartuna 57
Romsdal 58
Roosval, Johnny 57
Roskilde 56, 58
Rossetti, Christina Georgina 43
Rossetti, Dante Gabriel 43
Rossetti, William Michael 43
Rossi, J.B. de 1, 2
Ruether, Rosemary Radford 11,
    17
Rydbeck, Otto 57
Råby 57

Sahlgren, Jöran 56
Saint-Germain-des-Prés 5
Samsø 57
Sancta Dorothea virgo 30
Sandar 62
Sands, Tracey 56
Sapricus (*alias* Capricius,
    Fabricius) 8
Saxony 27, 29
Saxtorph, Niels M. 48, 56, 57
Scandinavia 17, 18, 47, 48, 53, 57
Scania 57
Schachner, Heinrich 18, 26–28,
    30
Schade, Oskar 6, 20, 21
Schrade, Michel 25, 26
Schreiber, W.L. 45
Schreiner, Klaus 9
Schwaben 25
Sebastian, Saint 18
Seip, Didrik Arup 64
Serjeantson, Mary S. 37
Seybolt, Robert Francis 8, 74
Sharp, William 43
Shook, L.K. 74
Sicily 12
Síða 60
Siena 46
Sigmundur Matthíasson Long 63
Sigurður Jónsson 63
Sigurjón Einarsson 62
Sixtus V, Pope 6
Skagafjörður 60
Skara 47
Sköna Dorothea, Den 56
Soest 45
Somerset 46
Sophia, Saint 16, 60
Sorunda 57
South English Legendary 34
Spain 46

Spengler, Franz 29, 54
Spes, Saint 16, 65
St. Gall 25
St. Gall Abbey 5
St. Georgen 25
Staður 60
Stadler J.E. 7
Stammler, Wolfgang 20
Stede der Vrouwen 33
Steingrímur Thorsteinsson 61
Strängnäs 47
Sunte Dorotheen passie 21, 24, 27,
    38, 75, 76, 78, 84
Surtees, Virginia 43
Sweden 34, 47, 58
Swinburne, Algernon Charles 43,
    44
Switzerland 5
Swithun, Saint 34
Syriac Breviary 2
Södermanland 57
Søholm, Ejgil 29, 53, 54

Teitur Þorleifsson 59
Tensta 57
Thalbacher Legenda aurea, Die 18
Thea (*alias* Theodora) 10, 20, 21,
    29, 56
Thecla, Saint 49
Theodora (*alias* Thea) 20, 21, 23,
    27, 38, 40
Theophilus 34
Theophilus, Saint 1, 2, 7, 8, 10,
    19, 21, 23, 25, 28, 30, 31, 39,
    40, 42, 44, 45, 50, 54–56, 61,
    75, 77, 79, 82, 84
Thomas à Becket, Saint 34
Tierp 57
Tilmann Riemenschneider 45
Titus, Saint 1
Tjæreby 48
Toldberg, Helge 29

Tortuna 57
Transitus Mariae 60
Trastevere 1
Trevelyan, Pauline 44
Tyrol 9
Tönnies, Eduard 45

Þorlákr, Saint 59

Ukena, Elke 27, 28
Ulldal, F. 57
Unger, C.R. 64, 74
Uppland 57
Uppsala 47
Urban VIII, Pope 6
Ursula, Saint 37, 57
Usuard: *Martyrologium* 5, 6
Utro Hustru, Den 55

Vadstena 50, 56
Valö 57
Vatican Council, the Second 1
Venturi, A. 46
Venus 42, 44
Vesta 12
Vienna 4, 46
Vincent of Beauvais: *Speculum his-*
    toriale 33
Virgin Martyr, The: see Dekker,
    Thomas
Visdoms Spejl 38, 48, 78, 79
"Vísur af Dorotheu" (*alias Doro-*
    theudiktur) 61
Visio Pauli 60
Vitae patrum 30
Vitus, Saint 18, 48
Vitz, Evelyn Birge 79
Vogelsang, Willem 45
Von Sent Dorothea 23, 27, 75, 76
Västerås 47
Västmanland 57

Wandalbert of Prüm: *Martyrologium* 4
Wallin, Sigurd 57
Wegener, Philipp 20
West Pennard 46
Westminster 35
Widding, Ole 74
Willenberg, Gotthelf 21, 39, 40, 75
Williams-Krapp,W. 8, 18, 20, 21, 23–26
Wimmer, E. 9, 27
Wimmer, Otto 1

Wolfram von Eschenbach: *Parzival* 23
Woodforde, Christopher 46
Worcester 34
Wrangel, E. 56
Würzburg 45

Zealand 56, 57
Zell, Ulrich 20
Zeno 7
Zwickau 27, 28

Åbo 47
Ålborg 58